The Racial Integrity
of the American Negro

by

A. H. SHANNON, A.B., B.D., M.A.

ISBN: 978-1-63923-851-4

Printed: March 2023

Published and Distributed By:
Lushena Books
607 Country Club Drive, Unit E
Bensenville, IL 60106
www.lushenabks.com

ISBN: 978-1-63923-851-4

TABLE OF CONTENTS

INTRODUCTION

THE AUTHOR of this book has been for some years a close observer of race relations and a student of those problems growing out of racial contacts. As Chaplain of the Mississippi State Penitentiary, he was called upon to minister to several hundred Negro prisoners, thus gaining a measure of intimate knowledge of the Negro criminal. As a teacher in the employ of the Imperial Government of Japan, he was privileged to make a brief study of an Oriental civilization. Here was gained a measure of knowledge of the Eurasian problem, so acute in some of the Asiatic countries and in evidence wherever contact of East and West has occurred.

The chief interest of the author in the Negro problem has centered about the matter of racial intermixture—the mulatto problem—and most of his writings have had to do with this evil. The present study, while endeavoring to ascertain and to state facts impartially, necessarily gives a large measure of personal reaction to certain of the problems involved in present-day contacts of the two races, the black and the white, in the United States. Whoever really understands conditions now obtaining in this area is prepared to understand the situation wherever two dissimilar races occupy the same territory, or wherever casual racial contacts occur—as is now the case throughout the greater part of the world.

There is a conscious, an intentional, limiting of this study largely to those features of the situation which may well tend toward discouragement, if not toward hopeless pessimism. Since it now appears fashionable to approach the Negro problem from the standpoint of the invincible optimist, resolutely ignoring or consciously discarding those facts which, fairly faced, would shatter so many pleasant theories, it is well that someone should present the darker side of the picture, for there is a distressingly dark side. The reader, once the situation is clearly analyzed and its elements indicated, may be trusted to interpret aright the issues unquestionably involved. Americans, white and black alike, are not awake to the real situation confronting them, a fact clearly evidenced by more than eighty years of silence and indifference touching the vital issue of race amalgamation and the conditions under which this is still occurring.

As an answer to the ever-ready charge of ministering to, if not creating, racial antagonisms and hates—a charge behind which there sometimes lurks more of moral laxness and of intellectual inertia than some good people are aware of— there is to be noted the difference between a clear statement of fact, a clear-cut challenge to the self-respect of each of two groups, and a maligning of one group by another. If it has come to the pass that a calm facing of fact, a thorough analysis of a given situation, must be opposed because it reveals the destructiveness of an inherited unreasonable and unreasoned program, there should, at least, be a clear understanding of the attitudes displayed and a close scrutiny of the motives behind these attitudes.

Both races in America, especially in the United States, are confronted by facts demanding careful consideration; by problems the solution of which depends primarily upon thorough analysis as the basis for a full understanding of what is involved. Various organizations, secular and religious, are in the field, voluntarily endeavoring to carry out programs which they are free to make what they will. Most of these will resent the charge that they are contributing directly to moral confusion and to racial degradation. Most of them will resent the charge that their work and the attitudes upon which it rests constitute the most destructive influence against which the fullblood Negro must contend at the present time. Can it be shown that such charge is unwarranted? If only there could be a general and an honest, dispassionate inquiry, bringing these matters into the realm of conscious thought and reasoned program, there would be hope of constructive action. If this study assists the reader to break with traditional lines of thought and the attitudes and the programs based upon these lines of thought, thus promoting independent analysis and rationally constructive programs, it will serve a useful and a timely purpose.

The author is forced into a position which is essentially unpleasant. It becomes necessary to point out the grounds of criticism, the delinquencies, of those who, holding positions of leadership—political, educational, religious—have failed to see, or seeing have failed to meet, or have met with utter indifference, the problems here discussed. Upon the part of the leaders of both races there has been, at best, a very incomplete understanding of the trust reposed in their leadership. No further evidence is necessary to establish this fact than to call attention to present conditions and to the manner in which these conditions have, without effective protest or warning, become established and that they are now generally accepted, without analysis, and without intelligent evaluation of their logical, their inevitable results.

There are three fairly distinct divisions into which the population of the United States, with a few relatively insignificant exceptions, falls:

I—THE WHITE GROUP, completely overshadowing all others and in position to decide all matters of collective control. This group is, however, so confused in thought and in opinion and so divided in practice as to lose many of the possibilities inherent in its favorable position. The protection of its racial integrity, the preservation of its blood purity, seem to give this group vastly less concern than does many another interest of relatively trifling significance.

II—THE FULLBLOOD NEGRO GROUP, now numbering several million but largely inarticulate and wholly lacking in fullblood leadership. This group is also without those racial ideals and that racial self-sufficiency and racial self-respect necessary to preserve it as a race; and

III—THE MULATTO GROUP, now numbering in the millions and, through various means, dominating completely the fullblood Negro, to the serious injury of the other two groups. This group is divided further into the *initial increment mulattoes,* or those born of white and Negro or mulatto parentage, and the *diffusion mulattoes,* or those born of Negro-mulatto or mulatto parentage. Since all mulattoes have the same general markings, this distinction is of little practical value.

Many books have been written dealing with the situation created in the United States by the presence of the Negro. This situation is usually spoken of as the race problem. Magazine articles, discussing various aspects of this situation, have been quite numerous. It appears that, at least with a class of writers and the thoughtful element of the reading public, there exists a measure of interest in the present situation. There is, however, little agreement in reference to fact and even less attempt to deal constructively with present vital issues.

Anthropology, ethnology, ethnography, craniology, etc., are brought into this discussion and each yields its quota of information—too often subject to the personal equation of the investigator, or that of the writer using and interpreting what is accepted as fact. Science seeks to answer the question, "What is?" leaving to the moralist the question "What should be?" Yet the moralist needs, desperately, the help of the scientist. The second question cannot be answered intelligently until the first has been answered with reasonable fullness. The character and the intelligence of both races should be brought to bear, definitely, directly, and energetically, upon the moral and the religious aspects of the race problem.

The fundamental assumption in this study is that the Negro is human, and that the same principles which are applied to other races in preserving their higher interests, especially a pure home life based upon uncompromisingly high moral ideals and religious sanctions, are equally essential to the Negro. This is a forgotten or an ignored fact in the dealings of the white group in the United States with the fullblood Negro here. It is equally forgotten, or ignored, within the Negro group. When all the adverse details of his present situation are considered, it must appear clearly that the fullblood Negro in America is decidedly the chief sufferer from existing conditions, attitudes, and policies.

It is the purpose in the present study to deal primarily with the moral and the religious aspects of the Race Problem as these are related to the matter of the racial integrity of the American Negro. Other aspects are dealt with largely as they bear upon this central theme.

In the appendix will be found a brief list of books dealing with the race problem.

CHAPTER I

BASIC FACTS: A STATEMENT OF THE CASE

ACCORDING to the Census of 1940, there were at that time in Continental United States 12,842,024 Negroes. Of this number, 187,226 were returned as residing in the District of Columbia or, as the two are identical, in Washington City. The total "non-white" population of the United States is given as 13,454,405. For 1947 the total non-white population of the United States is given as 15,017,000, of which the Negro constituted 95.6 per cent, or 14,366,252. For 1950 the Negro population is given as 14,918,860. The findings of the census of 1950 are not yet available in detail but will, doubtless, furnish much valuable information, showing the present trends in the development of the race problem.

In recent years there has been a pronounced migration of Southern Negroes into the cities and into the industrial centers of the North and of the Northeast. The enumeration of 1950, when available in detail, will prove of special value in showing the distribution of the Negro migrants throughout the formerly white states. The race problem can no longer be considered a Southern issue exclusively. New York City, Philadelphia, Chicago, Washington City now pose problems even graver than do New Orleans, Birmingham, and Atlanta. The presence of a large foreign element in the Northern cities and industrial centers must be reckoned with, an element not prominent in the South except in New Orleans. The latest figures available give the non-white population of Washington City as 255,930. This figure is apparently based upon the annual enumeration made by the police department and is for the year 1948.

11

The above finding does not include a very considerable number of Negroes residing near but outside the District, many of whom are employed in the city. There are also a number of Negroes who are employed or present temporarily in Washington City—a constantly changing group—for whom even the police are unable to secure a complete enumeration. Many of the Negroes leaving the South for the northeastern section of the United States pass through Washington. Of all the cities of the world, New York City, Chicago, Philadelphia, and Washington City are the four having the largest Negro population.

In order that the situation in the District of Columbia may be brought clearly before the reader and that some basis for comparison of this situation with that existing in continental United States as a whole may be provided, the following tables are offered. These are taken in part from the United States census returns and in part from the reports of the health authorities of the District. Free use is also made of the enumerations conducted by the police department. There are numerous minor differences between the census figures and those of the health department bulletins, and even between those of the departments as repeated from year to year. Such slight discrepancies as exist, however, may be explained and do not affect adversely the value of these sources of information.

Table I gives for the whole United States the number of each race reported decennially from 1790 to the present. The earliest reference to the mulatto is found in the census of 1850. From the standpoint of the white race there is but one encouraging feature of the situation in so far as numbers are concerned. In 1790, Negroes constituted 19.3 per cent of the total population of the United States. in 1920 the census returns show 10.4 per cent of the total population as Negroes. The time may come, however, when a vastly increased number of Negroes and mulattoes will constitute no more than 10 per cent of the total population!

TABLE I [1]

Year	Total Population	White	% White	Negro	% Negro
1790	3,929,214	3,172,006	80.7	757,208	19.3
1800	5,308,483	4,306,446	81.1	1,002,037	18.9
1810	7,239,881	5,862,073	81.0	1,377,808	18.4
1820	9,638,483	7,966,797	81.6	1,771,656	18.4
1830	12,866,020	10,532,060	81.9	2,328,642	18.1
1840	17,069,453	14,189,705	83.2	2,873,648	16.8
1850	23,191,876	19,553,068	84.3	2,638,808	15.7
1860	31,443,321	26,922,537	85.6	4,441,830	14.1
1870	38,558,371	33,589,377	87.1	4,880,009	12.7
1880	50,155,785	43,402,970	86.5	6,580,793	13.1
1890	62,947,714	55,957,714	87.5	7,488,676	11.9
1900	75,994,575	66,809,196	87.9	8,833,994	11.6
1910	91,972,226	81,731,957	88.8	9,827,763	10.6
1920	105,710,620	94,820,915	89.6	10,463,131	10.4
1930	122,775,046	110,661,275	...	11,891,143	...
1940	131,669,870	113,214,872	...	12,865,518	...
1950	149,866,000	124,947,140	...	14,918,860	...

Table I supplies the fundamental facts in reference to the Negro problem in the United States in so far as numbers are concerned. In the following table will be found similar information concerning the District of Columbia.[2] Here, however, the annual status is given while percentages are not given. The inclusion of all other than white persons under the general classification of "non-white" introduces some confusion here, and elsewhere. The inclusion of other non-whites along with the Negroes probably involves slight error in so far as the Negro is concerned but does not materially affect the value of the census findings. We have here the most dependable information available concerning the relative number of the two races residing in the District after the year 1876. So far as we have been able to ascertain, Table I gives the only authentic information available for the period 1790 to 1870.

[1] Figures are from census reports. Inaccuracies due to elements of population not included.

[2] A number of near-whites are now attempting to classify themselves as Indians, or as whites of Latin extraction. This tendency is sufficient to affect totals concerning Indians as returned by the United States Census.

TABLE II

White and Negro Population District of Columbia, 1876 to 1950

Year	Total	White	Negro	Year	Total	White	Negro
1876	157,600	106,741	50,859	1914	363,664	256,049	97,615
1877	162,375	109,505	52,870	1915	357,749	258,904	98,809
1878	167,300	112,340	54,960	1916	359,997	260,854	99,143
1879	172,337	115,247	57,130	1917	395,947	293,329	102,618
1880	177,638	118,236	59,402	1918	417,405	312,806	104,599
1881	183,060	121,300	61,760	1919	455,428	340,796	114,632
1882	188,653	124,441	64,212	1920	437,571	327,595	109,976
1883	191,980	126,300	65,680	1921	454,026	341,662	112,346
1884	200,000	130,700	69,300	1922	454,326	341,476	112,514
1885	200,000	130,708	69,300	1923	475,966	359,569	116,397
1886	205,300	136,000	69,300	1924	486,936	368,915	118,021
1887	210,000	140,000	70,000	1925	497,906	378,261	119,624
1888	225,000	150,000	75,000	1926	528,000	402,100	125,900
1889	250,000	170,000	80,000	1927	540,000	403,100	136,009
1890	250,000	170,000	80,000	1928	......	......	......
1891	250,000	170,000	80,000	1929	......	......	......
1892	260,000	175,000	85,000	1930	......	......	......
1893	285,000	195,000	90,000	1931	......	......	......
1894	285,000	195,000	90,000	1932	......	......	......
1895	272,337	185,191	87,146	1933	......	......	......
1896	275,562	187,827	87,735	1934	......	......	......
1897	277,728	189,457	88,325	1935	......	......	......
1898	283,100	193,900	89,200	1936	......	......	......
1899	288,500	198,400	90,100	1937	......	......	......
1900	294,000	203,000	91,000	1938	......	......	......
1901	299,600	207,800	91,800	1939	......	......	......
1902	305,400	212,600	92,800	1940	663,091	474,326	187,266
1903	311,300	217,600	93,700	1941	......	......	......
1904	317,200	222,600	94,600	1942	......	......	......
1905	323,123	227,428	96,695	1943	......	......	......
1906	326,435	231,417	96,018	1944	......	......	......
1907	329,591	233,403	96,188	1945	......	......	......
1908	339,403	241,920	97,483	1946	......	......	......
1909	343,003	245,861	97,657	1947	......	......	......
1910	348,400	250,803	97,657	1948	898,000	642,070	255,930
1911	349,659	251,409	98,159	1949	......	......	......
1912	352,936	254,260	98,676	1950	......	......	......
1913	353,297	255,153	98,144	....	......	......	......

Table II gives an approximately correct numerical statement of the white and the Negro population of the District
of Columbia for seventy-four years. Statistics earlier than for
1876 are incomplete, there being no Health Department
Bulletin earlier than for the year 1851. The next is for the
year 1854. Then there are none available until the year
1872. Since 1876 a fairly complete annual bulletin has been

published. This reflects every advance the city has made toward achieving its present high standing in the matter of sanitation and along other lines, making this at present one of the cleanest and most healthful cities in America.

It is matter for regret that there are not more complete records for the earlier history of the city. Such records as exist are to be found chiefly in reports by, or to, the War Department, in newspaper files, and in information but indirectly and imperfectly supplied by other agencies. The years omitted involved the handling of those problems incident to the Civil War. Of these none was more serious, or more exacting, than the management of the large group of Negroes escaping from slavery and finding refuge in the District.

Another matter of regret is that information in reference to the mulatto as a distinct element of the population is consistently omitted from the records kept by the Health Department, as well as by other agencies. While giving information concerning the number and the percentage of illegitimate children born of each race, the reports furnish no information concerning the number of such children who represent initial amalgamations, i.e., those born of Negro-white or of mulatto-white parentage.

It is necessary here to emphasize the fact that in any reasonably complete consideration of the problems due to the Negro population of the District of Columbia, due account must be taken of those Negroes residing in the states of Virginia and Maryland but near enough to Washington City to affect vitally its social and its industrial interests. Many of these are actually employed in the District, but no means is at hand by which to ascertain the number so employed. It is quite safe, however, to place the total Negro population of the entire area—the resident group, the transient group, and the group in adjacent areas—at a minimum of three hundred thousand, an increase of approximately 100 per cent since 1930.

The Negro element in the total population of the United States, as previously stated, grows relatively smaller. In 1790 it was given as 19.3 per cent; in 1920, as 10.4 per cent. Numerically, however, the Negro element is increasing very rapidly. From 757,208 in 1790 it increased to 10,463,131 in 1930, and to 14,918,860 in 1950, this for the entire nation. It is probable that the inclusion of both whites and Negroes forming the groups in areas adjacent to the District would not materially change the figures for the city alone in so far as the ratio of white to Negro is concerned.

The foregoing gives a sufficiently full and definite statement of the Negro problem in the District of Columbia and in the United States as a whole in so far as numbers are concerned. The succeeding chapters will present certain details of the situation more fully, giving attention especially to those features affecting the moral life and outlook of both races as reflected in the progress of race amalgamation and in the attitudes of each race toward its racial integrity.

While many details of the race problem must be left for discussion in subsequent chapters, or not presented, it is well to indicate here certain facts and certain tendencies inherent in the figures already quoted and to present other matters of vital importance. All conclusions and all opinions concerning the future of the two races in America, if to be of any value, must be based not upon visionary theorizing but upon fact. Others have presented the facts in reference to the progress of the Negro group in education, in the mastering of trades, in the acquisition of property, and in other fields. None have shown how much of all this is to be attributed to the mixed-blood and how much to the full-blood Negro. Even the most casual observers must recognize a difference here, although they may not fully agree with Professor Reuter, who formerly reached the conclusion that the difference in the two, as measured by success and by positions of leadership achieved, is thirty-four to one in favor of the mulatto. In a later publication he goes much further, giving the black child's chances as compared to those of the mulatto child as one in forty to fifty, and again as one in fifty to one hundred.

The student who undertakes a study of conditions now prevailing must note the rapid increase of the mixed-blood people. Here the color of the mulatto renders racial intermixture apparent to all, even the most casual observer. Although this is true, very few are found in either race who have manifested any desire to ascertain the real status of amalgamation or the conditions under which it is occurring. Yet no statement of conditions now obtaining in Washington City or in the United States as a whole is complete without due reference to racial intermixture. Briefly stated, the findings of the Census of 1870 must be accepted as the most nearly complete and the most dependable statement available concerning the intermixture of the two races during the whole of the slavery period, the period of the Civil War, and the first five years of freedom. The Census of 1870 gives the results of 250 years of contact of the races, the first Negroes having been brought to Jamestown, Va., in 1619 or 1620. The first brought to America were landed in the West Indies by the Spaniards in 1501.

˙ The first Census enumeration to furnish information in reference to the mulatto was that of 1850. The figures furnished by the Bureau of the Census and dealing with the intermixture of the Negro and the white in Continental United States are given in Table III, as follows:

TABLE III

Year	Total Negro Population	Negro	% Negro	Mulatto	% Mulatto
1850	3,683,808	3,233,057	88.8	450,751	11.2
1860	4,421,830	3,833,467	86.8	588,363	13.2
1870	4,880,009	4,295,960	88.0	584,049	12.0
1890	7,470,040	6,337,980	84.8	1,132,060	15.2
1910	9,827,763	7,777,077	79.1	2,050,686	20.9
1920	10,463,131	8,802,577	84.1	1,660,554	15.9

It will be noted that the whole of the slavery period—1620 to 1865—with the first five years of freedom added, resulted, according to the Census of 1870, in 584,049 mulattoes. The last decade of this period witnessed the demoralization incident to the Civil War and the disorders consequent upon this war and the presence of large bodies of troops throughout the South. Under existing conditions an accurate enumeration was not to be expected in 1870, yet the figures of the two succeeding enumerations show results quite consistent with its findings. *The startling feature lies in the fact that twenty years of freedom, 1870 to 1890, virtually duplicated the results of the whole period of slavery, with the first five years of freedom added; while the second twenty-year period of freedom, 1890 to 1910, virtually duplicated the results in racial intermixture of the whole preceding time the races had been in contact—two hundred and seventy years!*

For a fuller discussion of the Census returns of 1920, manifestly incorrect in so far as the mulatto is concerned, see page 30. It is sufficient to point out here that it is impossible that the returns for 1910 and those for 1920 should both be correct. Those for 1910 are quite consistent with those of the two preceding enumerations and are, therefore, presumably correct. It is wholly unreasonable to assume that an element of population which had virtually doubled in each of the two preceding twenty-year periods should have decreased 390,132 during the ten years between 1910 and 1920. The Census Bureau frankly admits error here in so far as the mulatto is concerned.

Just here some personal estimates and opinions are of interest. Professor M. J. Herskovits, quoted at page 332 of the September, 1926, number of the *American Journal of Sociology,* holds that "only about 20 to 30 per cent of American Negroes are pure-blooded." About the same date Professor Kelly Miller asserted that 40 per cent of the Negro population then showed an infusion of white blood.

In the absence of definite findings by the Census Bureau for 1950, two calculations may be made by which the expectation for 1950 may be found. By dividing the number of mulattoes reported as of 1910 by the number reported for 1870 the rate of increase for this forty-year period is found to be 3.511. Multiplying the number of mulattoes for 1910— 2,050,686—by this rate the expectation for 1950 is found to be 7,199,958. A second method for arriving at this expectation is by use of the ratio-proportion formula, viz.: 584,049: 2,050,686::2,050,686: (?). Solving, the result is 7,200,276. The relatively small difference shown here would have been reduced had the decimals above been carried further. As to the validity of the expectation for mulattoes in 1950, reached by the above method, there seems no reasonable doubt. The calculations are based upon the existing Census returns, and they seem final.

Professor Herskovits emphasizes one fact that is of importance. Not all the slaves brought from Africa were of pure Negro stock. Those from South and those from East Africa had absorbed much Semitic blood and this was manifest in their color and in their physique, especially in the shape of their skulls and in their cranial capacity. The bulk of the slaves were true Negroes and came from the west coast of tropical Africa.

Another matter calling for careful study and investigation, but one upon which very little trustworthy information is available, is that of initial amalgamation, or the number of children born of white and Negro or of white and mulatto parentage. A careful examination of a number of Children's Bureau Publications brought to light but two references that could be made the basis for a calculation indicating the total number of such cases. In the city of Baltimore four cases of initial amalgamation were registered in a total of 706 illegitimate births reported in one year. The Negro population of Baltimore was given as 84,749. Four cases of initial amalgamation in this number of Negroes would give, among the

19

total Negro population of that date, approximately 564 cases of initial amalgamation in the United States annually. For the present, this number must be at least doubled. Even so, the figures are too low. No account is taken of mulattoes born of married women of either race. Bulletin No. 144, page 19, reports six white mothers who gave birth to illegimate colored children. Two of the four cases mentioned above involved white mothers. Are these cases sufficient to warrant the conclusion that the lowest stratum of the American white woman is joining the ranks of the racial traitors? Heretofore the integrity of the white race has been regarded as safe in so far as the white woman is concerned.

The only conclusion warranted by the inadequate data at hand is that, while there is no means by which to arrive at a definite statement concerning the prevalence of cases of initial amalgamation, such cases do occur in considerable numbers. The percentage of such births is certainly much higher at present than it has been at any time in the past. It is morally certain that there were a number of unreported cases in Baltimore and that the number actually reported should be increased, probably several fold. There are sections of the United States in which conditions are certainly worse than is indicated for Baltimore.

Much of the current thinking upon and discussion of the race problem assumes that this initial increment is now negligible. Professor Kelly Miller says: "There is not likely to be much further infusion of white blood into the Negro race." He sees, as the status to be achieved in the next three or four generations, a disappearing of the fullblood Negro except in "remote black belts of the rural South," while the near-whites "will have crossed the line, found a place and recognition in the white group or bred backward upon the color scale. A new Negroid race will have arisen." There seems to be here an asumption upon the part of Professor Miller that this drawing apart into two groups will, in some way, settle permanently the race problem. This, however, cannot be the case. The same vicious elements will continue to exist in the white race, subjecting the "yellowish-brown" or the "brownish-yellow" womanhood to the same, but intensified, unfair and unjust stress as must be met by Negro womanhood at present, while the incentive to "breed upward" instead of "backward" must be intensified. The hope, therefore, of two races living together in completely protective self-respect and in mutually protective respect for each other, has, and can have, but little basis in reality. What basis can there be for such a hope in a future in which the process of amalgamation has been, even by diffusion, carried to the point where the lawlessness of individuals of the two groups has achieved the anticipated change in the color of the entire Negro group? Will this group then, all the members of it, be satisfied to remain permanently "yellowish-brown" or "brownish-yellow" when the methods of "bleaching"are no longer abstract theory but show abundantly demonstrated achievement? The in-centives, the urge, to "cross the line" must logically increase as the individual, or the race, approaches sufficiently near to that line to bring such "crossing" within the range of reason-ably possible and speedy achievement. Meantime, race pride and racial self-respect must diminish.

Another factor, then, which must be dealt with in the mat-ter of the preservation of racial integrity is the attitude of the less advantageously situated group toward such preservation. Those groups which are distinguished by racial pride and loyalty, by racial self-respect, have every advantage over those lacking these characteristics. Those who are familiar with the racial history of mankind, with the struggles of various groups to maintain their existence as groups, know how difficult this struggle is even under the most favorable circumstances. Such are prepared to accept the statement of Professor Miller that: "The integrity of a self-despised race has never been, and never can be, preserved." It should be equally apparent that no group which has attained a high degree of economic de-velopment and of leadership is secure. Such groups formerly

21

invited their own destruction through the slaves introduced and later absorbed. Even today any such group may invite its own destruction through vast numbers, upon a lower plane of development, introduced as servants or as industrial workers.

All clear thinking concerning the mulatto in the United States must distinguish between initial amalgamation and the diffusion of white blood within the Negro group following its introduction through acts of initial amalgamation, necessarily involving a fullblood white and a fullblood Negro or a mulatto. Except in the small number of cases of interracial marriage in those states permitting this—a number relatively so small as to be almost negligible—initial amalgamation uniformly involves illegitimacy. On the other hand, mulattoes of this origin and their descendants may conform to all requirements as to legal marriage with fullblood Negroes or with mulattoes, their white blood becoming diffused more and more uniformly throughout the entire Negro group. But for continued cases of initial amalgamation, diffusion would ultimately result in a fairly uniform degree of intermixture in which neither the near-black or near-white would be in evidence and a fullblood Negro would be virtually unknown.

Very many of the mulattoes who have attained prominence in the United States have been those known to be both of illegitimate birth and also the product of an act of initial amalgamation. Such origin was formerly given special prominence in autobiographies, biographies, and in historical sketches, it being considered to the credit of the hero that he overcame this obstacle and to the discredit of a social system under which illegitimate racial intermixture could occur. The whole range of antislavery writings illustrate this, especially those of the decade immediately preceding the Civil War. Illegitimate birth and a white father proved a help, rather than a hindrance, to many mulattoes during the later years of slavery and have continued to be a distinct advantage under freedom. Outside the South, such origin has afforded

22

a ready-made appeal to popular sympathy and a command of those advantages based upon such sympathy. With better understanding of what is involved, less prominence is given to such origin and, in latest writings, reference to mixed origin tends to disappear altogether or is made in a more guarded and discreet manner. This is a hopeful indication, but does not, and cannot, obscure the fact that very many of the outstanding mulattoes of the past were the product of initial racial intermixture occurring in contravention of good morals. In scarcely less degree, this is true of those mulattoes now in positions of leadership. With the passage of time and the increase of mulattoes, it is to be expected that leadership, while remaining largely in the hands of the mulatto, will pass more decidedly into the hands of the diffusion mulatto rather than remain in the hands of the initial increment mulatto. Unfortunately there can be no distinction made at this point that will protect the ideals of the Negro group. The mulatto, whether directly the product of lawless racial confusion through initial intermixture or indirectly through diffusion, is not a Negro, and the finer his character, the more creditable his achievements, the more marked his ability, the graver the menace he becomes to the fullblood Negro. This is the tragedy of the mulatto feature of the race problem, a tragedy which must remain and which will, unquestionably, gain in intensity with the awakening of the fullblood Negro and of the white groups to existing facts and attitudes.

There can be no doubt but that the Census returns for the mulatto population in the District of Columbia, and for the United States as a whole, are too low. Of a large number of observations—made by the "random sample" method—the results were uniformly higher than the figures given for that area by the Census Bureau. Indeed, it is a very rare instance when any considerable group of Negroes in the District of Columbia does not show more than 50 per cent of the number clearly of mixed blood. Often more than 75 per cent show clearly the infusion of white blood. The percentage of mulatto to total Negro population here may have been lowered slightly by the recent influx of Southern Negroes. This, however is rendered less probable by the fact that a large part of the Negroes leaving the South are those of mixed blood.

Washington City has received its full share of those Negroes leaving the South in recent years. This influx of Negroes has affected the city in many ways. It has largely driven out the unskilled white laborer. It has created a grave housing problem. Certain areas have been given up to Negro occupancy and others, in large measure, have passed into the use or ownership of Negroes. Churches, schools, business properties and residences have passed into their hands as Negroes have come to predominate in a given area. The white people remaining permanently on such areas as have come to be occupied chiefly by Negroes are not, as a rule, helpful to the Negro. These people, especially in the larger Northern cities, are largely foreigners or that class of native born failing to make better provision for themselves and their families. As a rule, these foreigners lack race pride and often care little for American ideals. The native white American remaining permanently in the midst of a Negro quarter in any of the larger cities is not likely to prove fairly representative of his race.

On the whole, conditions of housing for Negroes in the District, as elsewhere, have improved. Certainly they have improved for a class of the Negroes. At an earlier period the custom of keeping horse and carriage prevailed quite generally among the wealthy of Washington City. This usually involved a building facing the alley and used as stable-carriagehouse-servant's quarters. With the passing of the horse, these buildings were, quite generally, converted into dwellings and rented, chiefly to Negroes. Thus grew up in the older sections of the city what is known in Washington City as the "alley" population, a situation not yet wholly corrected in parts of the city. Thus it came about that on the same lot there existed a home of culture and wealth and a

24

hovel of poverty, even of degradation. With the giving over to Negroes of sections of the city, the alley population remained, the wealthier Negroes succeeding to the homes vacated by the whites and becoming landlords to the alley dwellers. This situation has attracted much attention and is still acute in parts of the city. Similar conditions are reported from other Northern cities.

It seems to be the case everywhere that a group on a lower plane can supplant one on a higher plane where the decision lies with that element of the higher group whose interests demand, or seem to demand, labor at once cheap and subservient, thus inviting exploitation. Supplanting the higher type laborer, the home that would logically fall to him becomes useless unless occupied by the lower plane man. It seems to be the case that the Negroes are able to displace the whites in any section where they are permitted to secure a residential foothold or to compete with unskilled white labor. The District of Columbia affords multiplied examples of such displacement.

Certain areas of the District and of the adjoining lands are protected by provisions in the deeds against the property ever passing into the ownership or occupation of Negroes. This is not, however, sufficiently general to secure complete separation of the races in point of residence. Other forces are active, tending to bring about residential separation of the races, although this is opposed by Negro leaders because of its social implications. The higher interests of both races, especially the independent racial development of the fullblood Negro, are best promoted by such separation as is possible only as separate areas are occupied wholly by each race. Even so, such areas lie adjacent to those occupied by the other race, and there is always the possibility of friction. Washington has had its serious race riots in the past. There are those who are convinced that it would not be difficult to bring about serious racial clashes here at the present time.

When the Negro secures a foothold in any section of a city,

25

representative whites are no longer attracted to that area, while those already there begin to move out. Soon the white group comes to be represented, in the main, by those not helpful to the Negroes. Much friction has, in the past, grown out of the unwillingness of the whites affected to give up their homes thus. No one feature of the contact of the races has created a more intense or a more abiding bitterness than has this displacement of the home-owning white by the Negro. Even when the Negro pays an excessive price for the property, as he often does on first purchases in a given area, resentment upon the part of the remaining owners and residents usually includes both the seller and the Negro purchaser. A far more general resentment follows when the white laborer is displaced by the Negro laborer or when the white laborer, in order to secure employment or to hold his job, is forced to accept a lower wage and the correspondingly lower standard of living.

A general statement of the situation in the District of Columbia or in the whole of Continental United States as created by the presence of the Negro, therefore, necessarily involves some reference to racial contacts as determined by the areas occupied by each of the two races. In a general way the races are separated residentially, but it is not a separation *en masse* due to each race occupying wholly a given area. It is rather a separation by settlements, sometimes relatively small and removed from one another. The Negroes now occupy part of the older section of the city, with the more exclusive residential sections lying beyond and reached from the business section, theaters, offices, hotels, etc., only by passing through a Negro section. This, together with the numerous disconnected areas given over in part to the Negroes, necessitates contact of the races in virtually all street cars, busses, etc. At the present time this situation does not often result in clashes between white and black. It does sometimes provoke deep feeling. This feature of the situation had much to do with bringing on the race riots in Washington City some

26

years ago and it greatly increases the danger of racial clashes at the present time. Such danger is increased by the fact that there is no separation of the races in public conveyances. Only tact and mutual forbearance, not universal characteristics of any race, can prevent future clashes, here or elsewhere.

Turning from the race, as such, to the grouping of the Negroes according to occupation, intellectual progress, social stratification, etc., some very interesting and instructive facts are quickly forced upon the observer. Some of these may be stated briefly here, reserving fuller discussion for the chapters that are to follow.

In Washington City, as elsewhere, the fullblood Negro is usually found in unskilled labor and but rarely in higher occupations requiring prolonged training and a high degree of specialization. There are exceptions to this statement. A limited number of fullblood Negroes have qualified for the more exacting fields of endeavor, and a few have made good in these fields. The number of such exceptional cases is not sufficiently large, as yet, to disprove the above statement nor to impair seriously its force. The fullblood Negro is often found working under the immediate supervision of a white foreman, often with a white man charged with the immediate oversight of each small group of Negroes employed at a common task. Much of the work of cleaning the streets is done by fullblood Negroes. Here, as elsewhere, the gravest injury to the white group falls upon the unskilled, unorganized white laborer. The white woman has the same disadvantage in domestic service and in other employment where she must compete with the Negro woman.

Again, in Washington City, as elsewhere, the mulatto element tends toward one extreme or the other. Either the mulatto rises above the average of the Negro or shows a marked tendency in the opposite direction. In the Government service he is very prominent and holds many desirable positions. Indeed, it is the mulatto who monopolizes much that is intended for the Negro. Theoretically, the two are grouped together, without discrimination. In reality, it is the mulatto who gets the benefits and who achieves position. This fact often obscures the large element of mulattoes who do not make good. There is such an element. The infusion of white blood carries with it some degree of the outlook of the white race and a share in its ambitions. Unrealized and unrealizable aspirations may result in a hopeless outlook, frustration, defeat. The position of the mulatto woman is deplorable.

In concluding this chapter a further word concerning the mulatto in Washington City may be added. There are here very few fullblood Negro teachers. The writer formerly made the acquaintance of two fullblood Negro teachers occupying important positions and doing highly creditable work. There may be, doubtless are, others; but the major part of the teachers belonging to the Negro race and employed in the District show clearly the infusion of white blood. There are very few fullblood Negro preachers holding important pastorates in the District, or elsewhere. This is especially true of the stronger churches. What is true of the ministry and of the teaching profession is equally evident in all the professions and other activities of the race. The so-called Negro problem in Washington City, as everywhere else in Continental United States, is really the problem of the mixed blood; a mulatto problem.

CHAPTER II

THE MULATTO

NO FEATURE of the race problem throughout the Americas is more important, or more insistent, than is that of racial intermixture. Yet, notwithstanding its vital importance to each of the three races primarily involved—the Indian, the Negro, and the Caucasian—there has been no persistent and no effective effort to bring these races to understand what is actually occurring or to comprehend its significance. Without such understanding, constructive action is improbable, if not impossible.

Concerning the Indian, little need be said. Undoubtedly there has been a slight ragged fringe of immorality as between the white and the red in the present territory of the United States. Elsewhere, this has been much more marked. Here a relatively small number of Indian-Caucasians owe their origin to such immoralities. Others in this Indian-Caucasian group have had as parents those who have had due regard for the conventionalities. A somewhat larger group, relatively, has arisen from the intermixture of Indian-Negro blood, with little attention paid to the conditions under which this mixture has occurred. In some instances, especially among the "red-bones" of the Atlantic seaboard and along the Gulf Coast, a very inferior type of white has been involved. The effort of the near-white to make the impression that his origin is Indian-Caucasian rather than Negro-Caucasian, is now pretty generally recognized as belonging among the ancestry myths.

In the preceding chapter there is given a statement of the number of Negroes in the United States at various dates in the past. Also a statement of the number residing in the District of Columbia, and an estimate of the number residing outside but near enough to the District to affect its social and its economic interests. Some reference was made to the mulatto, the mixed-blood element of the District population. In the present chapter this feature of the race problem is to be discussed more in detail and in national scope. The Negro problem in Washington City, possibly to a degree not fully duplicated anywhere else in the world, is complicated by the fact that so large a percentage of the Negroes here show an infusion of white blood. Even with the mulatto element eliminated, the problem would still present many difficulties, for the fullblood Negro would still create the economic ills involved in the competition between the Negro and the white laborer. But the mulatto is present—cannot be eliminated—and there is no feature of the present situation of the fullblood Negro, in the District of Columbia, or elsewhere, more hurtful or involving graver ills for the future than this dominance of the mulatto. It is the mulatto, rather than the fullblood Negro, who extends the range of interracial competition to those working in fields other than manual labor.

The Census returns giving the total Negro population of the United States; the number of fullblood Negroes; and the number of mulattoes from 1870 through 1920 are as follows:

TABLE IV

Year	Total Negro	Negro	% Negro	Mulatto	% Mulatto
1870	4,880,009	4,295,960	88.0	584,049	12.0
1890	7,488,676	6,337,980	84.8	1,132,060	15.2
1910	9,827,763	7,777,077	79.1	2,050,686	20.9
1920	10,463,131	8,802,577	84.1	1,660,554	15.9[1]

It will be noted here that the first three enumerations, beginning with that of 1870, show a fairly uniform rate of increase in mulattoes, both numerically and in percentage of total Negro population. It is clearly impossible, however, that the number of mulattoes should have increased from 1,132,060 in 1890 to 2,050,686 in 1910—918,626—and then decreased from 2,050,686 in 1910 to 1,660,554—390,132—between 1910 and 1920! The Census Bureau frankly admits

[1] See Bulletin No. 129, p. 15, Table II.

error here. The enumeration of 1920, is, therefore, worthless for the purposes of this study, as it has doubtless proved misleading to many who have not investigated the situation carefully. With the rate of increase of the preceding forty years maintained during this ten-year period, nearly 3,000,000 mulattoes would have been returned in 1920. Even so, the returns would probably have been too conservative.

The Census figures dealing with the number of mulattoes in the District of Columbia are given in the following table. The Census Bureau makes no effort to give the number of mulattoes after 1920.

TABLE V

Year	Total Negro	Negro	Mulatto	% Mulatto
1870	43,404	35,372	8,032	18.5
1890	75,572	55,736	19,836	26.2
1910	94,446	61,954	32,952	34.9[2]

A question arises concerning the accuracy of the Census returns dealing with the mulatto. The only possibility that an individual can form an opinion of value in this matter is by the use of some form of what is known as the "random sample" method of investigation. As applied in this case this method of investigation involves a study of various groups of Negroes and the classifying thus of a large number of individuals as accurately as possible. In these studies three divisions were made, as follows:

I—Negro, or those showing no infusion of white blood;

II—Mulatto, or those showing clearly the infusion of white blood; and

III—Doubtful, or those whose appearance, color, etc., are such as to indicate a slight intermixture. In such cases definite classification cannot be made without either a careful inspection—usually impossible—or a knowledge of the ancestry, which is likewise impossible in most cases. Here it is necessary to deal with two types of marginal cases. The first is composed

___

[2] Neither the reports of the Health Department nor the annual enumeration made by the Police Department returns mulattoes as such.

of those so nearly black as to present but few evidences of intermixture. These involve no serious interracial problem peculiar to themselves but are universally regarded as Negroes. Many of these may have a very light strain of white blood, acquired since their ancestors reached America, or their African ancestors were of mixed blood and their tribal color, therefore lighter than that of the typical Negro. Professor Herskovits evidently had this situation in mind when he wrote: "Only 20 to 30 percent of American Negroes are pure-blooded."

The second type is composed of those so nearly white that it is difficult to be sure that there is blood mixture. There are many instances in which dark-skinned Caucasians are darker in color than are some of the near-white mulattoes. Washington City affords many examples of this fact. These, with other kindred facts, render it very difficult to recognize, with any degree of certainty, some of the people composing this class and make it possible that fullblood Caucasians, of dark complexion, may be regarded as mulattoes. Where, however, a generation or two of a given family may be observed, it is usually possible, by observing for cases of atavism, to arrive at a fairly definite and dependable conclusion concerning the racial status of the group, and thus of the individual.

Applying the "random sample" method of investigation in the District of Columbia in 1914, it soon became evident that the Census figures were then much too low. Similar investigations, made in 1926 and again in 1949, lead to the same conclusion. It is very rarely the case that an observation made on the streets of Washington fails to reveal more than half the cases considered as of mixed blood. In some instances as high as 75 per cent of those observed were clearly of mixed blood!

In applying the "random sample" method here, some marked differences are to be noted when employment groups are studied. Fullblood percentages run very high where unskilled manual labor is being performed. On the other hand,

very few fullblood Negroes are found among the clerical em-
ployees of the Federal Government. The same is true in
reference to the City Government. As typical of the whole
field of Government service, the findings for the group employed at the Bureau of Printing and Engraving may be
offered. Of 597 Negroes observed entering or leaving the
premises and evidently employed there, 486, or 81.4 per cent,
were mulattoes; 105, or 17.58 per cent, were fullblood
Negroes; while 6 were classed as doubtful. This observation
was made in October, 1926. It is fairly representative of
similar observations made during the same year.

Observations made in 1949 show conditions unchanged
except for a more decided dominance of the mulatto over the
fullblood Negro, and a much more complete monopoly of
certain fields of employment by the Negro or the mulatto.
The 255,930 Negroes residing in the District in 1948 leave
little enough for the unskilled whites!

In reference to the mulatto, then, this much may be regarded as established fact. The mulatto now constitutes a
large portion of the total Negro population of the United
States as a whole, and a much larger portion of the total Negro
population of the District of Columbia. For the entire area of
Continental United States the mulatto now constitutes above
30 per cent of the total Negro population, but this statement
may be far too conservative. In the District of Columbia
at the present time (1949) the mulatto constituted a minimum of 50 per cent of the total Negro population. Personal
investigations show conclusively that the Census figures are
too low for the District of Columbia. There is every reason
to believe that the figures given for the whole of Continental
United States are sharply below the present status. Using the
term *mulatto* to include all Negroes showing any degree of
infusion of white blood, the Census figures for both areas are
certainly too low. Still, whether regarded as a minimum, or
even as a maximum, statement of the case, the Census figures
reveal clearly the seriousness of the situation.

Elsewhere attention is called to the distinction between those mulattoes who represent initial amalgamations and those who are "diffusion" mulattoes, or those born of mulatto, or of mulatto-Negro, parents. Carrying out this classification through the entire list of mulattoes who have achieved distinction, it is found that very many of the outstanding men and women of this group represent initial amalgamations. It has also been pointed out that, in so far as the ideals of the Negro are concerned, the distinction between the initial increment and the diffusion mulattoes is not generally made and, even if it should be made, it would prove of doubtful value. The yellow face tells the story of racial intermixture, and the yellow face cannot be permanently concealed.

Arising largely from those social conditions inevitably involved in his leadership, or in his prominence otherwise, there are certain limitations upon the usefulness of the mulatto as a factor in the uplift of the Negro race, as such. It is impossible to conceal racial intermixture as between the white and the black. Whether the individual mulatto be the product of an initial amalgamation or a diffusion case, the blood mixture is manifest to all and the effect upon the Negro masses is necessarily evil. It cannot be emphasized too often or too emphatically that the Negro is in need of right ideals so mediated as to create a social atmosphere compelling attention to primary moralities and forcing upon him an honest effort to protect his own race! *The mulatto, in direct proportion to his ability, his excellences morally, his achievements, becomes a menace to the fullblood Negro.* Here is the tragedy, the inescapable tragedy, of the mulatto problem. Behind the mulatto stand the masses of the Negro group, a fact which must be recognized if truly constructive work is to be done.

As a matter of fact, under existing conditions, the Negro and the mulatto alike encounter no effective inhibitions discouraging amalgamation. As the really successful element of the race, both must recognize a very limited number of men and women in outstanding positions of leadership and quite

34

generally proposed as examples for emulation. An examination of the color of the local representatives of this group, or the color of the members of this group as a whole, reveals the fact that the fullblood Negro is conspicuous chiefly for his absence. Almost all are mulattoes. Hence there arises for the thoughtful members of the race a powerful incentive to breed away from the true racial type. Negatively, this will involve reprobation, social disadvantage, for neither mother nor child. Positively, disregard of social conventions, of moral considerations, will place the resulting child in a class in which the chances of achievement in life are vastly greater than in the case of the fullblood Negro child. One of the most careful and accurate students of the Negro problem had formerly reached the conclusion that *the chances of the mulatto are thirty-four times those of the fullblood Negro child.* (See page 36.) *Some years later he changed his figures to 50 to 100 to 1 in favor of the mulatto.*[3]

For those interested in the uplift of the Negro a question arises here. How, in the face of this situation and in view of present racial contacts, is it possible, can it be possible, that the ideals of the Negro race here, or the ideals of the individual Negro, should be brought to a high standard or, where high, be preserved? The situation demands thorough study, exhaustive analysis; yet no feature of the race problem has been more persistently or more completely ignored, especially so by those white people actually engaged in educational or religious work intended for the uplift of the Negro race. In every interest of the race the mulatto now dominates completely, and where position, salary, or honor is involved, he has a practical monopoly. This is a fact of prime importance, one to which frequent reference must be made. It is well, at this point, to note in some detail the more important of the causes and the conditions producing and fostering the evil of amalgamation.

In the United States the mulatto, equally with the Negro,

[3] *Race Mixture,* E. B. Reuter, p. 126.

has been denied admission into the white race. From the beginning he has been classed with the race of the mother rather than that of the father. Even the negligible number of mulattoes born of white mothers have been, together with their offspring, considered as belonging to the Negro group. Where the Negro has fared well, the same has been true of the mulatto; where the Negro has fared badly, the mulatto has shared his hardships. On the other hand, the exceptional mulatto has, within the Negro group, achieved leadership to the extent of domination in the business, the professional, the educational, and the religious interests and activities of the race.

The extent of this domination is not generally recognized, nor is its significance realized by either race, nor has it been possible as yet to arouse even the thoughtful element in either race to a realization of what the present situation involves for all concerned. As a consideration of the status of the mulatto and of related features of the race problem is essential in any comprehensive study of the causes and of the conditions affecting the racial integrity of the American Negro, some pertinent facts may be offered.

Reference has already been made to the work of Professor E. B. Reuter. With great care and thoroughness he has gathered information concerning members of the Negro race in the United States who have achieved any marked degree of prominence along worthy lines. In a table entitled "Relative Prominence of the Negro and the Mulatto in Selected Fields of Endeavor"—twelve in number—he gives 2,129 names as worthy of mention, 1,844 men and 285 women. Of the men, 206 are listed as black and 1,638 as mulatto. Summarizing his investigations upon this point, covering 4,291 cases of those prominent enough to merit consideration, he finds 447 blacks and 3,844 mulattoes. At page 314 he writes: *"On the basis accepted for the purposes of this study, the chances of the mulatto developing into a leader of the race are thirty-four times as great as are the chances of the Black child."* [4] The italics are ours. This quotation merits the highest possible emphasis.

The figures quoted above make clear two vitally important points: *First, that there are fullblood Negroes capable of leadership; and second, that the mulatto, rather than the Negro, now holds the leadership of the race.* These and similar facts bring the student to the heart of this matter. All that has been done in behalf of the Negro has been done upon the individualistic basis—with a strange disregard for the ethical interests of the individual—rather than in view of the interests of the two races as such. This has led, in so far as the Negro is concerned, to a general suspension of those moral and ethical principles which, enjoined upon the individual through religious sanctions, constitute an impelling force for the conservation of the ideals of the white race, especially as these ideals pertain to its family life.

In order to grasp the full significance of this situation the student of the race problem should acquaint himself with the activities of the race and with its leadership in as many fields as possible. Everywhere, he will find the mulatto in control— usually exercising a leadership unchallenged by the fullblood Negro. Here again Professor Reuter's work is invaluable. Frequent reference will be made to it as furnishing concrete facts supporting and illustrating our contentions. For convenience, we may deal with the activities of the race under four general divisions: Business, Politics, Education, and Religion. It is not possible to assign each individual exclusively to one of these divisions, for the activities of some cover two or more spheres. This feature of the situation, however, does not alter the facts of leadership.

The Mulatto in Business

It is not possible to deal as definitely with the group of Negroes who are engaged in some form of business as it is

[4] In a later study this advantage is given as 50 to 100 to 1 in favor of the mulatto. See *Race Mixture*, E. B. Reuter, p. 126.

with those of other callings. Increasingly, the Negro group is owning and operating farms, mills, groceries, etc. There is reason to regard this group as containing a higher percentage of fullblood Negroes than may be found in any other similar group; but the relative prominence of the mulatto seems to increase as the simpler and less significant forms of business are passed and the more exacting fields are considered.

Of a general list of names of Negroes preëminently successful in business, 158 in number, twelve are classed as black and 146 as mulatto. Of thirty-nine bank presidents whose racial status is known to Professor Reuter, four were classified as black, and thirty-five as mulatto. The National Negro Business League is, perhaps, the most important business organization of the race, and its ethnic composition is correspondingly important. For 1914-1915, its officers are given as one black and eleven mulatto; its executive committee, fourteen in number, was composed wholly of mulattoes. The life members numbered 235. Of these, the classification of sixteen was not known; seventeen were black, and 202 were mulattoes!

It is quite manifest from these figures that *there are full-blood Negroes capable of managing business interests successfully,* but that the number achieving marked success under existing circumstances and conditions is relatively insignificant. A contributing cause for this poor showing made by the fullblood Negro in business may be found, in part, in conditions existing in the schools of the race. No general effort in behalf of the fullblood Negro has been made. It is certain that the business situation in general involves no compelling force leading the race to prize, or to preserve, its racial integrity.

Turning from this rather general survey of the relative prominence of the Negro and the mulatto in business to a necessarily incomplete reference to conditions in the District of Columbia, the following may be noted:

There are quite a few Negroes engaged in small business enterprises; but these depend largely upon the patronage of

38

their own race for success. There is progress in reference to the ownership and the operation of various enterprises, but certain limitations are manifest. There is evidence of insufficient coöperation; and, in most cases, where success has been achieved, it has been due to a dominant personality, the permanence depending too much upon the personal element. Negroes in the employ of the Government—exclusive of soldiers and sailors—are said to receive more than $60,000,000 annually. A very large part of this huge sum is paid to Negroes in the District, and this is sufficient to support quite a volume of trade and to support quite a bit of professional patronage. The partial segregation existing in the District unquestionably gives to the Negro businessman and to the professional Negro a better opportunity to live by the patronage of Negro people. Segregation has this value for the Negro business and professional men everywhere.

Particularly in the cities there is a manifest tendency for certain classes of foreigners to locate in, or near, the areas occupied by the Negro or where there is a large rural Negro population. Jewish merchants are especially in evidence, as are tradesmen of Mediterranean origin or extraction. There is little competition between the Negro merchant and the older American white stock everywhere. There are, however, numerous instances in which the latter have been driven out of business by both the Jew and the Italian.

In reference to the business situation in general and to the Negro's participation in business enterprises, this general statement may be made: The Negro is, in increasing numbers, entering the field of business. Lack of capital and lack of business experience exercise a restraining influence, and lack of credit forces many who attempt to develop a business to operate on a small scale and with little risk through credit extended to customers. In a general way it is true, despite a few exceptions, that the mulatto is far in advance of the full-blood Negro in point of commercial interests, and that, except in simpler enterprises, the same advantage seems to lie with the mulatto here as elsewhere. Something of this may be due to the fact that the mulatto predominates so completely in the schools open to the race and that he, rather than the fullblood Negro, has received the training requisite for success in business, as well as in the professions.

Should the time come when the American Negro, wearied with the struggle here, sets for himself the goal of a country of his own, a chance for his race, that element of the race which has experience in commercial affairs will be in position to render a service of most vital importance. If segregation, proscription, race prejudice, added to racial self-respect, increase the number of those thus prepared beforehand for racial service, the value to the Negro race of these supposedly destructive forces will have been demonstrated. It is this feature of the situation, whether in Washington or elsewhere, which gives to the Negro in business and in the professions his chief interest and value. Aside from this interest, this hope of ultimate autonomy of race, the rewards to the business and to the professional Negro will probably prove circumscribed, if not unduly meager. The Negro merchant, especially in the rural districts and in the smaller towns, due to lack of adequate capital and to lack of adequate buildings and equipment, does not, as a rule, conduct a creditable establishment. At little expense, the typical Negro merchant exercises in his sphere the same depressing influence of racial competition noted in other fields of endeavor. The very high percentage of mulattoes found in the successful group of Negro merchants, as in all other Negro groups, is the central fact of the present situation for all who are concerned for the welfare of the two races, as such.

The Mulatto in Politics

Elsewhere will be found a fuller treatment of the political aspects of the Negro problem, especially as these affect racial intermixture. Some reference should be made here to past political activities and to their results. Both the present and the future have their roots in the past, and only as the past is understood may there be hope that constructive effort may prevail. It is in the District of Columbia that the political aspects of the Negro problem may be studied to best advantage.

The Negro became a disturbing element in the life of the nation long before he was aware of the fact that he was of the least political significance. His participation in political activities dates from his emancipation and began under circumstances and conditions which would have proved very difficult for a people with far wider experience and far greater preparation than the Negro of 1865-70 possessed. He found himself between two powerful groups of white people just emerging from a bitter prolonged Civil War. The victorious North promised much to the Negro and stimulated impossible hopes. The defeated South, knowing the Negro better than did the North and confronted by the problems he created not as abstractions but as grim realities, was driven, largely by Northern intervention, to otherwise needless extremes. Dominated by white men, whom none now defend, the Negro's brief period of ascendancy in parts of the South was marked by conditions so horrible that this section still remembers them in connection with the Negro in politics. It is needless to say that the typical Southern white man does not look kindly upon the Negro politician, and it is only in rare cases that such are able, or have the opportunity, to serve their people in a constructive way.

Much of the acute racial antagonism since 1865 has grown out of politics, and there is still, wherever the Negroes vote in any numbers, a probability that they may, by voting as a group, wield the "balance of power," a contingency which has, so far, prevented the South from developing a second political party of sufficient strength to make an appeal to the Negro vote worth while. Walter White claims that the Negro now holds the balance of power in at least "seventeen states with 281 votes in the electoral college." [5] There will likely

[5] *A Man Called White*, Walter White, p. 262.

be some disturbance to party lines in those sections of the North into which large numbers of Negroes have recently gone. The race riots and the racial antagonisms in the North preceding the outbreak of the first European War will probably recur, with added complications and intensity, should business depression ever again reach the point of too severe a struggle for existence. The "poor white" of the South has never known anything other than the competition of Negro labor, slave or free, and has accepted the low standard of living involved because inherited. The white laborer of the North and of the West will not voluntarily consent to the necessary lowering of his standards when brought into competition with cheaper Negro labor, and should not be forced to do so. The political party, therefore, which appeals to the Negro vote in these sections will probably not be able to hold the vote of the laboring class of the white group.

In the political field the leadership of the mulatto has, from the beginning, been quite as pronounced and as complete as in other fields. Here, again, the work of Professor Reuter affords the detailed statement of fact. Of the two Negroes who have been members of the United States Senate, one is classed as a mulatto and the other as a Croatan Indian—Negro-Indian? Of the twenty members of the Negro race who have held seats in the National House of Representatives, three were black and seventeen were mulattoes. Of nineteen members of the race who were otherwise prominent during Reconstruction, four were classed as black and fifteen as mulattoes. Of six Lieutenant Governers furnished by this race during Reconstruction, all were mulattoes. Under President Taft, according to the *Negro Year Book,* there were fourteen "more important political positions" allotted to this race, all of which were filled by mulattoes. Later National Administrations have been quite liberal in their dealings with the mulatto.

These facts are quite sufficient, understood in all their bearings, to show *how the Federal Government has thrown*

42

the weight of its influence into the scale against whatever effort the Negro might have made to preserve his racial integrity. This has been done—is still being done—through the distribution of patronage at the disposal of the victorious party, especially when this party is the one making the stronger historic appeal for the Negro vote. The mulatto dominates completely the political organizations of the Negro. He is, therefore, in position to control the share of patronage allotted to the Negro race. Whether it be on account of superior ability found in the mulatto group or for some other reason, *it is unquestionably true that virtually all the more important government positions set apart for the Negro race in the United States fall to the mulatto.* The figures are not available, and it is, therefore, not possible to give a definite statement of the relative number of Negroes and mulattoes in government service. It is manifestly true, however, that except in less important positions and in those requiring little more than manual labor, fullblood Negroes are virtually not employed in government service. (See page 36.)

Conditions in Washington City afford an easily grasped demonstration of the closing statement of the preceding paragraph. A tour of any one of the Government buildings will furnish a concrete example, especially any building in which a considerable number of Negroes are employed, as is the case in the Bureau of Printing and Engraving. Doubtless this predominance of the mulatto in Government service has attracted mulattoes from every part of the United States and has made this city especially attractive to the mulatto.

The Mulatto and Education

The educational interests of the Negro race in the United States are as completely dominated and monopolized by the mulatto as is the case in the business and in the political spheres. As a force in shaping its ideals and in determining its outlook, the educational interests of the race are even

43

more important than are its business and its political interests and activities.

The public schools are not designed to produce or to train
leaders. This is, necessarily, left to higher institutions—high
schools, technical schools, colleges, and universities. The
State is under obligation to furnish at least elementary educational opportunities for all its youth. Already burdened
with the absolute necessity of maintaining separate schools
for the two races, the Southern States are unable to make
separate provision for the mulatto group. With those schools
founded by private philanthropy or by religious organizations, the case is different. These have, throughout their
existence, but especially in the earlier years of freedom,
been in position to choose their students. They have, therefore, been in position to make an effective stand for the
highest social, ethical, and religious ideals. Through the
educated teacher and minister, the ideals and the sanctions
obtaining in the higher institutions influence, through the
local schools and churches, the ethical practices and the
ideals obtaining in the local communities.

The understanding by the Negro people of the problems
confronting the Negro race depends largely upon its teachers.
The attitude toward race purity, in so far as it depends upon
the teachings of the Negro public schools, is likely to be the
counterpart of the teachings and the practices of the higher
institutions of learning. The vital point to be noted, and
guarded, in reference to the Negro public school in its relation to the racial integrity of the American Negro is that
whatever ideals and practices prevail in these higher institutions will, sooner or later, obtain in the grade schools
and, through these, in the local Negro communities as well.

*The higher institutions of learning maintained by, or for,
the Negro are dominated by the mulatto, both in teaching
force and in their student groups.* Reference to Professor
Reuter's work will again afford a working basis of fact for
this part of our study. At page 271 he gives the results of an

44

investigation of conditions obtaining in twenty-five Negro colleges and universities. In 1916 there were enrolled in these institutions 9,172 students, of whom 7,567 were classed as mulattoes and 1,605 as "black," not necessarily all full-blood Negroes.

Turning to individual institutions, Morgan College, of Baltimore, is credited with 450 students, *all mulattoes.* Wilberforce University is credited with 450 students, of whom 394 are classed as mulattoes and forty-six as black. Of twenty-nine Negro educational institutions of college or university grade and presided over by other than white men, three had presidents classed as black, while twenty-six had mulatto presidents. Of seventeen state agricultural and mechanical colleges, "one had a white president, one a Negro president, and fourteen had mulatto presidents," with one unclassified. Tuskegee Institute has had one fullblood Negro as president, a man of ability and one of the finest type of his race—Major R. R. Moton. This institution was, however, founded by Dr. Booker T. Washington, an initial increment mulatto, the son of a white man and a fullblood Negro woman. Of the teaching force of this institution, Professor Reuter has this to say: "This school has a teaching force of approximately two hundred. Of this number, nine, none of whom are in high position, are Negroes, who generally pass as full blood. One hundred and eighty-four are persons of mixed blood." [6] See also footnote quoting Mr. William Archer, a distinguished English writer, as follows: "Indeed, I saw no one in high position at Tuskegee who would not, with very little lightening of hue, have been taken without question for a white man." [6] This was written during the administration of the late Dr. Booker T. Washington. The late Major R. R. Moton, who succeeded Dr. Washington, was unquestionably a fullblood Negro, a man of fine character and unquestioned ability. Professor Carver, noted industrial chemist, a fullblood Negro, was also employed at

[6] *The Mulatto in the United States* E. B. Reuter pp. 250 to 309.

Tuskegee. Moton and Carver show what might have been accomplished had fullblood Negro youth of recognized ability been sought out and trained for racial leadership.

Tuskegee Institute, together with the Hampton Normal and Agricultural Institute, Hampton, Va., stands for the practical training and the industrial development of the race and deservedly occupies a foremost place among the institutions upon which the race must depend for the training of its industrial leaders. The above facts are given as furnishing an example of what is true, even more decidedly, in the higher literary institutions maintained by, or for, the Negro race in the United States.

There can be no questioning the fact that the higher grade institutions for the education of the Negro race are dominated, practically monopolized, by the mulatto both in the composition of the student body and, where Negroes are employed, even more decidedly in the composition of the teaching force. It is, therefore, evident that in the future, even more decidedly than in the past or the present, the race will, in its educational interests, its intellectual life generally, be under the domination of the mulatto unless a definite, and successful, effort is made to train a fullblood Negro leadership, carefully selected from the more highly endowed fullblood Negro youth and given that type of training demanded for successful dealing with the problems now confronting the race. *The relatively few fullblood Negroes who have, even under prevailing conditions, made good in various callings, demonstrate the fact that a sufficient number of capable fullblood Negroes may be found.*

Conditions here pointed out are such as may well discourage utterly the thoughtful, aspiring fullblood Negro, especially the fullblood Negro student. Correct evaluation of the situation and the despair incident to an understanding of conditions existing in such educational institutions have been expressed to the writer by several fullblood Negroes. In most cases, however, the personal element, approaching jealousy, was uppermost in the minds of such fullblood Negro students rather than the racial significance of this predominance of the mulatto.

The gravest need of the present time in Negro education is for a well-equipped, well-endowed, well-manned institution for the training of the leaders of the race, and to which only fullblood Negroes may be admitted. Such an institution might well become the means of promoting worthy race pride and racial self-respect, thus becoming most helpful to the race. *The fullblood Negro does not have a fair chance in those institutions where the teachers are wholly or partially white and the student body overwhelmingly mulatto.* This is equivalent to saying that the fullblood Negro does not really have a fair chance at any of the higher educational institutions maintained by, or for, the Negro race in America. Even though the situation wholly escapes his notice and the fullblood Negro remains, therefore, unconscious of its significance, *his education fails dismally in the matter of implanting personal and racial self-respect.* It is a sad commentary upon eighty years of effort in behalf of the Negro that this, the most vital issue involved, has had virtually no place in the program followed and that little or no thought is now given to it by those seeking to assist the race! Under the circumstances, it was wholly unreasonable to expect the ideals of the Negro to rise higher than the standards set for him by his white teachers, or for his practices to go beyond that which was accepted by his white teachers and his white religious guides!

The Mulatto and Religion

Closely allied to the educational interests of the Negro race, but in many respects of even greater importance, is the field of religion. Great numbers of Negroes who have had but meager educational advantages, if any at all, have been definitely influenced by some form of church life and religious teaching. In most instances Negro churches are now

47

independent of the white and undoubtedly serve, in addition to distinctly religious ends, to help the race toward racial self-sufficiency. Other of their churches and religious organizations are more dependent upon the various white churches—and white purses. In the earlier period of the freedom of the race, dependence upon the various white agencies was excusable, and it is to the credit of the race that, with its advance along other lines, it has voluntarily gained independence along religious lines.

It is undoubtedly true that the earlier years of freedom brought not only opportunity to assist the Negro but also, for those voluntarily undertaking the task, the responsibility of fixing the ideals which were to prevail among the Negro Christians, if not with the entire race. The vital mistakes of this period were made, not by the Negro—he was virtually helpless—but by white people, and were due to a strange lack of foresight in the matter of the protection of the Negro in his race life and in his home life. The more deplorable his condition in reference to home and family life under slavery, the graver the need for right instruction *and for right example* at the beginning of his freedom. This feature of the situation, instead of being met fairly as the outstanding need of the Negro of 1865, seems rather to have been treated as justification for excusing the race from the struggle to rise to right ideals and correct practices. Specifically, *bastard origin, openly known and unquestioned, was not only not allowed to militate against the individual; it was actually in his favor.* In thus dealing with this early situation, precedents were established, and attitudes based upon these have prevailed until, in the face of the millions of mulattoes, protest now seems novel, if not radical!

The activities of all the churches in behalf of the Negro are open to the same criticism as are those of individuals and of other organizations, whether philanthropic or religious. So far as we have been able to learn, none of these, North or South, makes, or has ever made, any distinction between the Negro and the mulatto. As a result of this "hands-off" policy, this failure to protect the race at this vital point, the domination of the mulatto is quite as marked in the religious interests of the Negro race as in any other field. Without inquiry into family history, mulattoes, even those representing flagrant initial amalgamations, are employed as teachers in those institutions under control of the churches and also as preachers!

A few references to Professor Reuter's comprehensive investigations will show how complete is this domination of the mulatto in the various Negro churches, especially in administrative affairs. In 1914 the nine bishops of the Colored Methodist Episcopal Church were all mulattoes. Of the eleven general officers of this church, nine were mulattoes, with two unclassified. Of twenty-seven bishops of the African Methodist Episcopal Church, four were classed as black and twenty-three as mulatto. Of the eight bishops of the African Methodist Zion Church, two were classed as black and six as mulatto. The officers of the National Baptist Convention (Colored), twelve in number, are all given as mulatto, as is the case with the five general officers of the New England Baptist Convention (Colored).

It is not necessary to give details further, as is done in the thorough and complete presentation characteristic of Professor Reuter's work. His "study has brought together the names of 643 members of the Negro ministry. . . . When the names previously mentioned have been removed there remain 580 persons. Ninety-five of these are considered full blood, and 485 are known to be mulattoes." Let it be remembered that these figures deal with virtually all the most prominent representatives of the Negro ministry in the United States. Here, again, the mulatto greatly outnumbers the fullblood Negro, but the ninety-five fullblood Negroes who are worthy of mention in a group so small, relatively, are quite sufficient to demonstrate what might have been

49

accomplished had right ideals prevailed and had practical effort been made to realize such ideals.

As in all others who enter upon a careful study of conditions existing in the ministry of the Negro churches, much is found by Professor Reuter that is distinctly discouraging to the friends of the race. He writes: "The Negro preachers, on the average, are not a particularly superior class of men. As a rule, they are uneducated and frequently profoundly ignorant. Morally they are perhaps inferior to any group of professional men among the Negroes." Yet, with the mass of the race it is true that the Negro preacher, good or bad, is one of the most potent factors in the situation.

There is, however, an instinctive recoil from statements which condemn indiscriminately. There are Negro preachers who are wholly unfit, and some are, undoubtedly, grossly immoral—possibly, in view of all the antecedents, nonmoral is a more accurately descriptive term. It is also true that various organizations, especially those local in character, representing the religious interests of the race, often prove unable, or unwilling, to eliminate the offenders and the undesirables. Yet there are Negro congregations keenly alive at this point, and there are Negro ministers who are morally above reproach and who are doing a work sane and effective in behalf of their people. These must, however, do their work under unfair conditions, all but driving them to compromise, or silence, upon vital racial issues or to lose their pulpits. Few Negro preachers could attack the mulatto problem without disastrous consequences to themselves. The same is true of many white pastors whose work is located in districts where there is special need for plain speaking.

What Professor Reuter, in common with many others who have written upon this feature of the race problem, fails to stress duly is the underlying causes producing these conditions and results so justly subject to adverse criticism. The results, the adverse conditions, are quite apparent and subject to scientific analysis and classification. It is easy to

attribute to antecedents, to race, to social status, to ignorance, results which cannot be wholly explained in this way.
Until the relation of the mulatto to the fullblood Negro
as an individual and to the Negro problem as a whole is
understood in all its bearings and its influence made plain,
especially to the fullblood Negro himself, there is little
prospect for improvement.

Discussing the racial integrity of the American Negro
some years ago, the following was written: "So far as we
have been able to ascertain, no religious organization, North
or South, makes, or has ever made, any consistent distinction between the Negro and the mulatto. Without reference to family history, mulattoes are employed as teachers
and as preachers. The result is what might be logically expected. The mulatto avails himself of the opportunities
offered. What type of morality can he inculcate? Will not
every success achieved and every honor won react unfavorably upon the Negro? If the reader will take the pains to
ascertain the complexion of the ministry of any of the
religious organizations of the Negro he will find that, where
the Negro's greatest need lies, the least foresight has been
exercised in his behalf, and that the moral and regenerating
forces of Christianity have been largely neutralized by the
object lessons thus furnished. Religion should give a wholesome moral atmosphere, as well as correct moral ideals.
Otherwise, what is built with one hand is torn down by the
other. Certainly religion should not vie with political
parties for the first place as patron, if not promoter, of racial
destruction. Here, as elsewhere, patronage must be considered as virtual endorsement."

Again: "Mistakes have been made in the past and are still
being made, and the interests of both races demand that
such changes shall be made in dealings with the Negro race
as shall hold it rigidly to the same moral and ethical standards as are applied in other races. In our judgment of the
moral lapses of the Negro there is call for abounding charity,

along with discriminating insight. Lacking the latter, in the exercise of that type of charity in evidence in the past the friends of the race, as well as others, have vitiated the moral standards of the race, robbed Christianity itself largely of its moral and regenerating power for the race, and have left but little to furnish that imperative incentive to right living of which the race, as a whole, stands so much in need. With the moral and ethical standards actually suspended in reference to race and family in the case of the Negro by those attempting to conduct his education and his moral training, it is not strange that the Negro himself suspends them—on occasion. With mulattoes as its political leaders, as the teachers of its youth, and dominating its pulpits, we see no hope whatever of any marked improvement or moral uplift in the character of the race—as a race."

These paragraphs were written more than twenty years ago. At that time the effect of this strange attitude of its white friends upon the race in the particular matter of its racial integrity was chiefly in mind; but it becomes increasingly evident that this suspension of standards in the sex life and in the home life of the Negro influences the race throughout the whole range of its interests. There are those who rise above these unfavorable conditions, but these conditions and the attitudes associated with them undoubtedly make the struggle of the race for the preservation of its racial integrity infinitely difficult.

Major Earnest Sevier Cox, Richmond, Va., makes this statement: "The most subtle, as it is the most dangerous, miscegenationist trend in the South at the present time operates under the cloak of Christianity." Other thoughtful writers are being driven to the same conclusion. There is, indeed, a grave danger that, as this situation comes to be more generally understood, the moral leadership of the churches will suffer because of this failure to deal constructively with miscegenation. Against one of the gravest wrongs possible, a wrong that cannot be concealed, has been interposed only silence. Is this the silence of ignorance of the true situation, or is it the silence of indifference, or is it the silence of those who see and understand but purposely ignore? No one need question the honesty, the sincerity, of those members of the white race who have sought to assist the Negro race, but their insight, their activities, must be evaluated by the results actually produced. *The outstanding result is the failure to give to the Negro race a sane racial pride and outlook, together with a compelling religious zeal for its racial preservation.*

The generally recognized characteristics of the race, together with the experiences through which the American Negro has passed, make it all the more necessary that those details of right living, which may be safely left to the individual conscience in other groups, should, with the majority of the Negroes, be explicitly taught both by precept and by example, especially by the latter. The matter having never been laid upon the conscience of the race, directly and unequivocally, it is not just to hold the race as solely to blame for existing conditions. Censure must fall upon those, North and South, who have, in matters vital alike to character and to constructive religious faith, vitiated the ideals of the Negro by tacitly accepting and virtually approving his moral lapses instead of impressing, by energetic disapprobation of their breach, fundamental moral principles.

The figures already quoted and the facts given and discussed indicate, with sufficient fullness and definiteness, the completeness with which the mulatto dominates the business, the political, the educational, and the religious activities of the Negro race in the United States. Conditions in the schools, especially in the colleges and universities devoted to the education and the training of leaders for the race, indicate that the leadership of the Negro here must quickly pass even more decidedly and completely into the hands of the mulatto unless radical changes are made and these institutions brought to render practical assistance in the matter of the preservation of the racial integrity of the Negro. *Under present conditions, especially under present leadership, there is little to convince the fullblood Negro that his racial integrity is worth preserving. There is much to convince him it is not worthy of serious consideration.*

From this general survey of the situation of the two races in the United States, it may be seen that the influences radiating from our political, our educational, and our religious activities and institutions, so far as these affect the Negro, unite in forming a subtle, but constant, menace to Negro character, as well as to the racial integrity of the Negro, a menace none the less destructive because largely negative, or indirect. Too much has been credited to "race and previous condition of servitude," forgetting that, in so far as these had proved confusing to Negro thought and degrading to practical conduct, the need for clear-cut ethical instruction and correct moral example was indicated. Race, social status, and its past history are still accepted in certain quarters as sufficient to excuse most of the wrongs to which the Negro race is especially prone. *Thus its ethical code, primitive enough at best, is vitiated; religion becomes for the mass of the Negroes painfully near to being nonmoral; and the great body of the race loses the elevating effect of an all but compulsory effort to realize high moral ideals in daily living.* Every detail of the wrong thus done the Negro reacts with pitiless directness upon the white race.

It is difficult for any white person to ascertain the exact point of view, the social ideals, or the ethical standards of the individual Negro, or those of the race. It is, therefore, difficult to ascertain definitely the extent to which a different standard is consciously recognized by the Negro as quite proper for himself, although it is clearly manifest that a decidedly lower standard is applied by the white race in its requirements of the Negro than obtains, theoretically, within the white race, and is actually achieved in representative circles of this race.

54

It is also difficult for the untrained white person to measure accurately the effect upon his race of the presence of the Negro race. It is inevitable that, due to the presence of the mulatto group in the United States, our whole civilization must be subjected to an abnormal stress. The facts fully warrant the assertion that all our moral, social, and religious safeguards are proving utterly inadequate for the complete protection of either race. The cumulative nature of the evil of amalgamation involves graver difficulties for the future than have been encountered in the past. It seems now that, in many cases, if not generally, *race prejudice, rather than reason, or even religious conviction, affords the more effective protection for the Negro race in the United States!* To what may the white race look for protection?

Professor Reuter has pointed out, clearly and definitely, that the mulatto child has a very decided average advantage over the fullblood Negro child. To what extent is this situation understood by Negro and mulatto motherhood and to what extent does it account for the initial increment of racial intermixture?

It may be true that in the great majority of instances of initial racial intermixture the persons involved are too low in the moral scale and in the social scale—often intellectually as well—to be concerned with the dictates of reason, but are led by unbridled passion. Yet among the forces promoting amalgamation a large place must be given to the desire of Negro and of mulatto motherhood to improve the condition of the offspring. It is not claimed that this purpose is always present, nor that the influences mentioned are always positive, nor that they are consciously felt and followed in every instance of initial amalgamation. There are indications, however, that this is true in an increasing percentage of such cases. The fact that no conscience has been developed definitely and specifically concerning this evil; that the evil has been, and still is, approved in so many practical ways— these and other factors have left the evil free to take whatever course it would, or have given it effective encouragement through actual approval and manifest endorsement.

That conditions here discussed have produced unfortunate attitudes, and that this desire to improve the chances in life of the offspring is responsible for much of the initial increment of amalgamation, is the opinion of other students of this aspect of the race problem. It is plainly stated by Thomas, as follows: "That Negroes have a conscious sense of degradation, which they falsely attribute to their color, is shown by their eagerness to get as far away as possible from black shades. *It is this craving for a light color and better hair for their offspring which is responsible for many of the illegitimate children of Negro motherhood.*" [1] The italics are ours. For further expressions of similar opinion, a large number of quotations and references might be given. Indeed, it is hardly fair to the intelligence—the intellectuality—of the race to assume that it is incapable of grasping the facts concerning amalgamation, or that it is incapable of understanding their significance, or that its leaders have failed to do so. The white group in America is here attributing to the Negro its own brand of insight!

It will be noted that Thomas, himself a diffusion mulatto, places the incentive on the basis of the physical characteristics of the offspring—color, hair, etc. Other considerations are certainly present. Beyond mere physical characteristics, Negro and mulatto motherhood is certainly seeing possibilities before children of mixed blood which are practically denied to children of pure Negro descent. More or less generally, *Negroes, and especially mulattoes, are coming to look upon racial intermixture as a means of thwarting the exclusiveness of the white race. Upon the part of many of these, present conditions and especially the status of racial intermixture are cause for open exultation.*

In the face of this rapid increase of mixed bloods, the few who have given the matter any thought whatever have usually

[1] *The American Negro*, Thomas, p. 408.

assumed that this increase is now due to the diffusion of white blood throughout the Negro race by the natural increase of mulattoes and by the mixture occurring between the Negro and the mulatto. There is a widespread belief that racial intermixture, involving the fullblood white, has virtually ceased and that the initial increment of racial intermixture is now negligible.

An examination of the evidence available shows that this is not true. In some sections of the North, especially in a few of the larger urban centers, there are a limited number of interracial marriages, usually between Negro or mulatto men and white women. These white women who marry Negroes are rarely representative of any desirable status in their own race. A few are visionary theorists, or misguided religionists. The larger part belong to groups by no means a credit to their own race. Unfortunately, the vilest and the most degraded white man or woman, or black man or woman, as well as the misguided theoriest or religionist of either race, has in his keeping the ultimate results of racial contacts as registered in racial intermixture. The initial increment has never been relatively large as compared to this secondary diffusion, but it has been in evidence all the while and is now certainly larger than at any preceding time. No program ignoring this fact can conserve the higher interests of either race. Such a program may command the endorsement alike of religionists and of theorists generally and the resources of individual philanthropists and of "foundations," but it is essentially vicious in that it fails to bring to bear upon the evil of amalgamation, directly and unequivocally, the character and the intelligence of either race.

In the South the intermixture of the white and the black races has been wholly illegal. Further, it has occurred almost wholly through the white male and the Negro or the mulatto female. Had the purity of the two races here been in the keeping of the Southern white woman, the mulatto problem in the South would not now be a serious one. The writer knows personally of but one case in which a white woman in the South has given birth to a child by a Negro father. She was a poor, illiterate woman, of low intelligence, and not of previous chaste character. At the time of conception she was employed temporarily as servant in a rural home. The Negro man was a laborer on this farm and, permitted in the kitchen for his meals, thus came in contact˙ with this woman. Had there been no such privilege extended to the Negro, had the white woman been accorded the protection which her low intelligence and her deplorable moral status indicated, it is quite certain that this case would not have occurred. It is the ever-present threat of racial intermixture which justifies, or rather demands, racial segregation, especially separation of the lowest strata of the two races.

It is, in so far as the South is concerned, chiefly the immature and the immoral white males who have fastened the evil of racial intermixture upon America. In this evil a class of Negro and of mulatto women have proved more than willingly complaisant. Statements which include all Negro and all mulatto women in this class are quite as grossly unjust, and false, as are those which include all Southern white men. Yet there is, unquestionably, a very considerable number of such women, and they subject the unstable white man to a wholly unfair stress, a stress which is constantly present and which may at any time easily become destructive. Every white youth, whether he yield or not, runs the gauntlet of this class of Negro and mulatto women. They are present and their character is known. There is virtually no risk of legal penalty; there is too little risk of social penalty. There is a terrible hazard growing out of the diseases attendant upon vice. In the Northern cities the Negro man comes in contact with a class of white women who lack racial pride, as well as other desirable attitudes and characteristics. Some of these marry Negro or mulatto men. Others enmesh numbers of them in illegal and immoral unions or in temporary immoral associations. In many respects the race problem is now more serious in New York City and in Chicago than it is anywhere in the South.

Reference has been made elsewhere to the very limited number of mulattoes who have achieved leadership in the Negro race, and some reference has been made to the effect of such leadership upon the ideals of the race, especially upon the ideals and the outlook of the fullblood Negro. In order that the reader may realize the details involved, it is well to study a wide range of specific instances—in this case, prominent mulattoes. A typical case will suffice for our purposes. Very many such might be given.

Among the mulattoes who have attained marked success and who have to their credit worthy achievements, the late Dr. Booker T. Washington is an outstanding example and a study of this remarkable man may well illustrate several matters of vital importance. His autobiography, *Up From Slavery*, is a well-written book and presents very tactfully the story of his life. Throughout his life he accepted the classification which assigned him to the Negro race. His mother was a fullblood Negress, a slave; his father, a fullblood Caucasian. In point of race, therefore, he was neither white nor black, a fact which should be kept steadily in mind by all those who would keep their bearings in their thinking concerning racial matters? *To which element in his ancestry did he owe his ability and his practical efficiency?* This is a legitimate question in reference to every outstanding mulatto.

Dr. Washington, as was the case with several other prominent mulattoes of the past generation, was born a slave, a fact which must go far toward excusing the irregularity of the mother. In his earlier lifework his illegitimate birth was of great sentimental value to him and was used in such a way as to prove a great help rather than a hindrance, especially with Northern audiences and with his Northern supporters. He was tactful and skillful in the use he made of the outstanding facts of his life: his birth as a slave; his fullblood slave mother and the characteristics attributed to her; the unknown white father, who did nothing for him; and many other details. He was fond of picturing his mother, himself, and even the unknown white father as victims of slavery. Where should the responsibility for the greatly increased rate of racial intermixture under freedom be placed?

As one reads Dr. Washington's autobiography, so inspiring when only the surface is considered but so tragic to those who look more deeply, two questions may well arise: Could any white man, laboring under the handicap of known illegitimate birth, have accomplished so much? And what effect did the manifest fact of his illegitimate and bi-racial origin have upon his students and upon others of the Negro race who came under his influence? Glowing accounts are given of his numerous oratorical triumphs, especially those by which white people were influenced, and of his reception and of the social recognition he enjoyed when away from the South. Could any white man today, of known illegitimate origin, hope for such opportunities or, no matter what his ability or his personality, achieve such influence? In its last analysis, is not his career, as well as the careers of other mulattoes, educated and supported largely by whites, a rather sad commentary upon the race that did not, and does not now, furnish a sufficient number of fullblood candidates for such opportunities and privileges, and likewise upon the white group which did not, and does not now, seek out and train fullblood Negroes for such leadership?

The prevailing attitude of the white race, especially that of its leaders, toward the Negro race is in no respect more discouraging, or more disparaging, than in the readiness with which it accepts and practically approves this mulatto leadership here discussed, and in the utter failure to demand of the Negro race right ideals uncompromisingly applied in the matter of its racial preservation. It is exceedingly unfortunate for the Negro race in the United States that its earliest heroes and leaders were, almost without exception, mixed bloods rather than fullblood Negroes. Today relatively few fullblood Negroes anywhere in America occupy positions making them influential with any considerable group of their own race!

An experience coming to Dr. Washington in New York City has value as illustrating an important feature of race contacts where the two races occupy one building and affords material for a strong argument in favor of residential separation of the races. In an apartment house were both white and Negro tenants. It appears from current newspaper accounts that, on one of his visits to New York City, Dr. Washington was in this building and, while there, was assaulted by a white man of foreign origin. Evidently, antecedent conditions had been such as to place the white foreigner on guard and his act was, as he saw it, in defense of his family. Sectional attitudes certainly did not enter into this situation.

As a result of this incident, the usefulness of this noted mulatto educator was seriously impaired in the South, if not more widely. The incident would not have occurred but for the joint occupancy of this building by both Negro and white people. The South has insisted, wisely undoubtedly, upon such separation of the races as may, as far as possible, protect each from the other. This program is inadequate not because it is not the best possible under the circumstances, or because it is essentially unjust, but rather in the degree that there is failure so to apply it as to control the vicious and the degraded of the two races. It is manifest that no definite and energetic effort has been made to control this vicious element in either race. Racial separation unquestionably gives opportunity for race development, as well as removes largely the danger of racial conflict. Even a man of Dr. Washington's position suffered because of a too close racial association.

The astounding feature of such cases as that of Dr. Washington—indeed, of the whole group of mulatto leaders—

61

is that so few of either race have seemed to see beyond the present time or beneath the immediate surface. No one has seemed to realize fully the destructive effect upon the ideals of the Negro race necessarily associated with all outstanding examples of approved illegitimacy, especially those resulting in racial intermixture. It was largely those of such origin who were permitted to assume the leadership of the emancipated Negro. Yet behind the Negro people lay the primitive conditions of Africa; the "middle passage," with all its horrors: the years of bondage. They were desperately in need of anything and of everything calculated to strengthen and to purify their home and their family life. Out of the anti-slavery movement had emerged a small group of mulattoes, now recognized as the race leaders. This fact of a mixed-blood leadership, recognized alike by both races, necessarily had much to do with fixing the ideals of the mass of the Negroes. Continued adherence to the attitudes of 1865 is to be found everywhere. The yellow face is ubiquitous. In the face of these facts and these conditions, it is folly, or worse, to waste time and effort and energy in sectional recriminations while conditions, worse by far than prevailed even under slavery, are fostered and encouraged at the present time.

In concluding this chapter it is well to note, and to emphasize, the fact that it is not wholly fair to speak of present-day policies and activities as breaking down racial ideals and racial self-respect. Present policies and activities are rather a continuation of a course of action which has effectually prevented the development of right ideals and a genuinely constructive racial self-respect upon the part of the Negro, and which has so beclouded the thinking of the whites as to cause them to fail of any effective protest against existing conditions.

Essentially, *the interests of the mulatto are in irreconcilable conflict with those of both races*. This will appear the more clearly as the present situation is analyzed and studied in all its details. The situation should be so handled as to conserve, primarily, the interests of both the white and the black races, but this should be done with the least possible hardship to the mulatto. It should not be forgotten that the mulatto is the innocent victim of the sins of others!

An outstanding fact in reference to the mulatto problem is the utter indifference to it exhibited by the people of the United States as a whole. A survey of the books and magazine articles published within the past ten years and dealing with this problem reveals, upon the part of the writers generally, a wholly unsatisfactory grasp of the mulatto problem. There is little open sanction of amalgamation. There is little open, frank condemnation of it. There is, at best, but a superficial understanding or evaluation of its significance.

Another consideration which demands a place in any effort to state the more important facts entering into the race problem is that, on the average, a lower grade of white is now involved in racial intermixture than formerly. The same is true of the Negroes and the mulattoes involved. Unquestionably, there is a better element of the Negro group of women involved, dominated by a desire to improve the status of their offspring. In the main, however, the initial increment of racial intermixture is now encountered in the lower strata, if not in the lowest stratum, of each race.

Whatever his rank or his social status, no one can, for a moment, defend the guilty white man. Condemnation, contempt, is his just due. The higher his status socially, the greater his natural ability, by so much the more pitiless should be the scorn and the more nearly complete the social ostracism which should be visited upon him! Like all other moral and social evils upon which attention has been focused and concerning which conscience has been aroused, it is reasonable to assume that, in the main, in the matter of initial racial intermixture, a distinctly lower type of white man will continue this evil, while the higher types, in obedience to law and enlightened conscience and in respect for enlightened public sentiment, will refrain. In large measure this is true of the Negro group. Despite the incentives to racial intermixture involved in the prominence of the mulatto and in attitudes generally, resulting in cases in which the rule does not hold, a lower type of woman is, in the main, involved at present than was formerly the case. This is generally true; but, because of the stress put upon the race by present conditions, this rule is not without very many and notable exceptions. No stratum of Negro, or mulatto, womanhood escapes this stress wholly.

Another factor which deserves consideration is the situation of the Negro who has gone into the cities of the North and into the industrial centers. It is necessary to recognize the wide differences exhibited by these cities, but a few facts are, in some measure, characteristic of all cities, and especially of the larger cities of the North and the East. A large foreign element is present in each of these cities. Not only so, but in this foreign element are many who, by the hard training received before coming to America, are prepared to take advantage of the inexperience and the weaknesses of the Negro, or those of anyone else. A long list of adverse conditions is encountered by the Negro in such an environment, conditions for which his previous training has not fitted him and which, at best, involve the unsettled, if not destructive, conditions of a transitional period. It is not along the line of his financial interests, however, that the Negro suffers most. It is often the case that these are definitely improved. The stress involved has, of course, value in quickening mentality.

Among the foreign element in the larger cities, except in the case of the Jews, there is little appreciation of race and few of the loyalties which tend to produce satisfactory social conditions. In this atmosphere, racial intermixture thrives, and is often most flagrantly lawless. Few of the Northern States, now forced to deal with this situation, have any legal provision protecting race. Negro men are free to marry white women and, in so far as they do so, leave an element of Negro women unprovided for and, hence, under abnormal stress. Along with the better element of the Negroes in these cities is a class which yields to demoralizing influences. Fortunately, conditions are such as to limit the number of children born in such environment. It is also a fact, hard in itself but wholesome for the future, that the death rate among such children is abnormally high. Possibly the time may come when mankind will no longer countenance the crowding of multiplied thousands into city slums, there to fester and rot, while vast areas of unused land are available, some of which often lies scarcely beyond the city limits!

There is, quite generally, a disposition to augment personal importance and family status by claiming descent from the illustrious of the past. One needs but to reflect upon the vast numbers who claim descent from the Pilgrim Fathers, from Pocohontas, or from some European family of note, to realize the prevalence and the force of this trait among white people. A corresponding tendency exists among the Negroes of the United States. It may occasion surprise to learn to what extent these people still claim descent from some African chief or king. No other tradition may be cherished, but that of honorable descent grows stronger and more circumstantial with each passing generation.

Among the mixed bloods of the United States descent is frequently claimed as from some prominent white man. The diffusion mulatto especially, but also the initial increment mulatto usually, has a free field for romancing in reference to the white man originally involved in his blood mixture. Thus it happens that the white blood involved is quite frequently attributed to some outstanding white man or, at least, to some aristocrat of the old school. There are few names of those especially prominent in the earlier history of the South which are not now borne by mulattoes who, in very many instances, claim direct lineal descent from someone

65

bearing that name. The number of such instances is so great that there is scarcely a name prominent in Southern history which has not been appropriated by the romancing fancy of some mulatto. It would be a revelation to their admirers could they learn how widely traditions exist among the Negroes involving higher Northern officers prominent in the Civil War, and later. It is to the credit of Dr. Booker T. Washington that he made no such claim, but stated the facts concerning his paternity with no attempt at mitigation or embellishment.

It is probable that nowhere else in the civilized world today, certainly nowhere else in the Christianized part of the world, can there be found a group of people more unfortunately situated than are the mulattoes in the United States. The possibility that they can, in the presence of the full bloods of the white and the black races, find normal conditions under which to live and to rear children, is so remote that it is scarcely worthy of consideration. Only in so far as the white and the black races here suspend right moral principle and constructive social and racial attitudes may the mulatto hope to escape the hurtful elements of his present situation. A fair and full and honest consideration of the situation of the mulatto in the United States indicates that his own higher interests, as well as the higher interests of the white and of the black races, demand the separation of the white and the Negro groups. Such separation is possible and, to both races, would prove worth vastly more than its cost.

Only to the extent that fundamental principles are discarded completely or disregarded utterly by both the white and the Negro, may the mulatto hope for equality of status in the United States. It is useless to endeavor to conceal the fact that the race problem is now no longer bi-racial but rather involves three distinct groups. Behind the mulatto group lies disregard of fundamental moralities, and as this group advances in culture and in social and financial status, surpassing the fullblood Negro and thus becoming the leaders of the race, the possibility of the Negro developing along normal racial lines diminishes. The fullblood Negro is the victim of, the chief sufferer from, this prevalent suspension of those moral, ethical, religious principles which, observed, would make possible the "parallel" development of the races.

CHAPTER III

ILLEGITIMACY

IN THE investigation of any matter involving a large number of people a constant danger is that the investigator will fail to discriminate clearly between the various classes composing the group, and that he will fail to recognize the differences in outlook, in attitudes, and in conduct characterizing these various classes. This point should be guarded with special care in dealing with the subject matter of this chapter; and, since there are unquestionably different strata in the Negro population of the United States, the need for careful analysis is theoretically manifest. In actual contact with the problem of illegitimacy as it exists among the Negroes here, individual cases have not been and could hardly be classified from the standpoint of the status of the parent, or the stratum of population in which each case may have occurred. It is necessary, therefore, to deal with the Negro group for the present as an undifferentiated whole.

Among the Negroes themselves there are few if any aids available determining the status of the individual women involved. Surrounded by a white population which, in numbers, in power, and in achievement surpasses him decidedly, the Negro reaction is naturally a group solidarity highly unfavorable to lines of economic, of social, or even moral cleavage. It would simplify the problem somewhat if it could be determined that a large percentage of the illegitimate births registered for the Negro population of the District of Columbia—more than nine times that returned for the white population—occur wholly, or even in large part, among the lower and less privileged strata. Doubtless the evil is much more prevalent on such levels, but there are indications that it is by no means wholly confined to them.

Following, then, the example set by the United States

Census Bureau and by all other available authorities, no attempt is made to classify according to social status but the facts and figures are given for the race as a unit. The reader must reach his own conclusions concerning the conditions characterizing the different classes involved. The same is true largely in determining what share of responsibility lies with the individual offenders; what share should be credited to group indifference; to lack of group ideals; to lack of racial self-respect; and what share of reprobation falls justly upon extra-group ideals, attitudes, activities, and leadership.

Conditions in the District of Columbia may be taken as a basis for conclusions in reference to illegitimacy among the Negroes throughout the United States. Here records have been kept by competent officials and these records are now available. Since the year 1875 there has been preserved by the Health Department a very complete record of the births for each race in the District of Columbia. The number of births reported as illegitimate is also given by race for each year except two. Percentages, based upon these findings, are not provided here and so the figures only are given, as follows:

TABLE VI [1]

		Legitimate		Illegitimate	
Year	Total Births	White	Negro	White	Negro
1875	3,915	2,518	1,397	...	....
1876	4,285	2,568	1,717	75	505
1877	3,892	2,167	1,725	...	....
1878	3,421	1,839	1,560	44	170
1879	3,816	2,068	1,456	49	299
1880	4,095	2,241	1,456	56	342
1881	3,595	1,961	1,264	53	307
1882	3,391	1,747	1,277	53	314
1883	3,116	1,631	1,132	53	300
1884	3,224	1,648	1,196	63	281
1885	3,334	1,805	1,136	56	337
1886	3,516	1,936	1,184	65	351
1887	3,728	2,022	1,288	70	348
1888	3,670	1,964	1,262	71	373

[1] Compiled from several reports.

Year	Total Births	Legitimate		Illegitimate	
		White	Negro	White	Negro
1889	4,001	2,098	1,397	78	428
1890	4,070	2,171	1,341	75	483
1891	4,344	2,440	1,371	73	460
1892	4,614	2,581	1,447	67	519
1893	4,458	2,528	1,837	73	539
1894	5,042	3,007	2,035	77	539
1895	4,794	2,878	1,916	104	520
1896	4,706	2,886	1,920	100	517
1897	4,573	2,761	1,812	96	477
1898	4,709	2,737	1,972	96	518
1899	4,866	2,866	1,891	66	479
1900	4,641	2,790	1,851	90	387
1901	4,355	2,527	1,312	93	423
1902	4,932	2,984	1,390	102	496
1903	5,124	3,277	1,403	80	414
1904	6,218	3,390	1,676	104	518
1905	6,415	4,046	1,712	94	563
1906	6,529	4,216	1,713	114	486
1907	6,873	4,457	1,825	94	497
1908	7,040	4,723	1,745	112	462
1909	7,026	4,715	1,735	94	497
1910	7,031	4,555	1,916	84	476
1911	7,032	4,674	1,791	198	469
1912	7,007	4,734	2,273	109	496
1913	6,903	4,667	2,273	113	488
1914	7,130	4,925	2,205	90	422
1915	7,067	4,762	1,768	110	427
1916	7,388	4,961	1,813	119	495
1917	7,519	5,171	1,809	120	419
1918	8,221	5,978	1,814	85	344
1919	8,231	5,854	1,881	110	386
1920	8,898	6,240	2,127	129	402
1921	9,028	6,321	2,127	127	409
1922	9,121	6,371	2,180	129	441
1923	9,029	6,301	2,201	112	415
1924	9,357	6,404	2,365	121	465
1925	9,173	6,206	2,845	107	456
1926	9,004	6,159	2,845	126	440
1927	9,175	6,212	2,378	121	464
1928	8,994	6,066	2,332	135	461
1929	9,032	6,115	2,917	147	517
1930	9,443	6,391	3,052	133	582
1931	9,387	6,859	2,973	104	542
1932	10,184	6,859	3,325	175	604
1933	9,932	6,517	3,415	158	666
1934	10,023	6,592	3,431	135	680

ILLEGITIMACY

Year	Total Births	Legitimate White	Legitimate Negro	Illegitimate White	Illegitimate Negro
1935	10,850	7,163	3,687	145	770
1936	11,751	7,941	3,810	173	804
1937	12,248	8,246	4,002	192	864
1938	12,998	8,819	4,179	179	949
1939	13,981	9,547	4,434	220	979
1940	15,200	10,573	4,627	254	1,003
1941	18,130	12,869	5,261	261	1,229
1942	21,317	15,630	5,687	288	1,170
1943	23,352	17,483	5,869	385	1,233
1944	22,856	16,885	5,971	480	1,296
1945	22,954	17,125	5,829	483	1,471
1946	25,929	18,897	7,032	563	1,629
1947	28,622	20,285	8,337	532	1,717
1948	27,867	18,919	8,948	525	2,103
1949	.....	.....	....	421	1,992

Table VI, while making no distinction between the full-blood Negro and the mulatto illegitimate, and giving no information in regard to the prevalence of initial amalgamation, is probably the most accurate statement available concerning conditions existing in the District of Columbia. It is sufficiently inclusive and sufficiently accurate for practical purposes. This table necessarily forms the basis for certain calculations by which, in the absence of direct Census returns, conclusions are reached for the United States as a whole. Table VII, taken partly from page three of the Report of the Health Officer of the District for 1924-25, gives valuable percentages.

TABLE VII [a]

Illegitimacy in the District of Columbia, prevalence of, by years and by race, during the calendar years 1906-28, inclusive.

Year	Illegitimate Births and Stillbirths Registered W.	B.	Unknown	Total	Rates per Thousand Corresponding Population W.	B.	Total	Percentage of all Births and Stillbirths Reported as Illegitimate W.	B.	Total
1906-1910	110	572	..	682	0.5	5.9	2.0	2.3	22.1	9.3
1911-1915	111	541	67	719	0.4	5.5	2.1	2.2	21.7	9.6
1916-1920	112	452	52	616	0.4	4.3	1.5	1.9	18.1	7.2
1921	136	467	45	648	0.4	4.2	1.5	2.0	16.6	6.8
1922	135	493	54	682	0.4	4.4	1.5	2.0	17.4	7.1

[a] *Report District Health Officer, 1924.5, p. 3.*

	Illegitimate Births and Still-births Registered				Rates per Thousand Corresponding Population			Percentage of all Births and Stillbirths Reported as Illegitimate		
Year	W.	B.	Unknown	Total	W.	B.	Total	W.	B.	Total
1923	114	468	45	627	0.3	4.0	1.3	1.7	16.3	6.1
1924	130	511	47	688	0.4	4.3	1.4	1.9	16.8	7.0
1925	113	503	39	655	0.3	4.2	1.3	1.7	16.8	6.8
1926	132	489	48	669	0.3	3.7	1.2	2.2	15.8	6.5
1927	127	520	37	684	0.3	3.8	1.2	1.9	16.9	6.7
1928	141	505	5	651	0.3	3.9	1.2	2.2	16.3	6.8

There is information available, not contained in Table VII, concerning illegitimacy in the District of Columbia, but not subject to verification by official records. One such table is found at page 219 of *White and Black in the Southern States*, by Maurice S. Evans, of South Africa. Percentages only are given, and these run somewhat higher than the official figures quoted above. The source upon which Mr. Evans drew is not given. The table is here numbered as

TABLE VIII
Illegitimacy in Washington City

Year	% White	% Black	Year	% White	% Black
1879	2.32	17.60	1887	3.34	21.27
1880	2.43	19.02	1888	3.49	22.18
1881	2.33	19.42	1889	3.59	22.18
1882	2.09	19.73	1890	3.34	26.50
1883	3.14	20.95	1891	2.90	25.12
1884	3.60	19.02	1892	2.52	26.40
1885	3.00	22.28	1893	2.82	27.00
1886	3.28	26.86	1894	2.56	26.46

The three tables given in this chapter, except the third unquestionable in any vital detail, reveal clearly a feature of the Negro problem in the District of Columbia—and throughout the Americas—calling for the most careful study and for the most heroic remedies.

While the conditions obtaining in the District of Columbia are thus definitely indicated, no such statistics exist for the United States as a whole later than for 1920. The enumeration for 1920 is, however, descredited, so that 1910 is the latest date for which dependable returns are available for either race. A contemporary statement for the white race places the number of white illegitimate children born annually in the United States at from 32,000 to 38,000. If the percentage of illegitimate births reported among the Negroes in Washington City obtains throughout Continental United States, and there is every reason for believing that it is fairly representative, then there are virtually as many illegitimate births among the Negro population as occur in the whole white population. This means that *the illegitimacy rate among Negroes is approximately nine times as great* as that among the whites!

Too much stress can hardly be put upon the importance to any people of a pure and wholesome family life. Among the symptoms of group pathology, the illegitimate child must take an important place. Granting that the more experienced of abandoned women and the *sage femme* of modern life are not likely to appear in the lists of mothers of illegitimate children; and that the percentage of such births may, even does in large part, represent unsophistication upon the part of the unmarried mother; yet a high rate of illegitimacy, for the group or stratum in which it occurs, is an incontestable proof of low ideals and of inadequate family life and organization. The statistics available in reference to illegitimacy among the Negroes all agree in placing the percentage very high. Thus to the Negroes themselves and to their white friends and helpers is clearly indicated the point at which the need of the race is greatest and most serious; indeed, for a very considerable part of the race, most desperate.

The problem of the illegitimate child is one of the most serious confronting modern civilization. It is serious because of the number of such children born annually and because of the absolute necessity of determining their social status and of making provision for their support and their education. It is serious also because of their social significance and the threat involved for the family as the supreme social institution, and because of the necessity for a definite decision concerning the right attitude of society and its institutions, especially that of the Church, toward such individuals. *A program, reasoned or unreasoned, there must be.* Shall the policy be to conceal such origin, thus permitting the unfortunate individual to achieve for himself such station in life as he may, with the consequent perils to society? Or, shall the policy be that of publicity, sacrificing the individual for the sake of right ideals and the making of these effective in preventing demoralization from becoming general?

When both parents of an illegitimate child are of one race, concealment is not impossible. Indeed, the situation suggests this as the method of least resistance, promising relief for the mother and, in a measure, relief for the child. Thus very many illegitimate children in the past have, through the agencies of philanthropy and those of religion, grown up ignorant of their origin and among people equally ignorant of the facts in the case. Asylums, orphanages, and churches have followed the policy of concealment. Sometimes, in the effort to shield the unfortunate illegitimate child, the dependent legitimate child, through institutional associations, has the suspicion raised that he, too, is of illegitimate birth. Some institutions even refuse to permit the raising of the question of legitimacy.

When the parents of an illegitimate child are of different races, concealment is hardly possible. Not only is the child himself marked by color and by other manifest characteristics, but his descendants are likewise marked. In the case of two races between which intermarriage is not practiced, the implications of such intermixture as does occur are patent to all. Hence, either the ideals of society must be suspended in such cases, with the resultant confusion of moral sanctions, or a measure of social disadvantage, expressive of disapprobation of promiscuity, must be visited upon the offspring. This, viewed as an unrelated phenomenon, excites horror. Viewed in its relationships and as a socially protective attitude, many justly regard it as a necessity.

In the treatment of the general illegitimacy it may be well to digress sufficiently to secure a grasp of this matter as it affects other parts of the civilized world, and of the reaction to it here and elsewhere. A brief reference to conditions reported for certain Old World countries has a logical place here. These figures are given not to excuse conditions in the United States but rather to emphasize the importance of concentration of attention upon the matter under discussion and upon the application of sane remedial agencies. Conditions in Europe may be studied with great profit, for there statistics have been gathered for a longer time and, on the whole, are possibly more thorough than are those gathered in America. That illegitimacy is a world problem is demonstrated by even the briefest reference to conditions in the most highly civilized parts of the world. The figures given in Table IX are, for the most part, for periods immediately preceding the first World War. The demoralization of two World Wars must be regarded as more or less temporary, while the table given reveals normal conditions.

TABLE IX [a]

Percentage births—live—reported as illegitimate:

Germany	8.7	Wales	...
France	8.9	Scotland	7.0
Sweden	13.3	Spain	4.6
Denmark	12.0	Netherlands	2.1
Austria	12.3	Japan (1915)	8.7
Hungary	9.4	South Africa:	
Italy	9.4	White	2.2
Russia	2.3	Bantu	11.2
England	4.0	Mixed Peoples	30.8

The figures given in Table IX cover a fairly wide range and show the official statements of prewar conditions in the countries named. Everywhere conditions are worse in the cities than in the rural districts. Often it is the cities which cause the percentage for a given country to be so high. This is due to several facts. In the cities enumerations are more complete. To the city also comes the country woman for the

[a] *Children's Bureau Publication No. 66*, pp. 13-17.

birth of her illegitimate child, seeking the advantages of hospital facilities, or better opportunities to conceal her shame. Living conditions for large numbers in the cities are very bad—a situation reflected in delayed marriage and in the large number of illegitimate births.

It is interesting to note that quite generally statistics for Europe show a marked increase in illegitimacy as the period of World War I is approached, as there was during the progress of this struggle and in the following disorganization. Table X is instructive at this point.

TABLE X [4]

Illegitimate births in Berlin, London, and Paris, as follows:

City	1912	1913	1914	1915	1916	1917	(Percentages)
Berlin		23.3	22.6	22.2	23.8	...	(First 5 months, 1916)
London		..	4.5	4.8	5.4	6.8	
Paris	23.8	26.5	23.9	26.8	30.8	31.7	(First 38 weeks, 1917)

Table XI gives the average percentage of live births annually reported as illegitimate for the cities named for the period 1905-1909. Here again we avoid the war period.

TABLE XI [5]

Berlin	18.1	Paris	25.5
Budapest	26.3	Prague	28.7
Copenhagen	25.5	Rome	16.5
Dublin	3.5	Stockholm	33.3
Leipzig	19.2	Vienna	30.1

The figures quoted here concerning conditions in Europe are of vital interest. They indicate that an increasingly high percentage of children born in Europe are of illegitimate origin. This may be explained in part by the increased care and thoroughness in collecting data; in large part by the demoralization incident to the World Wars; and in large part by the spread of Communistic and atheistic teachings directly attacking the Christian home and the principles upon which Christian civilization is founded. In some cases

[4] *Children's Bureau Publication No. 66*, pp. 15-16.
[5] *Children's Bureau Publication No. 66*, pp. 15-16.

these figures may reflect the conflict between civil and ecclesiastic control of marriage, the State requiring civil marriage and reporting as illegitimate the issue of all other unions.

It is to be noted, however, that conditions in Europe were growing worse before the beginning of the war period. The widespread failure of religious conviction and of ethical sanctions based upon religious faith constitutes one of the most interesting and most instructive features of the period immediately preceding the World Wars. The "war baby" was, possibly, the logical consequent, as the illegitimate child of the postwar period is certainly the logical consequent, of relaxed standards quite as much as of the stress of war and the disorganization immediately following the war period.

Stockholm, Sweden, has the unenviable distinction of standing at the head of the list in the percentage of illegitimate children born—33.3 per cent. Why this should be true, no explanation is given. A seaport city, it has to do with detached seafaring men, but not in the proportionate numbers found in many other seaport cities. There is something of the cosmopolitan element in so far as population is concerned, but this fails elsewhere to produce so serious results as are here indicated. A city well to the north and situated in a country by no means noted for immorality, the figures for Stockholm are not explained. Personal inquiry elicited the information that the high illegitimacy rate in Sweden does not indicate that moral condition, the social laxities, the sex promiscuity usually associated with a high rate of illegitimacy. Taxation method was given as the cause here. Unmarried people pay on their individual income. The income of a married couple is treated as a unit and is taxed at the rate levied on the larger sum. To avoid this higher tax no civil ceremony is had. Although family life is quite the same as when the civil marriage is performed, the government lists as illegitimate children born of unions not based upon the civil ceremony. There is here, then, an

77

extreme case of resistance against a method of taxation, not a case of moral delinquency.

Conditions now existing in Europe, and especially those in South America, Central America, the West Indies, and in South Africa, should prove a warning to the United States and to Canada. Certainly no relaxation of effort, no lowering of ideals or of social standards is suggested to us by the reflection that we, as yet, even with our race problem, are not quite so unfortunate as are some of our neighbors and contemporaries. Because 33.3 per cent of all births in Stockholm are registered as illegitimate, or because "between 60 and 70 per cent of all recorded births" in Jamaica are illegitimate, cannot excuse the lethargic indifference to illegitimacy existing in the United States. Conditions in Europe, however deplorable they may be, do not generally involve racial deterioration. In the Americas, it is race, rather than the individual, that is at stake!

In the present study some notice should be taken of the matter of historic attitudes toward illegitimacy and the efforts made to control this evil. Like many of the earlier laws of England, those dealing with bastardy were very harsh, even more severe than were the laws of ancient Rome. In cases of illegitimate birth the Common Law of England "does not recognize a legal relationship even between the mother and the child and it does not allow legitimation by subsequent marriage. The bastard is described as 'filius nullius,' a child of no one, and this designation characterizes his status from the standpoint of property." [6]

Later statutory enactment has made the policy of England much milder and has changed many of the customs based upon the Common Law sanctions.

In the earlier period of American history, English attitudes and customs prevailed. The placing of the illegitimate child, and especially his mother, at such disadvantage as might, with frank brutality, serve to sanction and to pre-

• *Children's Bureau Publication No. 42,* p. 9.

serve right standards, was quite generally recognized as necessary. Within recent years, however, there has been a tendency to break away from the older standards and ideals. This is most noticeable among professional charity and welfare workers. In the presence of individual cases and definite concrete situations, all practical welfare workers are in danger of forgetting the wider signifiance of illegitimacy, especially the threat it involves in reference to the home and family. This tendency is clearly exhibited in a number of government publications giving the views and the methods of men and women engaged in caring for illegitimate children and for their mothers. A few quotations may be given as illustrations of this tendency, viz.:

"Together with the effort to secure complete and accurate birth registration must go concern that no record shall be so used that the child's future happiness may be in any way endangered." [7]

"Others contend that the law should, as far as lies in its power, wipe out the difference between legitimate and illegitimate birth." [8]

"Every effort should be made by law to relieve the child of the stigma that attaches to illegitimate birth." [9]

"Are we not, in the course of the next generation or two, gradually going to come to the point where the child born out of wedlock will be treated more or less as it now is theoretically in North Dakota, the child having just as much right as the child born in wedlock?" [10]

"Fair opportunity asks for the child a removal of all moral stigma that attaches to its birth. Such a mark must not be allowed to stand as a handicap in its path." [11]

". . . humane sentiment that organized society is now showing toward the problem of illegitimacy." [12]

[7] *Children's Bureau Publication No. 66*, p. 20.
[8] *Children's Bureau Publication No. 77*, p. 27.
[9] *Children's Bureau Publication No. 77*, p. 33.
[10] *Children's Bureau Publication No. 77*, p. 72.
[11] *Children's Bureau Publication No. 77*, p. 111.
[12] *Children's Bureau Publication No. 77*, p. 111.

". . . the traditional harsh attitude toward the unmarried mother and her child is sensibly moderating." [13]

It is only fair, however, to point out that even among professional charity and welfare workers there are those who stand for the highest ideals theoretically upheld and practically enforced; who see clearly that it is a mistake to sacrifice society for the sake of the individual. Two tendencies are operative: One leads to unreasonable severity, and is best pictured by Hawthorne in his treatment of this matter in *The Scarlet Letter*. The other leads to the suspension of moral and ethical safeguards, if not to their destruction. The problem, in both races, is how to protect those complying with right standards and to strengthen and enforce right practices without undue severity toward those necessarily involving dangers to the fundamentals of social order. The illegitimate child is, and must remain, an innocent sufferer, a tragic figure.

There is still, even among the professional charity and welfare workers, a conservative element. The following quotation is fairly representative of this group and of their views: ". . . and (3) that the stigma which rests upon the mother and the child is inseparable from society's respect for monogamy. As for this stigma—just so long as it adds to our self-respect to think of our own parents as having observed custom and moral law, just so long will it be impossible for us to feel an equal respect for those persons whose misfortune it is to have had parents who did not observe the moral law." [14] The personal element here, as contrasted with abstract principle, is given possibly too large a place, but the attitude is wholesome and commands attention.

Through this survey the reader may understand something of what is involved in the problem of the illegitimate child, and something of the magnitude of the problem of illegitimacy. The question of the racial integrity of the American

[13] *Children's Bureau Publication No. 77*, p. 147.
[14] *Children's Bureau Publication No. 77*, p. 99.

Negro cannot, in the nature of the case, in the matter of acts of initial amalgamation, be put upon the same basis as individual cases of bastardy within the white race, or within any other race. Vastly more is involved when the evil is interracial, rather than intraracial.

It is certainly an error to ascribe to the Negro race as a whole, possibly even to its more privileged classes in the United States, the attitudes and the ideals of the white group here concerning illegitimacy. Slavery gave ideals far superior to those of Africa; but slavery was not designed to teach morals. Conditions under freedom have not involved any compelling stress holding the race to high ideals as these affect marriage and purity of home life. It is certain that this lack of higher ideals and the distinctly lower moral plane upon which many of the Negroes live, make bastard origin much less a handicap and much less hurtful to a Negro child than it is to a white child. This is well and clearly expressed in *Children's Bureau Publication 66*, at page 22, as follows: "Illegitimacy among Negroes is a phenomenon which must be studied by itself in its relation to the social and the economic conditions surrounding the race at the present time and in its past history. Unfavorable economic conditions and lack of educational opportunities have resulted in laxness in marriage relations among the Negroes of many localities, and consequently in a high illegitimacy rate. However, illegitimacy as it prevails among the Negroes in these localities is not comparable with the same conditions among the white population. Regardless of the status of colored children, they are usually provided for by the mother or her relatives, and the child born out of wedlock has very much the same advantages and disadvantages as a child born in "lawful marriage." [15]

The author here quoted does not give a complete analysis of the situation. What is said is true of the fullblood Negro child. It is not so manifestly true of the mulatto child. *Here*

[15] *Children's Bureau Publication No. 66*, p. 22.

bastard origin does not prove a handicap. Often it seems a help, bringing enlarged opportunity. A long list of names might be given in support of this statement. After an exhaustive study, covering virtually all the more prominent Negroes and mulattoes of the past and the present, Professor Reuter reached the conclusion that "The chances of the mulatto child developing into a leader of the race are thirty-four [his latest figures are 50 to 100] times as great as are the chances of the black child." [16] Thomas also recognizes this advantage of the mixed blood, especially in desired physical characteristics, as a factor very influential with Negro motherhood. He gives one of the clearest and most comprehensive statements available concerning the influence of present conditions upon the ideals and upon the morality of that class of Negro and of mulatto women who are sufficiently advanced to be able to evaluate rationally this feature of the race problem. His statement is quoted in full at page 56.

The quotation to which reference is here made does not fully state the case. Unfavorable economic conditions there have certainly been, and such still exist. Lack of educational advantages, everywhere apparent, has had its influence. Racial heritage, less stimulating than that of any other race, involving less of ethical restraint and discipline and these operating through a shorter period of time than has been the case with other races, constitutes a grave handicap. The most destructive forces the Negro in America has had to face, however, have grown out of the universal suspension of fundamental moral and ethical principles, especially as these apply to his home life and his racial integrity. The fact that Negro illegitimacy is greatest in cities, where educational facilities for the race are far superior to those available in smaller towns and in the rural districts, indicates that more than education is required for the protection of the races. The situation in Washington City is especially instructive at this point.

---

[16] *The Mulatto in the United States,* Reuter, p. 314.

When all the details of fact and of attitudes are considered, it is not strange that, in every case in America where statistics have been collected, the illegitimacy rate among the Negroes is very much higher than that among the whites. In the District of Columbia, the paradise of the mulatto, this rate is about nine times that of the white. In Alabama it is about fourteen times that of the white. In Maryland, about nine times that of the white. In Baltimore, about ten times that of the white. These facts indicate clearly the direction which should be given efforts made to assist the Negro race, as well as those made to protect both races.

Because of the attitude of the white toward illegitimacy among the Negroes, an attitude painfully reflected in the morals, in the ideals, and in the outlook of the Negro, there is unquestionably an unfavorable reaction upon the moral sense and the moral perception of the masses of the whites and, especially of the leadership of the white group. In how far reaction to the conditions existing in the Negro race throughout the Americas thus affects the white population, especially that of the United States, is matter for speculation. It is inevitable that a people, grown accustomed to disregard illegitimacy in another race, with which close association exists, should, within their own group, lose something of that keenness of appreciation of its significance which might otherwise exist.

The prevailing attitude of the white educators, the white philanthropists, the white ecclesiastics of the United States toward the amalgamation of the white and the Negro races here must react upon the clarity of their own moral vision. Voluntary assumption of leadership carries with it an inescapable obligation to ascertain accurately what is involved and to know definitely what ends are sought, as well as the means to be employed in reaching these ends. Otherwise, it is a case of "the blind leading the blind" into hopeless moral confusion. It is quite certain that this situation is, in part, an explanation of the indifference of the white people of the

United States to conditions resulting in more than 40,000 illegitimate white children being born annually. Through the whole period of freedom—85 years—the natural guardians of morality have largely failed both races.

The ideal of the family, as this has come down to the present age through the Hebrew-Christian Scriptures and from Norse-Germanic sources, is the best in existence. Followed consistently, this ideal would leave unsolved few problems, personal, social, or racial, falling in its field. The insistent nature of evil, however, has manifested itself everywhere in insidious attacks upon this the most sacred institution given to humanity.

These attacks have been both theoretical and practical. In the present generation, as was the case during the French Revolution, certain groups are attacking the principles upon which alone pure homes may be founded and maintained, thus threatening to rob humanity of a priceless possession. Russia, closely paralleling a most unfortunate feature of the French Revolution, has fostered a movement calculated to substitute other ideals. Such ideals, however, involve consequences so dire as quickly to discredit them with all right-thinking people. It is not, however, philosophic immorality, communistic or otherwise, that is most hurtful. It is rather the unrealized perversions of recognized moral principles in their practical application. There is a most dangerous tendency to accept conditions as they are, and to wrest moral and ethical principles, and even religious sanctions, to the approval of existing conditions, rather than to bring these conditions up to the ideal.

The chief value of this chapter lies in the fact that it calls attention to two vitally important matters: Illegitimacy in general and illegitimacy as a distinctly racial problem. The Health Department of the District of Columbia has rendered a service greater perhaps than is yet realized in including in its records data bearing upon illegitimacy as this occurs in the District. It is a matter of deep regret that no information is available in reference to initial amalgamations. It is now claimed that the phenominal increase of mulattoes here, and elsewhere, is due to the natural increase of the mulatto group through the interbreeding of mulattoes and of mulattoes and fullblood Negroes, the latter tending to increase greatly the extent of the infusion of white blood while diminishing its degree in individual cases. It lies within the range of possibilities for the Health Officer of the District to secure fairly accurate information concerning initial amalgamations occurring here. As a contribution to accurate and complete knowledge of the race problem, this information would be of prime importance.

Absolutely accurate classification as to degree of mixture is not possible for several reasons. One of these is due to what is known as *atavism,* now generally recognized by scientists. This is also known as *reversion to type,* and it is well established that where cross-breeding has occurred, some of the progeny will bear the impress of one strain of the ancestry and others that of the other strain. Thus it happens that the children of mixed-blood parents sometimes show marked variation, one being almost white while another will exhibit many of the characteristics of even the fullblood Negro. Atavism is likely to occur indefinitely, certainly through several generations. Where this is not understood, a mixed-blood woman, or a fullblood woman married to a mixed-blood man, may be subjected to unjust condemnation by reason of the color or other characteristics of the offspring. Atavism is probably most likely to occur where both parents are mulattoes, the offspring of fullblood parents. There is always a possibility of error in the case of the near-white when only one generation of his family is considered. Where several generations are taken into account, especially when collateral relatives are included, the presence of even a trace of Negro blood is virtually certain to be indicated clearly.

The facts set forth in this chapter reveal a situation which is most deplorable. The attitudes assumed toward these facts and toward this situation by different individuals and by different groups will doubtless continue to vary widely, determined largely by the bias of previous affiliations, and by the force of fixed institutions and accepted practices and precedents. Utter indifference is now a widely prevailing attitude. Of the great number of educated, cultured, and intelligent white men and women in the District of Columbia, as is the case throughout the nation, very few have given any serious thought to the matters here discussed, especially as these matters affect the Negro. Upon the part of the leaders of the white group, political, educational, religious, no evidence is given showing any thorough comprehension of conditions confronting them. Certainly there is no definite or specific effort to correct the manifestly unfortunate features of the situation. The Negroes, both leaders and led, are likewise silent in reference to the mixture of the races and, especially, in reference to the conditions under which this is occurring. They are likewise silent concerning the high rate of illegitimacy prevailing among them.

That illegitimacy among the Negroes in the District of Columbia has decreased from a very high rate—Evans tells us that 27 per cent of the Negro children born in the District in 1893 were illegitimate—to 15.8 per cent in 1926 and to a somewhat lower rate at present, is very encouraging. Possibly had the matter been, from 1865 to the present, dealt with specifically and energetically, the standards of the Negroes, as well as their practices here, as a group average, would now be much nearer to the ideal. When all the elements entering into the situation during the past eighty-five years are considered, this rate of improvment possibly surpasses reasonable expectation. It is doubtful if, under the same conditions and circumstances, any other race would have done better. Still, 15.8 per cent is a distressingly high rate of illegitimacy. It should be remembered, also, that the figures of the Board of Health measure illegitimacy but approximately as occurring out of wedlock. It is not possible to secure figures measuring accurately that element of illegitimacy due to marital infidelity. It is reasonable to assume that there is an unreported element of illegitimacy occurring in both the unmarried group and in the married group of Negro women. The family still functions very imperfectly, if at all, with a considerable element of Negro womanhood.

There are doubtless those who regard the problem of illegitimacy among the Negroes in the District of Columbia, and among those throughout the United States, as distinctly a matter for the Negro's consideration, one concerning which the white need not concern himself. For several reasons Negro illegitimates do concern the whites. Among the children of this origin occurs practically the whole element of initial amalgamation. It is here, therefore, that the gravest menace of the Negro to the white race in America lies. It is equally true that here the gravest menace of the white to the Negro race in America lies.

The Negro came to America—not willingly—from a country very backward in civilization and wholly without our ideals of either morality or of the family. Negroes are now assumed to have achieved the same standards as have the whites. Their illegitimate birthrate is one of the manifest measures of the indifferent success achieved upon the part of the white, during this long contact, in mediating the ideals, the morals, of Christianity to them. When, in the most favored situation in which any part of the race now finds itself, one in each six children born to this group—it was less than one in four in 1893—is officially reported as illegitimate, the case is desperate and calls for immediate, strenuous, and constructive attention and action.

As is the case in reference to the general matter of racial integrity, illegitimacy, as a menace to the Negro in the United States, has not been adequately considered, nor has it been laid, definitely and effectively, upon the conscience of either race. The thoughtful Negro should awake to the significance of this evil for his race—to the necessity of extending the family ideal to every stratum of his race. He should make diligent inquiry concerning the attitudes of race leadership, evaluating each by its practical effect upon his racial integrity. Why are not Negro institutions—schools, secret orders, social organizations, press, churches, and etc.—outspoken at this point? Is not the real reason to be found in the fact that all these institutions are now completely dominated and largely monopolized by the mulatto?

If the moral insight and the social ideals of the American white have suffered—it is certain that they have—because of this failure to impose upon the Negro right ideals and right practices, what of the effect upon the Negro? Unquestionably, the answer is to be read in the high rate of illegitimacy, some of which is certainly due to initial amalgamation, prevailing in the District of Columbia, as shown by official reports, and which must be assumed to prevail among Negroes throughout the United States. A much higher rate of illegitimacy is known to prevail among the Negroes in other parts of America. We listen, almost in vain, for an outspoken word of constructive understanding from either race!

At no point is the American Negro more desperately in need of help than in reference to his family life, in his need to develop pure and wholesome homes as the basis of his racial integrity and of his racial progress. At no point has the white race in America, in its dealings with the Negro, shown less of foresight. At no point has it imposed upon the Negro here influences more destructive of right and wholesome ideals, or more certain to prevent the development, the achievement, of such ideals. There is little ground for hope that this situation will improve greatly while the two races are in contact.

CHAPTER IV

THE NEAR-WHITE

IN THE matter of slight racial intermixture as between the white and the Negro in America, two marginal groups must be recognized. There are those whose infusion of white blood is so slight as to render careful expert observation necessary in order to establish the fact that any infusion of white blood has occurred in a given case. As all such individuals—the near-blacks—are, in the United States, recognized as Negroes, no serious problems arise concerning them as apart from the Negro group. In the great majority of such cases originating in the United States the infusion of white blood is remote and has been followed by a breeding back toward the Negro stock. Much of this infusion of white blood occurred in Africa centuries earlier than the introduction of the Negro into America. Such intermixture has occurred in Abyssinia and along the eastern and the southern coasts of Africa. Egypt and that part of Africa lying north of the Sahara Desert have seen the absorption of much Negro blood, but from neither of these areas were slaves brought to America in considerable numbers, if at all. Many were, however, brought from the eastern and southern coasts of Africa and few, if any, of these were of pure Negro stock. The white elements involved were chiefly Semitic, and the color of these people is not the typical black of the true Negro but rather the lighter hues characterizing the mixed blood.[1] Professor M. J. Herskovitz is quoted as holding that only 20 to 30 per cent of American Negroes are now pure-blooded,[2] his figures manifestly dealing with the infusion of white blood both before and after the coming to America. Since the entire group of near-blacks is uniformly classed as Negro, we may dismiss

[1] There are evidences that, during the reign of King Solomon, 1015-975 B.C., gold was secured from the southern part of Africa, as well as from Abyssinia.
[2] See *American Journal of Sociology*, September, 1926, p. 332.

it with merely calling attention to the fact that it is not of unmixed Negro stock.

The second marginal group is composed of those who have, since coming to America, so far mixed with the white as to have lost most of the markings of the Negro. This group of near-whites does constitute a very grave problem. Many of these now have so slight a trace of Negro blood and exhibit so few of the physical characteristics of the Negro race that they are attempting to "pass" as white and, in certain sections, are meeting with some degree of success. There are, however, certain facts which cannot be changed and from which there cannot be a permanent escape. "Crossing the line," passing over into the white race in the sense of losing entirely and permanently the markings of the Negro, is physically impossible.[3] A personal acquaintance with several families in which there is a remote trace of Negro blood, as well as some knowledge of the history of other families of like ancestry, leads to the conclusion that, as between the Negro and the white, racial intermixture, however slight, cannot be permanently concealed.

There is in genetics a principle known as *Atavism,* or reversion to type. This characterizes not only the human race, but all animals as well. Scientists have observed this matter of reversion to type until they have been able to formulate certain laws in reference to it and are able to advance these with confidence. These laws cover certainly the immediate future, as they interpret both the immediate and the remote past. How far into the future amalgamation must have been carried before Atavism will cease to operate and the group involved come to be a real unity, is a matter for speculation. There is warrant for placing this at a date too remote to be worthy of consideration in dealing with present-day problems. Atavism will certainly, through occasional, individual rever-

[3] An article in *The World,* New York, of July 28, claims that 5,000 near-whites are crossing the color line and entering the white race annually. Others give much larger numbers. Walter White gives the number as 12,000 annually.

sions to type, keep alive indefinitely the knowledge of racial intermixture wherever this exists.

Since, then, the knowledge of racial intermixture must abide with and upon the near-white, the question arises as to whether or not the significance of amalgamation is to remain the same as at present or whether it is to grow more, or less, hurtful with the passage of time. This will depend upon many contingencies, but principally upon the fate of the full bloods of both races, especially upon the ideals characterizing the full bloods. Since there is no arbitrary protection of race and no effective elimination of the mixed blood individuals, there is reason to believe that the racial groups must ultimately undergo permanent change, for neither of two groups can ever be the same that it was before the mixture occurred. One group may apparently disappear completely, but in reality it does not do so. Both undergo change. There are steps which, once taken, can never be retraced, and blood mixture is such a step.

There are, then, abundant instances of the near-white in the United States. His difficulties and his disadvantages need little study in order that something of their significance may be realized. A few cases may be given, chosen from many others because of their illustrative value. A number of such cases may be found in literature. Cooper's use of this situation in *The Last of the Mohicans* has an interpretative value and may serve to bring a realization of what is involved, for there is here what is typical of the situation of the person, especially the woman, who nurses the secret of her Negroid origin. Despite her strength of character and her nobility of soul, Cooper could do no better for his near-white heroine than to let her perish!

A number of cases of *Atavism* have come under the personal observation of the writer, and many cases have been reported which he could not investigate personally. Three may be offered as typical.

The first of these cases of infusion of Negro blood occurred in the early days of a section of the South settled by the French and in which the Latin,[4] as opposed to the Teutonic, sanctions had prevailed. The mixture affected but one of the married couple in question and was very slight, so attenuated that few knew of the presence of Negro blood. In the course of time a large family of children were born to this couple and, with a single exception, these showed no sign of racial intermixture. One son, however, a typical case of atavism, showed clearly the presence of Negro blood. With advancing years, the physical characteristics of the Negro became more marked and, in later life, he came to associate with Negroes and was regarded as Negroid.

A second case has likewise great illustrative value. In the remote past of a section similar to that mentioned above, a free mulatto woman settled and accumulated a stock of cattle. A white man from another section passed that way and became interested in this woman. Whether or not a formal marriage occurred is not known. A son was born to this couple. He, with the property prestige, married a white woman and reared a family, all of whom passed for white; but, in two instances, the children had perceptible Negroid characteristics, these becoming more pronounced with advancing age. The facts in reference to the racial status of this family became known in recent years and proved utterly destructive to the political ambitions of a grandson of the original couple. The family of the grandmother, residing in an adjoining county, has all the while been recognized as Negroid.

A second case, stemming from this grandmother, was a very pronounced example of atavism. A woman of the third generation and showing virtually no Negroid markings was married to a man concerning whose status as fullblood white there could be no question. A son was born who had all the markings of the mixed blood. Although the percentage of Negro blood in the mother was very small this son had the physical markings of the mulatto born of white and fullblood

---

[4] "One drop of white blood makes a white man," is quoted as giving the Latin sanction.

Negro parentage. So pronounced were the Negroid characteristics of this son that the question of his paternity was inevitable. My own study of this case led to the conviction that
he was the child of this married couple but that this was the
most clearly marked case of atavism yet encountered. The
consequences for both mother and son were devastating.

A third case, with real tragedy involved and in which both
parties, a man and a woman, were wealthy and socially prominent, turned upon the discovery by the man, and but a short
time before the date fixed for the marriage, of the fact that
the woman had a strain of Negro blood. She was posing as of
Latin-American origin.

A bit of tragic history was written some years ago when
the records of the early parish churches were appealed to in a
section that had been largely Latin in the origin of its population. Forgotten facts were revived, and people who had regarded themselves as pure-white were found to be descended
from Negroid ancestors, F.P.C.s., or Free Persons of Color.

There is now to be noted a rather general movement of the
near-white people from those sections of the country where
they are recognized as of mixed blood, and where racial attitudes are uncomfortable for them, into such sections as lack
a knowledge of facts concerning amalgamation, or where attitudes are not discriminatory in such cases. Among the colored
people leaving the South to make their homes in the North,
there is, unquestionably, an element who seek to escape the
onus of racial origin and to be recognized as white, or who
fear that, in sections where familiarity with such cases greatly
increases the danger of publicity, some incident may precipi-
tate an avalanche of publicity. A change of residence, an entirely new situation, is usually sought by those who make an
effort to "cross the line." A large part of the finishing-off of
this process is, therefore, occurring in sections outside the
South.

There are other considerations which demand attention.
There are those who claim that cases of initial amalgamation

are now very rare, so much so that the race problem may now be regarded as permanently tripartite, with little passing from one group to another. The increase in mulattoes now actually occurring is by others regarded as explained by the natural increase of mulattoes, and by the diffusion throughout the Negro group of what white blood has already found place in this group, a process which may ultimately permeate the entire Negro group. This assumption has an element of truth in it, for such diffusion is now taking place. If, however, it were universally true, there would be no near-white problem, for with diffusion would come increasingly uniform distribution rather than cases at either extreme. There are, however, a considerable number of children born whose fathers are white but whose mothers are either Negro or mulatto women. As yet, the number of mulatto children born of white women is small but is rapidly increasing, especially in the large cities of the North and wherever there are numbers of low-type native or unassimilated foreign-born white women. Among certain foreign-born groups, race consciousness and racial self-respect are wanting, and a few Negro men are finding white wives from such groups. There is a type of Negro man who, flaunting the women of his own race, accepts the feminine derelicts of the white race, and doubtless feels that in doing so he is thwarting the exclusiveness of the white race; possibly that he is avenging the wrongs suffered by the women of his own race.

With the mulatto one of two attitudes must prevail: Either he must accept his classification as part of the Negro race, or he must reject this classification. Since this classification is made by all others, it is of no practical value to the mulatto to reject it openly. That this classification is not recognized as final by many mulattoes, and especially by the near-white, is doubtless true. In reality, the near-white is more white than black and would, in several of the Central and South American areas, be recognized as white. No one can censure the near-white woman in the United States, or elsewhere, for looking longingly across the color-line and wishing, if not for herself yet for her children, a place on the more privileged side of this line! This is a fact which must be reckoned with, a fact undoubtedly tending strongly to promote initial amalgamation. The mulatto man, shut out from all hope of further racial transition in so far as he is personally concerned, does nothing radical to restrain the Negro or the mulatto woman in her efforts to secure a better racial status for her offspring. In a lesser degree, possibly, the fullblood Negro man fails to impose upon the Negro or the mulatto woman an effective restraint. It is not known to what extent he endeavors to do so. Thus the preponderance of the influences now operating in the Negro group is practically on the side of race amalgamation.

The incentive thus supplied to the whole Negro race in the United States to breed away from darker shades of color is undoubtedly strong. The matter of relative achievement alone would have this effect. Professor Reuter has reached the conclusion that the chances of the mixed blood in the United States are thirty-four times greater than are the chances of the full-blood Negro child.[5] The Negro and the mulatto women are capable of understanding this situation and of drawing from it incentives which, reënforced by baser motives, hasten racial intermixture. These incentives have a potential force for the entire Negro group. They are certainly operative for considerable numbers.

There is no doubt that, once the process of amalgamation is begun, the incentives to complete it are intensified with each advancing step. To the mulatto the process is partially completed, the road to its consummation clearly pointed out. The nearer the goal, the greater the haste. With the near-white the prize is almost won and eager attempts to "cross the line" are the natural reaction to this situation.

What then should be the attitude toward the near-white? All the hurtfulness of the mulatto group as a whole is en-

[5] *The Mulatto in the United States*, Reuter, p. 314. Later this advantage is given as 50 to 100 to one.

countered here in greatly intensified form. The situation is greatly complicated. The interests of the white race are clearly indicated and should prevail. The interests of the fullblood Negro are likewise clearly indicated and, in fundamental aspects, coincide with those of the white race. The mulatto group, some millions strong, cannot be a negligible factor. There can be no escape from the problems created by this group. Refusal to recognize and to deal consciously and decisively and constructively with it and with the problems it creates means that the matter of racial integrity is left to take the course that chance, or worse, dictates, certainly the worst possible method of dealing with it. The near-white is now, like the Negro and the mulatto, one of the inescapable facts in American life.

As in the mulatto group as a whole, even more so in the near-white group, there are two extremes. There are those who, in the long periods of time involved, sink hopelessly. Often these are the more sensitive, the more highly endowed individuals. Possibly no other class of women is more unfortunately situated. On the other hand, it is in this near-white group that some outstanding examples of culture and achievement are found. There are indications that the tendency in this group is either to fall decidedly below, or to rise decidedly above the average of the Negro group as a whole.

As in the mulatto group as a whole, even more so in the near-white group, there is one fact which cannot be ignored. It is impossible to disregard moral and ethical principles in practice and yet maintain them by theory or by precept. Behind the near-white is a record that is quite universally most unfortunate potentially for the individual inheriting it. In order to reach such a racial status, there must have been several cases of initial amalgamation, each usually involving a fullblood white male and a female of a succeeding generation of the Negroid family. In no part of the United States has any relatively large number of cases of mixed marriages occurred. In many states, such marriages are illegal. If this situation is accepted without analysis—as it is accepted by many persons at the present time—its significance may not appear. If carefully analyzed, its significance is overwhelming. As with the mulatto, even more so with the near-white, outstanding achievement renders him the greater menace to the ideals and the practices of the fullblood Negro, and of the mulatto.

Here there arises again the problem of how to deal justly and constructively with the mixed blood and yet preserve the ideals and the racial integrity of both races. As yet, no one has furnished a reasoned program and secured its general acceptance and application; so that chance, or worse, has prevailed. The near-white is the logical, the inevitable, result of conditions which have obtained and of the attitudes and sanctions held by both groups.

The mulatto problem is very acute in the State of Virginia. The first Negro slaves brought to the English Colonies were landed at Jamestown late in 1619. A generous portion of all the Negroes imported during the next century were landed in this State or found their way into it for labor in the cotton or the tobacco fields, both these crops proving highly profitable under slave labor. In the main, the system of large plantations did not obtain in Virginia to the degree that it did later in some sections further south. Slavery here was more decidedly domestic in character, involving a closer association of the races than did the conditions on large plantations. Time, and this closer association, naturally resulted in an increased number of mixed bloods. Then, too, the demoralization incident to the Civil War fell most heavily upon this State. In no other State were so many men under arms, or under arms so long a time.

The Federal Census of 1870 reported 72,248 mulattoes in Virginia. That of 1890 reported 122,441. That of 1910, the latest dependable enumeration, reported 222,910, the largest number of mulattoes reported for any one State in the Union!

97

If this rate of increase is maintained, the Census of 1950 would return not less than 400,000 mixed bloods in Virginia! In addition to those residing within the State, many Virginia Negroes are now scattered throughout the North and the East. Many are located in the District of Columbia. It is quite probable that mulattoes compose a larger part of the migrants than do fullblood Negroes. In reference to amalgamation, in so far as numbers are concerned, conditions are worse in Virginia than in any other State. This, however, should not stigmatize Virginia. Conditions among the settled Negro population of this State are now those that will obtain later elsewhere. There are in this State several Negro schools, dominated by, and attracting, mulatto students. The Census of 1910 showed the percentage of mulatto in the total Negro population higher in fourteen other States than in Virginia.

While there are in Virginia at the present time a very large number of mulattoes, there is no means of ascertaining accurately what percentage of these belong to the marginal group of near-whites. The proportion is probably higher than elsewhere. There is also a class in this State known as "redbones," showing a mixture of Indian-white-Negro, but insisting upon being classed as Indian. Possibly the most valuable study yet made of this situation is that by Estabrook and McDougle, under the title: *Mongrel Virginians.*

The situation in Virginia and the efforts made to control miscegenation there are worthy of most careful study. As conditions are worse, numerically, than in any other State, so here has been developed a program for the protection of the white group. In reality, the policy of Virginia affords protection for both races, but its anti-miscegenation program, initiated two hundred years late, is frankly and avowedly for the protection of the white population.

In some sections of Virginia the situation is greatly complicated by the presence of a group claiming to be Indian. Such groups, carefully studied by Estabrook and McDougle, are unquestionably of mixed Indian-Negro-white origin but claim Indian descent, since this classification is the most favorable possible. *It is often the case that the near-white claims Indian descent.* This claim is sometimes made by typical Negroes and is now sufficiently general to affect the figures giving the Indian population of the United States.

Through the State Registrar of Vital Statistics the work of ascertaining and registering the ancestry and the racial antecedents of the near-whites of this State has been carried forward with gratifying thoroughness. Wherever there arises need to do so, local officials who issue marriage licenses must refer the case to the Central Office, with such references as will serve to identify both parties and must thus ascertain the facts before issuing the marriage license. Penalties are severe, but necessity for their infliction seldom arises. The near-whites are known locally and do not, as a rule, make application for license to marry fullblood whites when it is known that such application will not only be refused but will likely lead to wide publicity. The easier, and more prevalent, method with such people is to leave the State. There are now in the District of Columbia and further north a very considerable number of near-whites who have left Virginia, or some other Southern State. Some have gone as far as into Canada. Frequently these explain any peculiarities of color or features that may exist as due to Latin or Indian ancestry. The desire to "cross the line," and thus to find a place and recognition in the more favorably situated white race, may well be the determining motive impelling the near-white in this migration.

The Virginia plan, while harsh in some of its aspects, is the best yet devised for the prevention of amalgamation through legal intermarriage involving near-whites. It is deficient in that it does not deal with cases of illegitimate racial intermixture—initial amalgamations. That the plan should drive into the District of Columbia and into the cities and towns of the North and East much of the near-white element in the South is unfortunate for these sections.

Too much emphasis can hardly be placed upon the fact

that there has been, and still is, quite a general movement of the mixed-blood people from the South, where conditions and the significance of racial intermixture are better understood, into those sections where there is as yet no general knowledge of and no definite convictions concerning black and white racial intermixture. The finishing up of the process of amalgamation may logically be expected to occur largely in the Northern half of the United States.

New Orleans has a large element of near-whites. There is also a large element of Latin extraction and a large group of mulattoes. A considerable part of the city is occupied by such people.

There is no way to arrive at an accurate statement of the number of near-whites in the District of Columbia. It is certain, however, that there are many falling under this classification. In the main they do not attempt to pass as whites, but accept their traditional status. There are those, however, who endeavor to enter the life of the white group by denying or concealing their Negro ancestry. Certain conditions here are favorable to such efforts.

There are at present in Washington City a considerable number of people who, in color and in features, are nearer to the mulatto type than are some of the near-whites. Many of these are doubtless fullblood white people—Aryans—but only those who have made a careful study of such matters can be at all sure upon mere casual inspection that there is or is not black-white mixture in a given case. In the main there is little occasion for the average citizen to decide upon the racial status of another man. As a rule there are no prospective relations, business or social, outside the government service, that render it necessary to investigate the matter of racial antecedents, as most people would do before admitting a doubtful case into their circle of personal intimates. Occasional mingling with white people in public gatherings or in official or semiofficial social functions is relatively easy, but in the more personal and private social life of the city the

situation is different. So long as only public or official functions are involved, no one is likely to make inquiry or to
volunteer information. It would be easy to point out many
cases in which the near-whites are associating with white
people to the extent of eating in white restaurants and attending white theaters and white public gatherings generally.
In reality, the facts in such cases are reasonably certain to become known and to have their effect, both with the Negro race
and with the white group involved. Several such cases are
known to the writer in which the near-whites are associating
thus with white people, apparently believing that they have
"crossed the line," when, as a matter of fact, many white people are convinced that Negro blood is present. Such cases are
deeply tragic. The hurtfulness of racial intermixture seems
less in those cases where it is accepted and the life ordered
accordingly. This puts the individual life upon an honest
basis and removes the fear of adverse discovery.

It is among the near-white group that the greatest dissatisfaction with the present status exists. It could hardly be
otherwise. The mulatto has received, with his white blood,
something of the distinguishing characteristics of the white
race. As, by repeated infusions of white blood, the mulatto
approaches the blood status of the white man, he gains
something of the outlook of the white race. With its achievements and with its ideals there is vastly greater affinity than
there is with the Negro heritage. If, as Professor Reuter finds,
the average advantage of the mulatto child in prospective
achievement is thirty-four times that of the average fullblood
Negro child, then logically this advantage of the white child
over the fullblood Negro child is 68 to 1. It is equally logical
to treat the ascending scale of the infusion of white blood as
carrying with it increasing potentialities, so that the index
for the near-white would lie somewhere between 34 to 1
and equality with the white. This is, however, too largely
theoretical to be regarded as final in so far as exact figures are
concerned. There are factors other than race involved and

some of these are vitally influential, if not decisive. The achievements of the exceptional mulatto, especially those of the exceptional near-white, as contrasted with those of the fullblood Negro, unquestionably tend very strongly to promote amalgamation.

The statement is often made by Negro writers, and by others, that cases of "crossing the line," or passing over into the white race, by near-white mulattos are very numerous in the District of Columbia and elsewhere. There is doubtless exaggeration in such statements, yet there is enough of truth in them to give them currency and to make them a warning concerning attitudes. There are such cases, and those involved often exhibit shrewdness in playing their parts. They often mistake in reference to the insight of others. In some of these cases the dominating motive is that of outwitting the whites and thwarting their exclusiveness. In others there is an honest desire to share in the cultural life of the white race, especially so as the Negro has not yet reached the point where he can produce or support a satisfying cultural life. In other cases there is an earnest desire to escape from a race disparaged by its own members. Whatever the motive, or combination of motives, the burden these people bear is a frightfully heavy one, easily becoming a highly destructive heritage.

In concluding this chapter, regarded by the writer as one of the most important in this book, it seems especially unfortunate that a more detailed statement, a more accurate numerical statement, cannot be given. It is known that there is an increasingly large number of near-whites. It is also known that these are migrating northward. When considered from the standpoint of their own attitudes, these fall into two classes. There are those who make no attempt to conceal facts and who, whatever their personal feelings and attitudes, resort to no subterfuges or deceptions. However tragic the situation of such people, they deserve that credit and that consideration which sincerity and honor everywhere command. It is certainly true that this recognition of fact and this basing of the life upon ultimate fact goes far toward neutralizing certain otherwise destructive elements in the situation of such persons. Many near-whites are, however, taking the chances of "passing" for the sake of the advantages now available chiefly to, and through, the white race.

The second class of near-whites, then, consists of those who, occasionally or habitually, "pass" as white. They are thus, without racial discrimination, able to attend the social functions of a public nature and to participate in the public cultural agencies of the white group. It is sometimes claimed that such are able to mediate to the Negroes what they, by stealth, gain from the white groups they enter. This, however, may be questioned. No near-white may hope to pass for white and, at the same time, retain his place with the Negro, or even with the Negroid, group. The purpose of such persons is usually not the uplift of the Negro but rather to achieve escape from a race disparaged by the very attempt to escape from it. The hurtfulness of the situation, deplorable enough in the case of those meeting it honestly, is greatly augmented by the fact that the persons of this second class are consciously practicing deception, and such deception as must influence adversely moral character as well as self-respect.

Against their possible value as intermediaries between the Negro race and the culture of the white race, the hurtful effects of the mulatto—especially the near-white—must prevail. The depressing effect upon race consciousness and race loyalty must be considered. The fullblood Negro's race consciousness, his race loyalty, are correctly regarded as, in large measure, the product of his social position *and of race prejudice,* not of a clear grasp of fundamental principles involved. This is a vital, but a melancholy, truth in the great majority of cases in which race loyalty exists. Race prejudice upon the part of the white, essentially defensive, and the answering attitude upon the part of the whole Negro group, must be recognized as possibly the most potent force making for racial self-respect and for racial integrity. Christianity, as applied to this situation, is failing just where race prejudice becomes most constructive and most effective.

Virtually all who discuss the matter of race amalgamation neglect, or treat inadequately, the conditions under which this occurs as between the black and the white races in America. The biological aspects of the race problem are treated as if more important than the moral issues involved. The social and the political aspects receive more attention than do the moral and the religious problems involved. Relatively few legal intermarriages between Caucasians and Negroes have occurred. It is safe, therefore, to assume that, in the case of every near-white, there have been from three to five cases of illegitimacy—initial amalgamations—in the immediate ancestry. It is this fact which renders it impossible to deal with the near-white upon the individualistic basis without a most destructive influence upon the whole Negro group. It is here that we are brought face to face with the supreme, the inescapable tragedy of the near-white as found throughout the United States. *There is here one of the strongest arguments supporting racial separation.*

CHAPTER V

THE POOR WHITE

IN EVERY social order there are those who fail to achieve economic independence. That this is true is due partly to the organization of society and partly to the personal characteristics of the poor. Poverty is sometimes reprehensible; it is sometimes an inherited misfortune, carrying with it no just censure upon its unfortunate victim. The children of the incompetent, the thriftless, the vicious, the blamelessly unfortunate, do not have a fair chance in life. Social stratifications appear at their best when they surround the economically fortunate and the socially privileged with opportunity and when pride of birth and pride of position prove an inspiration leading to noble endeavor and to high achievement. Social stratifications appear at their worst when, because of heredity, poverty, ignorance, or from any other cause, they limit the field of opportunity or even destroy the ambitions of those unfavorably situated. Childhood and youth are most influenced by such stratification. There are, of course, numerous instances in which superior advantages fail in the production of either character or economic efficiency. There are other instances in which individuals rise superior to unfavorable environment and depressing antecedents. However numerous such cases may be in newer and undeveloped areas, cases of marked individual achievement tend to grow relatively infrequent among the underprivileged when a more advanced stage of industrial development has been reached and competition has grown correspondingly intense. In such a situation the tendency of inefficiency, of inertia, of lack of ability, is that the individual, together with those dependent upon him, is forced into a lower and less favorable classification. The "submerged tenth" of the slums of the larger cities is the outstanding example that our civilization affords of the operation of the principles applying here.

In situations where there is but one race to be dealt with, the problem of the poor is relatively simple. While the number of the poor may be large and their depressing influence great, the problem remains individualistic or, at worst, becomes a class problem. It does not become racial in scope. The situation is more likely to affect adversely those who are deficient in some vital respect determining natural ability, or in some personal characteristic determining efficiency or dependability. The problem of poverty is, therefore, quite different as between a uni-racial and a bi-racial or a cosmopolitan situation.

The most unfortunate bi-racial situations, as measured from the standpoint of the interests of the poor of the dominant race, are found, possibly, when the poor of the more advanced race, a race whose standards of living are high, must compete with the laborers of another race whose standards are lower and who can, therefore, if sufficiently numerous, drive out the laborer of the superior group, or reduce his standard of living, his possibilities, to the level of those characterizing the laborer of the less favored group. The burden of this competition falls at first upon the most defenseless stratum of the superior race. Later it extends to other strata. The slums of a uni-racial situation are essentially eliminative, in that they tend to limit, if not to destroy, the elements constituting them.

Through the operation of the laws and the forces involved in the contact of two races upon different planes, especially as these affect the poor of the more advanced group, then, there arises, in addition to that part of this group which would normally fail to achieve or to maintain economic independence, another group which might readily thrive under more favorable conditions but which, thus situated, sinks to the common level of those less highly endowed. Thus there is added to the handicapped element of the more privileged

106

group a class which, although possessing possibilities, is characterized by inefficiency, lack of ambition, and, ultimately, by shiftlessness. These are terms accurately descriptive of the lower type of the "poor white," as found in the South, and of the corresponding class in South Africa. It is highly suggestive of the existence of a general economic fact, or law, when similar conditions in widely separated parts of the world are found producing similar, if not identical, results. It is interesting to find students familiar with both situations using virtually the same terms in dealing with the "poor white" as are used in dealing with the "bywoner." Both are largely rural.

The similarity existing between the problems confronting the white residents of South Africa and the conditions in the United States is such as to render a study of South Africa highly instructive. The area is great and by no means uniform. In the older settled regions the natives have been in contact with the whites for more than three centuries. The first Dutch settlement was made in 1652, at which time they displaced the Portuguese. Van Riebeck, governor of the colony, had with him one hundred men and five women.

From the beginning of the settlement of South Africa, there was little reason to admit the poor white European. Native labor was abundant and the institution of slavery made it possible to use the natives for all the work required—farming and stock-raising. Conditions later became such that prohibitive conditions were imposed for the purpose of restricting white immigration. Only those possessing a minimum sum in cash were admitted. Yet a very considerable number of white people found their way into South Africa, people under the necessity of earning a living by labor or by agriculture and that in competition with the natives. In mining the unskilled labor was done by the natives. Mr. James writes of "five hundred thousand poor whites" [1] who lost their land, attributing this to their unwillingness to use improved

---

[1] *South of the Congo*, James, pp. 43, 112.

machinery or to break otherwise with established custom. Other students and writers are more sympathetic and recognize the fact of competition with the native as the chief factor in the all but hopeless state of the South African "bywoner."

South Africa is an immense area and different parts are now at different stages of development. Negro labor is, however, much the same throughout and involves much the same social and economic considerations. Everywhere Negro labor is cheap. For coarser tasks and for manual toil generally, native labor is now sufficiently intelligent and gives promise of further improvement. There are now cases of natives performing skilled labor and receiving for such labor a wage greater than is paid to unskilled white labor.

The white in South Africa has stopped tribal and clan wars and forays as between natives, thus ending great and wanton destruction of property and preserving alive many who would, but for this intervention, perish in the prime of life. Under the instruction of the white, and using the tools and the implements of the white man, an adequate and dependable food supply has been developed—an indispensable condition of population increase. Under the supervision of the white, the advantages of medical skill and of sanitation have been, to some degree, imposed upon the native. Indeed, the South African Negro owes every advance he has made directly to the white man. Lobengula, Dingaan, and other tribal chiefs were responsible for so many wars and such destruction of lives as to keep down the native population. As order was introduced, and enforced, and slaughter stopped, the immediate result of this supervision was a phenomenal increase in the native Negro population. The American Indian disappeared before the advance of the white settler in North America. The African native is not so accommodating.

On the other hand, the white man of South Africa has made free use of those expedients calculated to protect him-

self, his standard of living, and his civilization. He has even
given some attention to the matter of his racial preservation.
In the last respect he has shown an insight and an intelligence
sadly missed in America's dealings with the same problems.
One of the lines of defensive effort has been to hold the
native to unskilled labor, refusing to permit him to serve
such apprenticeship as would make of him a skilled laborer.
In the fields of unskilled labor his wage has been so low as to
render competition on the part of the white impossible. The
scheme of all skilled labor for the white and only unskilled
labor and menial tasks for the native has not, however, proved
a final solution for the situation. It is of interest that the
author of an article in *The Round Table*, despite the relative newness of South Africa and the abundance of the land,
finds that the "bywoner" class, the "poor whites" of South
Africa, number nearly one tenth of the whole European
population." [2]

Under the title "The African Labor Problem," the situation in South Africa is ably discussed in this issue of *The
Round Table* for June, 1928. Here it is pointed out that the
Negro ". . . is usually debarred from employment in the
skilled trades by custom, trade union interdict, and in the
mines by legislation." [3] It is further pointed out that the
"European worker is haunted by the fear of competition of
great masses of native laborers with their low standard of
comfort and consequent willingness to accept wages which
to the European mean degradation, if not starvation. . . .
Self-preservation is the first law of nature, and so the policy
adopted has been one of 'keeping the native in his place,' in
order that certain of the higher jobs might be retained as the
special preserve of the European worker. . . ." [4] Thus the
Trade Union Coordinating Committee states the situation.

Other authorities are even more emphatic. Sir Walter Hely
Hutchinson, Governor of Natal from 1893 until 1900, and of

[2] *The Round Table*, June, 1928, p. 505.
[3] *Ibid.*, p. 511.
[4] *The Round Table*, June, 1928, p. 512.

Cape Colony later, thus explains the situation in reference to the "poor whites" of South Africa: "Speaking of the poor white class, he says: 'Kaffir's work they will not do, skilled work they cannot do. They sink and sink and live in misery and wretchedness, the poor whites as they are called, objects of compassion, and, alas! of contempt even to the natives, relying, not a few of them, on the natives to preserve them from starvation. The poor white problem is one of the most pressing of South African problems. It is in a sense the direct result of native and coloured environment.' There is no ambiguity about the opinion of one of the able proconsuls Britain has sent to South Africa, and one whose opportunities for obtaining the fullest information, and forming a sound judgment thereon, were very great." [5]

"The presence of the persistent yet adaptive black man seems to set up a line of cleavage in the white race. Those who, whilst accepting the situation, accept it with all its responsibilities—responsibilities of government and of individual development, and thus retain their race fibre; and those who, accepting the easy conditions of merely animal life set up by the presence of a lower race, lose their fibre and degenerate." [6]

"In others we see various stages of degeneracy down to absolute indolence and familiarity with the native terminating in miscegenation. Once that is reached, the white man is lost. He may struggle and pretend that he still retains his self-respect and at meetings of men attempt to assert himself, but invariably the consciousness of effort is present, and a general coldness of those present accentuates it. But generally a misanthropic aloofness is characteristic of those who have fallen so far." [7]

"I suppose, in the opinion of the average South African (white) the admixture in blood of the races is the worst that can happen, at least for the white race, and possibly for

[5] *Black and White in Southeast Africa*, Evans, p. 221.
[6] *Ibid.*, p. 222.
[7] *Black and White in Southeast Africa*, Evans, p. 223.

110

both. . . . But he can see the degradation of the white man, the ambiguous position of the children, often the resentment of the native in cases of miscegenation: and he deplores it as the ultimate evil due to the contact of races. . . . The vast majority deplore and condemn, and with them I must range myself. Whatever may be the position of the woman, that of the man is one of degradation, and, if no other argument were possible, the anomolous position of the children should be sufficient warrant to make for utter condemnation." [8]

These quotations, from authorities of unquestionable standing, are offered here as the best statement available of the situation existing in South Africa in reference to the "poor white" and to the miscegenation of the races. The two are inseparably connected. The white man, deserted by his own race, deprived of employment at a living wage because a Negro will work for less, deprived of home and family ties because of this competition, may well curse the race which betrays him. Certainly, he cannot be expected to take pride in its perpetuation. His social degradation furnishes an atmosphere in which miscegenation thrives.

The effort of the white laborer in South Africa to protect himself has been but a partial success. Back in England have been missionary societies and churches and philanthropists, teaching equality and brotherhood—chiefly for foreign or colonial consumption—and commercial and governmental agencies sometimes more concerned, seemingly, for the native than for the colonial whites. Indeed, in the future scheme of empire as held by Europe, so long as Europe herself may be regarded as safe, little attention is given to the mongrelization of remote areas or to the loss to the white group of the whites involved. There is cause, however, for serious alarm upon the part of Europe. It is highly probable that a backwash of mixed bloods will ultimately find a place in Europe in sufficient numbers to affect the population even there.

Competition with Negro labor in South Africa has pro-

<hr/>

[8] *Black and White in Southeast Africa*, Evans, p. 223.

duced one result there that is very important and has its counterpart in the United States and elsewhere. *Labor is discredited,* and anyone performing certain types of manual labor, especially unskilled labor, loses caste by doing so. "These humbler occupations have been practically barred to the poor European by the sentiment that they are 'Kaffir's work.' Ordinary manual labor is beneath the dignity of the white man, because it reduces him to the level of the native and is rewarded by a wage which precludes him from maintaining a civilized standard of life." [9]

"If the white man becomes an unskilled laborer, his social superiority over the black race, to which he clings the more forlornly as he sinks in the social scale, is gravely menaced." [10]

"There are already a number of white men whose standard of living is definitely below that of the more advanced natives." [11]

Summing up the situation in South Africa, the article in *The Round Table* calls attention to the fact that the unionist "knows that he (the native Negro) will always be ready to do the same work for less money. To admit him, therefore, into the skilled occupations would simply mean the debasement of the standards which trade union action has succeeded in securing, with the ultimate degeneration of the white worker generally." [12] The present situation, however, does not warrant optimism in reference to the ultimate complete success of this plan. The native is improving and is gaining in the contest so that, in the opinion of this writer, ". . . equality of economic opportunity between the white and the black races is becoming inevitable." [13] The situation of the white laborer is the less hopeful since it is evident that in South Africa, as in the United States, the employers of labor, with few exceptions, are vastly more interested in dividends than in racial selection and preservation. This is especially true

[9] *The Round Table,* June, 1928, p. 504.
[10] *Round Table,* June, 1928, p. 505.
[11] *The Round Table,* June, 1928, p. 506.
[12] *The Round Table,* June, 1928, p. 508.
[13] *The Round Table,* June, 1928, p. 515.

of the large mining concerns. In South Africa, as in the United States, there is urgent need for intelligent supervision of the employers of labor, with special reference to the race and the quality of the people who are imported as laborers and to the relative needs of the higher, as contrasted with the lower, in the groups already employed., Uncontrolled corporations, employing large numbers of manual laborers, will usually turn to the cheapest labor available, whether that labor be European, Asiatic, or African. With such corporations, the present profit looms larger than the social conditions or the racial situation inevitably following. Had the corporations been allowed to carry out their plans, and the large land-holders of the United States been permitted to develop their holdings with cheap Oriental labor, the West would have been lost to the white race. This lesson now seems lost or forgotten. Mexicans, Cubans, and Puerto Ricans are finding places among us.

The references and the quotations given above indicate the situation in South Africa. The outstanding fact in reference to this situation is that there has been an effort upon the part of the white people involved to protect themselves. That this effort is not a complete success is evidenced by the existence of the present "bywoner" group, constituting 10 per cent of the white population. If the white cannot hold his own now in competition with the black worker, what will be the result when the natives, *and the mixed breeds,* greatly increased in numbers and, better trained and educated by the whites, assert their claim to the mastery of the country?

Both in South Africa and in the United States the white and the black races live side by side, but nowhere on general terms of social equality. In both areas there has developed this class of "poor white" much more numerous than can be accounted for on the ground of mental deficiences or moral delinquencies. In neither area has there been, upon the part of those entrusted with the supervision of affairs, civil, economic, social, moral, religious, any clear and complete under-

113

standing of this element of the population. Both in England and in America there has been exhibited, in circles usually not in intimate touch with bi-racial contacts, an utter lack of comprehension of the situation of the white who has had to make his place, and build his home, and rear his family in the presence of the Negro, or in competition with any other group similarly situated. Both in England and in America, therefore, there is, in the privileged circles, much more sympathy for and understanding of the Negro than there is of, or for, the "poor white." This class in the South, called by the Negro slaves "poor white trash," affords an illustration quite as valuable as does South Africa, quite as interesting and as illuminating an example, of what usually, if not inevitably, happens when an alien race, slave or free, performs the manual labor and the menial tasks of a civilization. There tends to develop a wealthy leisure class, a master class, composed of those born to privilege and of those who, through personal achievement, win recognition and this coveted social status. A strong middle class can hardly develop or maintain itself by honorable means under such conditions. We hear much of fair dealing, equal opportunity, and so on, coming from classes wholly removed from the intensity of the struggle for bread, a class often whose convenience, or pleasure, or profit, or leisure, depend upon a laboring class, which must submit to hard conditions and whose necessities hold them to service satisfactory from the standpoint of the employer.

In the United States there has been no effort to protect the "poor white" from the competition of the Negro, nor has there been upon the part of white labor, especially upon the part of the "poor white," any clear, far-reaching plan of defense against the inevitable tendencies of this competition. In the immediate struggle for financial success cheap labor is sought from whatever source available, while the future of the white race—the racial composition of the future population—is forgotten. Thus each area of marked achievement, instead of maintaining, or improving, its racial status, tends to become a magnet, drawing into itself elements calculated to reduce it to the common level.

It may be advanced as a general proposition that the white man, beaten down to a low standard of living and held there relentlessly, becomes either abject in his hopelessness and degradation or a social rebel. When native American white laborers are displaced by foreigners or by Negroes, crime usually increases, for thus are criminals made. The higher the spirit of the displaced group, the graver the danger of lawlessness. A liberal percentage of those thus displaced and of that greater number whose standard of living is forced down in order that they may be retained in employment, will, even though remaining law-abiding citizens, turn to radical theories, the tendency being, at best, toward socialism; at worst, toward communism or anarchy. Once driven to these groups; once the die is cast in favor of radicalism, recovery, economical or social, is unlikely. It is necessary everywhere to protect the poor white. He is not in position to protect himself. Often, after two or three generations, so complete is his lack of insight and his lack of outlook that he himself does not recognize his true status.

As an example of the features of race contact now under discussion, the following instance may have illustrative value. Some years ago there were employed on a farm in Middle Tennessee several laborers. Two of these were young white men whose wages did not exceed $15 per month. There were two Negroes employed, whose wages were supplemented by a cabin in which to live. There was also an elderly white man who, with his large family, occupied a small cottage and garden spot on this farm. His labor, with that of his family, was available in time of harvesting and in other times of stress.

It is not known what became of the two Negroes. One of the younger white men married and, with the family of his father, the elderly man referred to above, and that of a

115

brother-in-law, set out overland for Texas. Some years later he appeared in the State of Missouri, still a rover and still desperately poor. The other young white man soon left the farm and entered employment where there was no direct competition with Negro labor. He later became manager of the Western branch house of an important business concern, a man of recognized ability, and one commanding the respect of all who knew him. Had he not escaped the competition with Negro labor, his fate would not have been essentially different from that of the other two white men.

Possibly the most interesting and instructive of these cases were those of the young man who, through the influence and assistance of relatives, was enabled to escape the direct competition of the cheap Negro labor of that time, and the elderly man who finally gave up the struggle, put his large family and his few household effects into a wagon drawn by two inferior horses, tied the dog under the wagon and the cow behind it, and thus passed down the road and out of the life of the local community. Texas was the announced destination.

What is here said involved agricultural labor only, but holds good for all forms of manual labor, and especially for all forms of unskilled labor. Wages, wherever Negroes have been numerous, but especially in agriculture, have been so low that only Negroes, with their low standards of living, could render the service required. In recent years wages have been higher, but the cost of living has also risen and it is doubtful if there has been any material lessening of the hurtfulness of racial competition in so far as the poor white is concerned. In spite of the low wages prevailing at that time, the farm referred to above was not profitable. Prices for farm produce were likewise low.

The farm referred to above was that upon which the childhood of the writer was spent. Thus early in life he came into contact with a situation not then understood, one not yet understood by the American people, or even by those assuming the leadership of the American people. Labor organizations, in their opposition to the introduction of foreign labor, have made a near approach to a clear understanding of the significance of cheap foreign labor; but here the problem was one of immediate self-interest rather than of any farsighted view of the dangers of such competition in its inevitable results within the higher group. When the mobs, composed of white laborers employed in the construction of transcontinental railways, and of agricultural laborers, miners, and others rose against Oriental labor, and by violence stopped its use, the West was saved, for a time, at least, to a white civilization.

From the records of the past, it seems clearly established that no group of people, occupying a privileged position socially or economically, will hesitate to use the cheapest and the most subservient labor available. As long as possible it was the *slave* of an alien race preferably, but the *slave* even when he represented the poor of the same racial group as the master. The Hebrew Scriptures are very illuminative just here, especially the Mosaic law dealing with the institution of slavery.

The next higher step in mass progress is illustrated in *feudalism*. Here the dependence of the poor upon the feudal lord was scarcely less than that upon the master under slavery, there being little place except in outlawry for the detached "no man's man." The chief superiority of feudalism over slavery lies in the fact that it introduced an element of voluntary action in giving or withholding allegiance.

This, however, meant vastly more to the knight, to the socially privileged, than to the serf. Serfdom, possibly even more than slavery, tended to destroy the middle class, giving to the privileged classes such advantages as the underprivileged could not overcome. The nature of the arms and of the armor used was such as to confirm the privileges enjoyed by the knights. The invention of gunpowder and firearms destroyed knighthood and, incidentally, initiated the emancipation of the serf.

We are accustomed to speak of industrialism as if it were conducive to real democracy. Except for universal education and for other forces counteracting its logical tendencies, modern industrialism would quickly destroy individual freedom, for here the individual laborer is dependent for food, for shelter, and for clothing—everything he uses—upon his wages. Whoever controls the wage, controls the wage earner. Hence the power of the uncontrolled employer of labor. By bringing in or by employing a given type of labor, profound changes in population may be quickly made. The higher racial types of labor may completely disappear.

There appears, then, to be little place for the unfortunate of the superior race, or for those of the more privileged race compelled to live by toil, when the more privileged class of the superior race are able to secure the services of those belonging to a less favorably situated racial group. Indeed, this seems to be a general law of higher and lower group contacts, even when racial differences are not involved, but greatly intensified when such differences enter into the situation. A seeming exception occurs in those cases where a limited number of representatives of the more advanced group go into the territory of a less advanced group and there prosper in business or gain dominant status otherwise. It must be conceded, however, that such individuals possess initiative, or they would not leave their own group. They are really a select few and do not belong to that class in special need of protection. In spite of possible exploitation, these individuals may, and often do, prove helpful to the people among whom they go. They do not deal with the laboring class of their own race.

This need for protection upon the part of the poor of a given race, when in competition with another race, is a problem apart from the academic question of inferiority or superiority of one race as compared with another. The Japanese becomes the greater menace to the white laborer of America not because of any inferiority but rather because of his excellent qualities as a laborer, his perseverance, his dependability, his high intelligence, and his skill, coupled with his race inheritance from centuries of enforced practice of ultimate economies. On the other hand, as opposed to Chinese laborers, the Japanese needs protection, since Chinese standards of living are lower and the conditions under which the Chinese poor have lived for many centuries have schooled them in the art of consuming little while maintaining high productivity. The contest between the Chinese and the Japanese, the two great peoples whose standards of living for the masses are now lowest, is probably one of the greatest of the world problems at the present time, and destined long to remain so.

The responsibility for the existence of the "poor white" class, in so far as it is composed of subnormal individuals, need not be fixed. That is a task for the eugenists. In so far, however, as this class is composed of those capable of achieving economic efficiency and independence but fail to do so, the problem is more complex, and a large share of the responsibility must be placed outside the group failing thus to use their native endowment. A large part of the responsibility for the existence of the "poor white" class, therefore, rests upon those in the white race who, in position to promote a constructive program, through ignorance, through indifference, through shortsighted greed, through desire for mastery, or through any and all unreasoning attitudes, have been willing, for temporary gain or convenience, to depress and to repress the poor of their own racial group.

There are few instances in American history in which the employers of labor have acted with the ultimate results of their acts in view. The early settlers demanded, and obtained, Negro slaves; later, the industrial plants, the mines, and the railroads demanded, and secured, cheap European labor; the West is now demanding, and getting, cheap Mexican labor,

119

with a contingent from the Philippines. The West Indies—Cuba and Puerto Rico—with Jamaica—are at our southern border. Possibly since the landing of the first Negro slaves at Jamestown no graver crisis has confronted the white man in these United States than was involved in the threat of Oriental immigration, unless it be in the present threat of the West Indian and of the Mexican immigrant.

The privileged white, with the advantage of cheap service, and seemingly secure in his social and his racial status, is prone to forget the poor of his own race group—when he does not actually exploit them. The "poor white" of the South suffered most seriously under slavery, but competition with the Negro as a free laborer is scarcely less hurtful. Under slavery there were forces tending to prevent the development of a strong middle class in the white group. Only the newness, the undeveloped condition of the South, with the vast acreage of unused fertile soil and other resources untouched, counteracted much of the potential hurtfulness of this situation under slavery and has had a favorable influence since the emancipation of the Negro. With the increase of population and with the harder conditions of living; with the sharper competition and the greater intensity of the struggle for a bare subsistence, the advantage of the Negro over the "poor white" is more keenly real, and his power to degrade white labor generally is correspondingly increased.

There is in the United States, but not in South Africa, a rather general assumption that, in order to have the Negro cease to be a menace to the white race, he should be "elevated" in the sense of becoming a skilled workman, be admitted to the trade unions, and in every way be encouraged to enter the fields of higher paid employment. In considering this view, several considerations arise. In the first place, there are a sufficient number of white men—if trained and the present wastage corrected—to perform all the skilled labor required, or likely ever to be required, in the United States. In the main, these whites are not receiving technical training.

Why are the Negrophile philanthropists and religionists so concerned for the prospective Negro artisan but so utterly forgetful of those of their own race? This question every white man directly affected may well ask. For every Negro trained as a skilled artisan, a white skilled artisan, actual or potential, is displaced. For every such Negro who builds a home and rears a family, somewhere a white man is either deprived of the chance to build a home and rear a family, or is driven to contend with highly unfavorable conditions in his efforts to do so.

Here we have the crux of the matter as seen by the white laborer of South Africa. So far, the skilled laborer of South Africa has, by custom and by law, been protected. The fact that the "bywoner" there constitutes 10 per cent of the total white population indicates that the brunt of racial competition has been thrown upon a single class, and that the class least able to bear it. In America in the past as at present the brunt of racial competition has likewise fallen upon that element of the white race least able to resist it. In the two areas this disregard for the interests of the unfortunately situated stratum of the white race has produced similar, if not identical, results. The white group here has seemed quite willing that the burden of interracial competition should rest upon the poor, but the time has come when the interests of other classes are affected. The reaction of such groups is usually unfavorable to the Negro, but no constructive program has been agreed upon. The Negro schools are now training carpenters, bricklayers, cement workers, and like artisans. Every one of these Negroes will, in so far as he works at his trade, displace a white worker, actual or potential. These schools are also fitting Negroes for professional life. The support of the professional Negro must come largely from his own race, thus involving competition with the various professional white groups.

Agriculture has small place with the Negroes who have migrated to the North but throughout the South it looms large. In this field of activity there is less conscious competition between the races than in any other, possibly more of cooperation. Unfortunately, the one-crop system prevailing in parts of the South and involving Negro labor to a large extent has very little intellectual stimulus for either race. In other than the staple crops the average Negro is even less skillful in production and in marketing and thus tends to depress prices and to render the whole field of agriculture unsatisfactory.

When this whole situation is considered, one naturally asks: Is it possible that, by permanently restricting, or excluding, immigration, the injurious effects, at least the worst features, of racial competition may be avoided by furnishing to each and to every worker of both races employment that will be rewarded by a fair and adequate wage? Such is the dream of certain visionaries and, until carefully examined, the dream seems reasonable.

It is true, in the first place, that a very small percentage of labor finds employment in industries so well organized, and standardized, that they pay standard wages, or can afford to do so. Such industries absorb relatively few laborers, and only those with special training and who are skilled workers. This type of labor is usually further protected by labor organizations, and but few Negroes have as yet secured positions in such industries.

Another class of labor competes under much less favorable conditions and for less satisfactory wages. There is not the intensive organization among the laborers; and, if there were, the employers could hardly meet the increased demands and remain in business. In many instances the employer, operating a small factory, must secure cheaper labor, as well as efficient, or be quickly forced out of business. It is in this range that competition of Negro labor is possible, but in many respects the advantage lies with the Negro. It is here that the depressing influence upon white labor begins. The greater the scarcity of labor, the more nearly would all laborers approach to ideal conditions; but there must be an employer as well as laborers and, as soon as profits cease, demand for labor slackens. It is relatively easy to drive capital to cover, or to prevent its being invested in industry. The exhibition of an unreasoning independence—a disregard for the interests of the employer—upon the part of labor is certain to curtail investment and thus to decrease the demand for workers. Again, high wages quickly result in the mechanization of industry and this, in turn, eliminates the less skillful and the less dependable laborers. Here is a vital cause for the existence of a large class of labor falling below the median of economic income. The introduction of tractors and of improved machinery generally has already gone far toward eliminating the lower class of farm labor. It is to this class that rural Negro labor largely belongs.

There is, then, a class of workers dependent upon their labor for support but who fail to achieve satisfactory status or adequate income. Here labor is not generally protected by organization. This is the realm of the unskilled, unorganized workers, whose job is frequently temporary, or whose position in agriculture is that of the hired hand or the share cropper. Of these little is required except industry, brawn, *and docility,* nothing the uneducated Negro cannot supply. On this level is encountered the whole range of the "poor white" group. The class, if not created by Negro competition, is greatly augmented by it.

It may be pointed out that the organized champions of the Negro race and of the mulattoes of South Africa are found in certain missionary societies and certain churches in England. Likewise, the white champions of the Negroes and the mulattoes in the United States are found largely in certain philanthropic and religious organizations chiefly located in sections until recently removed from immediate personal contact and competition with the Negro. *In both England and in America,* in certain quarters, *zeal for black and yellow is joined with utter disregard for the "poor white."*

When will the "poor white" awaken and achieve such class consciousness as to cause him to understand and to evaluate the real attitude of his own race? When will the worm turn? What must be the thought of the white man or the white woman who awakes to the fact that, in the fundamental values of life, the race to which they belong has deserted them and forced them into competition with the Negro so sharp as to render the better things of life impossible for them? If, in the face of this situation, men and women become embittered and deliberately betray the group which, for its own leisure, its pleasure, its convenience, or for its profit, has deserted and betrayed them, there will, at least, be poetic justice in the outcome. There is ground for resentment and intense bitterness upon the part of the underprivileged white who endures this competition. The time may yet come when every individual and every organization, political, philanthropic, or religious, now disregarding the poor of the white group will stand out—leaders especially—pilloried, as is so richly deserved, as *traitors to their own race!* The "pride" which makes the "bywoner" unwilling to do "Kaffir's work" because, in the presence of the Kaffir, it involves lowered racial status; and which makes the "poor white" loyal to his race, although betrayed and deserted by the dominant elements of that race, is a heritage most precious, a quality conditioning the interests—even the blood purity—of that race which has shown so little concern for its own poor. Destroy that pride and all is lost!

Washington City affords excellent opportunities for the study of the effects of racial competition as between the laborers of the two races. Everywhere one notes the Negro doing the greater part of the unskilled manual labor. Usually a white man will be found directing a group of Negro laborers. Often it is a case of the white man doing the skilled work, with one or more Negro assistants. For this type of work it seems that the Negro is rather generally preferred to the white. The numerical aspects of the situation are revealed by the rapid increase in the Negro population of the District from 187,266 in 1940 to 255,930 in 1948. These 255,930 Negroes are displacing a very large number of potential white laborers. They have driven from the city many white laborers. In increasing numbers Negroes are extending the range of racial competition by entering the better paid ranks of skilled labor.

An opportunity was presented for observation of typical details of the labor situation here during the construction of a large apartment house. Very little of the skilled labor was done by Negroes except the laying of brick. Hardly a white man was employed at unskilled labor. It was usually the case that from twenty-five to seventy-five white men would be on hand at the beginning of work each day in the hope of being given a job, some of them remaining until the afternoon work was well under way. It was frequently the case that some of these men would be present for the evening service at the Union Gospel Mission, where a light meal and a free bed could be had by those unable to pay for food and lodging elsewhere. It is at such missions and at the Salvation Army stations, often at the jails, that one sees the real significance of conditions existing in Washington City, and elsewhere, as these bear upon the unskilled white laborer. This observation was made some twenty years ago but seems to apply equally well to 1949.

During these twenty years a great building program has been in progress in Washington City, a program not yet completed. The cost of building already done; that now in process of construction; and that in prospect runs into the fabulous millions. In all this there seems to have been, is now, very little place for the unskilled white laborer. It is the Negro who is doing this type of work. Occasionally Negroes and mulattoes are found doing high-priced skilled labor, usually bricklaying, plastering, cement work, etc.; but the great body of this interracial competition falls upon the untrained, unskilled white laborer, the man next in rank to what we have called the "poor white" and who, with very little depression, is in grave danger of falling into this class. In the matter of domestic service, the Negro woman exercises upon the white working girl the same depressing and destructive influence as does the Negro man upon the unskilled white male worker. Either the white girl must meet this competition in wages and in standard of living, *and in docility,* or seek her living in other ways—a situation putting upon her, at best, an unfair stress; at worst, an utterly destructive stress.

The outstanding significance of the 255,930 Negroes in the District of Columbia; the undetermined number located in the immediate vicinity of the District; and of the millions scattered throughout the United States, is that, in their struggle to live, a considerable number of them are forced to accept employment upon such terms as are offered, and thus little is left for that class of white laborers who are unskilled and whose natural ability or personal characteristics limit them to the performance of manual, if not menial, tasks.

For every Negro employed by the Government, a white person is displaced. This is true not only in the District of Columbia but throughout the nation. On September 8, 1928, there was released by the Department of Labor a statement showing the number of Negroes employed by the United States Government, the statement not including enlisted men in the Army or the Navy. The personnel total for the fiscal year ending in 1928 is 51,882, and the salaries paid these people reached a total of $64,483,133.

This matter of the "poor white," as a victim of Negro competition and association, should be recognized as one of the most serious problems of the present time. The practice of the privileged class of any race ignoring, or exploiting, the poor, the backward, of that race is unwise, although only one race is involved; it is vastly worse when a recond race, one on a definitely lower plane, is used as the destructive agent.

It is in this degradation of the standard of living of the

126

white laborer that competition with Negro labor works its greatest economic harm to the white race. Such competition forces an element of the white race, normally capable of efficient work, to a standard of living so low as to be destructive not, indeed, of life outright, but of the higher possibilities of life. It has power to paralyze the laudable ambitions of life. It certainly increases greatly the number of "poor whites," the "bywoners," those failing to achieve economic independence through industrial efficiency.

CHAPTER VI

ISABELLA AND JAMESTOWN
or
SPANISH AND ENGLISH COLONIZATION
IN AMERICA

THE FIRST permanent English settlement in America was made at Jamestown, Va., in the year 1607. Isabella, the first permanent Spanish settlement, had been made on the Island of Hispaniola, now known as Haiti, in the year 1493. It thus appears that the Spaniard was permanently located in the New World 114 years before the English entered definitely and successfully upon the colonization of this continent. The first Spanish settlement, made at La Navidad by Columbus on his first voyage, and the settlement located by the English on Roanoke Island proved failures, there being no survivor from either.

A chapter dealing with these early settlements and comparing Spanish and English methods of colonization and their respective results may seem quite remote from the situation in the United States some four centuries later. There are, however, certain contrasts very marked and very valuable in illustrating and in enforcing certain fundamental principles. Besides, we are now compelled to deal with the logical fruitage of the two systems. Out of these earlier settlements have grown, if not two diverse civilizations, certainly such differences as approach very nearly to such status. It is necessary, if we would be prepared to understand the significance of present contacts, that these differences be understood. It is inevitable that points of contact with the Latin-American peoples will increase. In increasing numbers citizens of the United States are going to the Islands and to the lands held by those who look back to Isabella as citizens of the United States look back to Jamestown and to Plymouth Rock. In increasing numbers these people are coming to make their homes permanently in the United States.

The unsuccessful settlement at La Navidad consisted of thirty-nine men left by Columbus when he returned to Spain after the discovery of America in 1492.[1] Scarcely had the ships of the great Admiral departed when dissension arose among these men. The Indians, friendly at first, were quickly driven to hostility by the behavior of these men. The site chosen for the settlement was unhealthful. When Columbus returned, in 1493, not one of the men left at La Navidad was yet alive. One feels, in reading the statements of the historians, that these men richly deserved the fate which befell them.

It is not the purpose of this chapter to enter upon any exhaustive study of Spanish settlement in America nor to contrast all its details with those of settlement here by the Northwestern Europeans. Upon a few vital points characterizing and differentiating the Spanish and the English as colonizers it is necessary to dwell at some length. Their attitudes toward the native Indians and their methods of dealing with them differed widely and in many respects, but agreed in that neither considered himself under any great obligation to respect the rights of the Indians. It was even held by some of the Spaniards that, since no mention was made of the Indians in Scripture, they were not human in the same sense as were those so honored.[2] The most marked contrast between the colonizing of the two peoples, however, lies in the dominating motive actuating each group, motives which give to the two movements very different methods and widely different results.

The Spanish settlement of Isabella consisted of 1,593 men. In so far as the records show, there was not a woman in the entire group. The dominating purpose was the immediate acquisition of wealth through mining or through trading

[1] *A History of Latin America*, Sweet, p. 37.
[2] This strange view prevailed widely, and even papal decrees did not wholly destroy it.

with the Indians. Agriculture was a later development and, to the Spaniard, a secondary consideration. Sufficient gold had been found among the natives to warrant the hope that, under Spanish supervision, vast quantities might be had for the digging. All Europe was eager to believe the tales of fabulous riches existing in the wilds of America.

As the conquests of the Spaniards and the Portuguese were later extended, the treasures of Mexico and of Peru, of Aztec, of Toltec and of Inca, found their way into the hands of the conquering Spaniard. Armor and superior weapons used by the invaders rendered the Indians helpless. Hispaniola, Cuba, Mexico, Central America, Peru, were quickly subdued, a small force of Spaniards being able to go where they pleased and to impose their will upon tribe after tribe of the divided and helpless Indians. Soon great numbers of Indians were toiling in hopeless slavery, working the mines and the plantations of the Spaniards.

Enforced labor, together with the so violent change in the manner of living and in conditions surrounding them, destroyed the Indians very rapidly. Las Cases, the historian of the period, has been accused of gross exaggeration in depicting the cruelties practiced upon the Indians, but there was, undoubtedly, a vast deal of cruelty inflicted, and the Indians, especially on the Islands where escape was impossible, perished with unbelievable rapidity.

It was in order to protect and to preserve the Indians that Nicolas Ovanda, in 1501, was given permission to import Negro slaves into Hispaniola. Las Casas, then an ordained priest and soon to win the title "Protector of the Indians," for some years advocated Negro slavery, but later, after noting its consequences, looked upon this as a capital mistake. Thus it came about that Negro slavery existed throughout the Spanish colonies long before the English colony at Jamestown was founded. Las Casas has been held responsible for its existence there, but unjustly so. It is true, however, that he for a time approved it and urged greater activity in securing Negro slaves in sufficient numbers to spare the rapidly disappearing Indians.

The Latin, as a Latin, proved, at best, an indifferent success as a colonizer. At the worst, he proved a failure because, in contact with native races, he quickly ceased to be Latin. Going out as an adventurer-exploiter-soldier and leaving his own women behind, he largely destroyed the native men and quickly produced the mixed-blood group, the beginning of that process by which some of the Latin groups in America have so quickly and so completely lost their blood purity and, because of this, have failed in the transplanting of Latin culture as they have ceased to be representative of the group from which they came. Thus Spain, Portugal, and France have sent out great numbers of men, weakening their home stocks by the removal and loss of possibly their most enterprising and energetic type of manhood. A backwash of mixed bloods has found place in each of these groups, thus producing, in varying degrees, a threat to the race purity of each. It is claimed that, despite later white immigration, only about 10 per cent of the population of several of the Latin-American countries is now of fullblood white stock. A racial intermixture of Indian-Negro-white constitutes, in several cases, the bulk of the population. Doubtless this fact explains the lack of stability and the lack of progress so long and so widely characteristic of these peoples.

The Northwestern European settlers coming to Continental North America did not, to any great extent, enslave the Indian. They did displace him and they did transfer their race and their institutions—especially the home and the home ideals—into whatever part of the country they came. The "Mayflower" brought over complete families; a fact the significance of which is realized more fully by comparison with Isabella and the social forces pent up in that womanless settlement, and with the Latin colonizers generally and their descendants. The original adventurers of the Jamestown settlement soon secured wives from England and founded

131

families not essentially different from the standards and the ideals of the England of that day. Nowhere did the Northwestern European send out a group of men to enterprise a permanent settlement without these men either taking along their wives and children or sending back for them quickly. *The place and the services of the pioneer white woman in the building of the civilization of the United States and that of Canada cannot be overestimated. It is she who has, thus far, saved these areas for a white civilization!*

The Northwestern European stock has, to a very limited extent, mingled its blood with that of the North American Indian, but in the present area of the United States, except for the recent introduction of some two million Mexicans, this intermingling of the Indian-white is to so small a degree that its results are relatively negligible. In more recent years the United States Census shows a marked increase in the Indian population. This is certainly due, in part, to a very considerable number of Indian-Negro-whites registering as Indians, the most favorable classification open to them. In a single group in the State of Virginia the classification of considerable numbers is thus changed between the years 1910 and 1920, a fact well known in the office of the Registrar of Vital Statistics of this state. Cases are known in which Negroes have claimed Indian descent when every characteristic indicated only a very remote infusion of white blood.

Elsewhere in this study may be found a statement of the extent to which the Negro in the United States now shows the infusion of white blood. The situation here is most lamentable, but is not so bad as is the case in some of the countries lying to the south and, especially, in the Islands of the West Indies. A statement covering conditions in many of these places is available. It was prepared by Professor Robert F. Foerster, of the Department of Economics in Princeton University. The purpose of the investigation and the report made to the Secretary of Labor was to secure information for the guidance of the United States in the matter of immigration from these areas. The value of this report as a sociological study is very great and is permanent. The conditions under which these investigations were made, the standing of the gentleman making them, and the purpose which they were designed to serve, give their results the highest value and entitle them to full credence. Here we deal with the results of 432 years of racial contact, 1492 to 1925.

Briefly summarized, the findings concerning these various countries are given as follows:

In Mexico: "The few Spanish women in Mexico became mothers of the pure Creole stock. . . . Beyond doubt the most frequent unions of the Spanish men were with Indian women. In the earlier days it was common to confer captured Indian women as spoils upon the soldiers. Some of these women were received in marriage by the men, some were taken as concubines, some became partners in irregular or occasional unions. Whatever the methods of mating, the result was presently the beginning of a new race of mixed Indian and white blood, called by the Spanish name of mestizo." [3]

"During the period of about two centuries prior to 1817, there was some importation of Negroes to be used as slaves. They were largely males, a part of whom subsequently united with Indian women. So far as the Negro stock persists today it is the so-called *Zambos,* the offspring of crosses between Indian and black, and it tends to be unrecognizably absorbed into the race stock of the country. Negro slavery as an institution ceased as far back as 1821." [4]

The population of Mexico is given by Professor Foerster as probably between 13,500,000 and 17,000,000. The Indian stock is placed at five to six million; the mestizo stock at seven to eight million; and the white stock at one and one-half to three million, the fullblood white constituting about 10 per cent of the total population. "The stock of the Mex-

[3] *The Racial Problems Involved in Immigration from Latin America and the West Indies to the United States,* Robert F. Foerster, p. 9. (A report submitted to the Secretary of Labor. Issued by Government Printing Office. Price, 10 cents. Quoted hereafter as "Foerster.")
[4] Foerster, p. 9.

133

ican people is, then, principally of mixed Indian blood." [5] Large numbers of Mexicans, chiefly of the laboring class, have recently come into the United States, in some sections the numbers being sufficient to create serious social and industrial problems. Due to their bi- or tri-racial origin, and to the conditions under which this racial intermixture has occurred, these introduce a very serious race problem. Mexico has not yet fully recovered from the demoralizing influences of the Spanish conquest, with its host of unmarried Spaniards, restless, unsettled, unrestrained.

Guatemala has a larger proportion of fullblood Indians than has any other of the countries of Central America. As an index to moral conditions, it is said: "The number of illegitimate births runs very high, being nearly half the total recorded." [6] In Salvador illegitimacy runs very high." [7]

In Honduras the number of white persons is very small. Negro immigrants have been numerous, and "illegitimate births equal or exceed legitimate." [8] In British Honduras, populated largely by "Indian and mestizo elements, about 40 per cent of new births in late years have been illegitimate." [9]

In Nicaragua there is the same confusion of races and the "illegitimate births are a large portion of all." [10] In Costa Rica the population is whiter but "illegitimate births are currently about a quarter of all." [11] In Panama "illegitimate births in some provinces run to more than half of all births." [12] The Canal Zone can hardly be regarded as possessing a fixed population, since great numbers of laborers have been employed there, drawn from many countries. No figures are given bearing upon the family life of those in the Zone.

South America shows largely a mixed population, with con-

[5] Foerster, p. 11.
[6] Foerster, p. 16.
[7] Foerster, p. 17.
[8] Foerster, p. 17.
[9] Foerster, p. 17.
[10] Foerster, p. 18.
[11] Foerster, p. 18.
[12] Foerster, p. 19.

ditions highly favorable to race fusion because of the absence of race pride, or other social force, opposing amalgamation. Conditions are worse because of the rather general custom of regarding the mixed blood as belonging to the white, rather than to the Indian or the Negro, group. This attitude, expressed by the dictum: "One drop of white blood makes a white man," is prevalent in some Latin circles and, together with the relative absence of race pride or race prejudice, greatly hastens the amalgamation of the races. As a general thing, the rate of illegitimacy is high in the countries of South America. The mulatto problem is most in evidence in Brazil, while Argentina possibly approaches more nearly to the Northwestern European and kindred American ideals than does any other South American country.[13]

Conditions in the West Indies are treated rather fully by Professor Foerster. So thorough was the destruction of the Indians in these islands by the early Spanish that the Indian element of the population is almost negligible, even as an element in blood admixture. It is in these islands that the influence of the womanless settlement at Isabella was most powerful, and it is here that the twin evils of amalgamation and illegitimacy, the gravest social conditions, must now be confronted. Concerning Cuba it is said: "About one quarter of the entire population were of illegitimate birth in 1919: Of the native whites one eighth were; of the colored more than half were illegitimate." [14] "There is no social disparity of white and black in Cuba" [15] and those who would destroy racial barriers between the white and the Negro in the United States should make a careful study of the absence of such barriers in Cuba. Also, of conditions resulting from the absence of such barriers.

In Jamaica less than 2 per cent of the inhabitants are considered white. The mixed bloods "are now more than ten times as numerous as the whites" and "illegitimate births are

[13] Foerster, pp. 19-34.
[14] Foerster, p. 36.
[15] Foerster, p. 37.

likewise high in number. Year in and year out they are between 60 and 70 per cent of all recorded births." [16] The Car-
negie Institute sent an expedition to Jamaica for the purpose
of studying the effect of race crossing. More than 60,000
examples, all mulattoes, might have been found at that time
within a radius of three miles of this Institute in Washington
City! Cromwell sent out many Irish boys and girls into virtual slavery to the planters of Jamaica. These gave rise to the
"Black Irish" of Jamaica.

These quotations from Professor Foerster's study are sufficient to indicate the fundamental difference between the
ideals, the institutions, and the social order having their
beginnings in the womanless colony at Isabella and the ideals,
the institutions, and the social order having their beginnings
in the Northwestern European colonies planted later in Continental North America. Even the fear of generating race
prejudice should not blind anyone to these manifest facts
nor to their logical consequences, now written large in the
racial composition of large numbers of people and in their
achievements and in their institutions. Among peoples of
confused racial antecedents, 25 per cent, or more, of whom are
of illegitimate birth, and few of whom can trace their ancestry three generations without coming upon an illegitimate
link, it is hardly possible that high ideals should prevail
among the masses. There is to be found in most such situations a small, exclusive racial group which, in reaction to conditions existing among the masses, maintains, within its own
limits, high ideals successfully reduced to practice. Sometimes, however, no such group may be found and natural in-
clination meets with neither barrier nor restraint. Among in-
dices of moral and social conditions existing in any nation, or
in any local group of people, a high illegitimate birth rate
must be regarded as indicating conditions exceedingly unfortunate, especially an absence of those ideals and of those
social sanctions upon which the family rests. Where any con-

siderable percentage of births are illegitimate, something is fundamentally wrong.

It is inevitable that the student who would make a thorough study of Latin America, especially of the beginnings of Spanish and Portuguese colonization in America, should give careful attention to the place of religion and to the type of religion prevailing at that time. This is a delicate matter, and one calculated to arouse serious antagonism. It is improbable, even after the passing of more than four hundred years and even with the revolutionary changes these years have brought, that many students will be found, impartial and able to lay aside personal attitudes and the bias inherent in affiliation with, or repudiation of, the great institution which so completely dominated the religious faith and activities involved. So sharply drawn were the lines between Catholicism and Protestantism after 1525 that it is still difficult to enter into a sympathetic understanding of all parties and of the beliefs and the claims of each as characterizing the sixteenth century. An age of splendid achievement in many fields, it was also the age of the Inquisition in Europe and of the religious wars which desolated Europe. The world has made great progress since 1493, and in no respect has this progress been more marked, or of greater value to humanity, than has been the case in the realm of religious freedom.

For more than four hundred years Latin America has been predominantly Roman Catholic in faith, and is still so. The unquestioned supremacy of this church and the acceptance of its moral and religious leadership necessarily involves a large measure of responsibility for racial conditions obtaining in Latin America, just as Protestantism in North America must be held largely responsible for permitting amalgamation of the white and black races here to progress at once illegally and unrebuked, even practically approved. In neither section has there been put forth any sustained effort to deal constructively with the racial problems confronting the religious leaders. The matter of lawless race amalgamation has been persistently ignored even where recognized.

Religion, as first mediated through the Spaniards, was represented by priest-chaplains who were attached to the military service, or closely associated with the civil authorities. Usually the military expeditions conducted by the Spaniards were accompanied by at least one priest. In the majority of instances such association was not conducive to the freedom and the independence of the priests. The character of those Spaniards in high position was not always of a type to approve high ideals and their temper was not always such as to brook restraint. The custom of seizing the property of the conquered Indians, especially any gold found in their possession, and that of distributing captured Indian women to the Spanish soldiers, must be judged in the light of that period rather than by the standards of the present. Occasionally an ecclesiastic or a layman was found who, in advance of his age or moved by a superior humanity, condemned the practices of the soldiers, but usually no voice was raised in protest. Occasionally a chaplain was found independent enough to condemn openly acts of treachery and of barbaric cruelty, or even to curse the perpetrators of such acts, as did Las Casas during the wanton massacre of a group of friendly Indians in Cuba. Those who wish a detailed account of conditions obtaining in the West Indies and in certain of the continental areas during the earlier period of Spanish settlement may find such an account in the writings of Las Casas.

The point of vital interest for the present study, and for comparison with conditions and ideals in the two Americas, has to do with the place given the home and with the estimate in which race was held in the two main streams of European peoples soon to pour into the New World. The fundamental weakness of Latin-American colonization, and also of the civilization founded upon and developing out of this colonization, lies ultimately in the absence of the Spanish or the Portuguese woman. In large measure both the Spaniard and the Portuguese failed to transplant to America the best, even the normal, type of home developed by them in Europe. Instead, there grew up a system destructive alike to the native and to the colonist.

It may be possible that a great civilization should arise and maintain itself without its people observing those moral and ethical principles upon which the purity of the home depends. It may even be shown that great civilizations have arisen and have prolonged their power and their influence without serious regard for the home. It is, however, believed by many who have studied carefully the rise, the career, and the fall of the empires of the past that decline follows invariably upon moral laxness and racial confusion, two characteristics of the closing period of each of the conquering empires. Rome sent her own sons to perish on the field of battle and received in their stead slaves of every blood and breed available.

The purest type of family life is that embodying best the Hebrew and the Christian teachings, with these reënforced by Norse and Teutonic ideals and institutions. From these sources have come the world's highest standards of personal morality and of civic organization. A careful study of Latin America and a comparison of conditions in the United States and conditions existing there, together with a thorough study of the forces which have brought about these contrasted conditions—these are of the highest importance at the present time. Large numbers of Mexicans are now in the United States. Excellent people though they may be, they differ essentially from us in race. Largely Indian, these people are, in part, Spanish and, in some cases, Negroid. Their ideals and their antecedents render them largely a nonassimilable population element and one calculated to lower the standard of living of the American labor with which they compete. The situation in reference to the West Indian immigrant is, except for numbers, even worse. Here the Indian long ago was almost eliminated, but his place was taken by the Negro, and the present inhabitants are largely of mixed blood, this mixture having taken place under conditions involving a severe stress upon right ideals and right standards. In his concise statement of conditions encountered, Professor Foerster has supplied the facts upon which Congress should act with energy and dispatch.

If there is a just ground in the rights of a people to maintain their industrial system through prospective tariffs, or otherwise, certainly there is no just ground for denying to any people the right to preserve their blood purity and thus to secure both the possibility and the opportunity of working out, intact, their group destiny. It is certainly the right of every people to secure a place where it may protect itself and thus secure the opportunity to realize its possibilities. Denied the right to exclude those whose standard of living is different; whose ideals are inharmonious; and who, in race, should be nonassimilable, unity cannot be achieved, or maintained, and every advance economically would merely invite an invasion, in overwhelming numbers, by those lacking the initiative to develop industries and thus make their own land both desirable and adequate. In maintaining this self-defensive attitude, it is not, primarily, a question of racial differences in the sense of higher or lower mental endowment. It is essentially a question of each racial group having an opportunity to work out its own destiny.

A recent writer has emphasized the tolerance and the lack of racial exclusiveness on the part of people who look back to Isabella as contrasted with those who spring from Jamestown and Plymouth Rock. At page 442 of *The Century Magazine* for August, 1928, Erna Ferguson says of the Mexicans now in the United States: "Never does one find the harsh Puritanical eagerness to judge and to condemn." It is probable that the statement might be made to include all Latin-American peoples, with the possible exception of the small percentage of whites who yet maintain their racial integrity. Is this attitude upon the part of the masses, certainly defensive, commendable?

There is, in reference to the moral and ethical sanctions affecting the family, a necessity for all people of mixed origin, when this mixture has occurred in contravention of good morals, to question the recognized standards thus ignored. This is often done not by consciously discarding these standards theoretically but by disregarding them in practice. Tolerance may be the expression of kindliness toward, and appreciation of, views opposed to those held by the person showing this spirit, and toward the person holding these views. It may be the result of a definite but sympathetic understanding of a given situation involving no essential wrong. What popularly passes for tolerance, and even for liberality, may, however, really be ignorance or indifference. It may also be an attitude essentially defensive. It is, therefore, all the more necessary that the United States— and Canada—should guard, with the utmost care, the purity of the white race. Every extension of racial confusion, and especially of illegitimate racial intermixture, carries with it a definite increase in the difficulties in the way of maintaining right ideals. *When the mixed blood and his offspring become sufficiently numerous, all hope of ultimately preserving more than a small and exclusive group of full bloods may as well be abandoned. This is the lesson of Isabella.* The process of amalgamation is much slower north of Mexico and Cuba. This is due to many differences, in addition to those here stressed. Yet *the United States is following the course of Latin America in the absorption of its Negro population.*

It is infinitely easier to destroy than to build up right ideals and right attitudes. *There can be no recovery for a destroyed race.* It is well to note that ideals have undergone radical changes since 1493. Along with every step of progress and every intellectual advance there comes a need for readjustments and the home, together with its sanctions, has sometimes been on the defensive; but when the confusion

141

subsides and the mature judgment of the age finds expression, it is an unqualified intellectual approval of Hebraic and Christian ideals and attitudes. Read and interpreted impartially, the history of Latin-American colonization and of the developments stemming from this source as these adversely affect race is possibly the world's potentially most important object lesson. There seems a cruel mockery in a situation which makes of religion a destructive rather than a constructive racial force.

The difficulties, involved in any and in all efforts to safeguard the white race in the United States as regards the mixed element in the Latin-American groups, may be readily appreciated. The ease of travel and the frequency of interracial contacts increase. The increasing numbers of white citizens of the United States and Canada and of Europe now coming to reside temporarily or permanently in Latin America greatly increase racial contacts. In increasing numbers these people are finding homes in the United States.

The contacts between the two peoples due to trade are also increasing. Here there is keen competition with the commercial interests of Europe. In Europe the mixed blood is not discriminated against, and there is little immediate danger that he will become a serious menace there. Conditions are such in Europe as to render it wholly unlikely, if not impossible, that any large number of Latin Americans should come to reside permanently in the industrial and the commercial areas of Europe. There may well be, therefore, upon the part of Europeans a disregard of race and of racial intermixture highly pleasing to the delicately sensitive temperament of the higher classes of these people. Merchants from the United States naturally desire a share in the trade with these countries. So of shipowners and of all other classes coming in immediate contact with them. Back of these stand the producers and the manufacturers of the United States, both anxious for markets, and the latter eager for raw materials. Trade groups are usually opposed to any step which may create or foster antagonisms, and all restrictions upon immigration from these countries and anything which emphasizes racial or social differences may be expected to curtail trade and hence to be opposed by the commercial interests of the United States. The immigrants from these countries now consist mainly of Mexican laborers and Cubans, with many from the West Indies. In Harlem there are several thousand Negroes from Jamaica and from Puerto Rico.

This chapter is essentially a digression. It is a far call from a settlement made 456 years ago on an island in the Atlantic Ocean to the situation in the United States in the year 1949. And yet the situation with which this chapter deals and the facts here given and those suggested are of vital importance. In considering the race problem, as it now exists in the United States, a wealth of valuable fact and constructive suggestion may be found in a careful study of the first Spanish settlement and the civilization growing out of it, and in contrasting this with the English settlements in Continental North America and the civilization growing out of them. By far the most important lesson of this comparison is to be drawn from the facts having to do with racial conservation and with racial intermixture.[17]

This chapter should furnish food for thought to those who would ignore race and the forces making for its preservation. Here, side by side, are two diverse groups, and it is possible to know the antecedents of each and the ideals and the social forces prevailing in each. Most important of all, it is possible to see, in present conditions, the legitimate, the inevitable, results of the ideals and the practices obtaining in each of these groups.

[17] For a discussion of the influence of the churches upon racial intermixture, see chapter on *Race and Religion.*

CHAPTER VII

POLITICS AND THE RACE PROBLEM

THE NEGRO became a factor in world politics long before he had made sufficient progress to enter into any situation as other than a helpless pawn, a "bone of contention" among the various antagonistic white groups, or nations, then ready to fight for the right of exclusive exploitation of any source of revenue. With the Negro offering no effective resistance, it became a mad race to determine who should exploit the available sections of Africa and the people inhabiting these sections. Every nation of Europe which possessed the requisite shipping was, at some time, engaged in this trade. First Portugal and Spain; then England and, later, the American Colonies engaged in the slave trade. Possibly England and the United States—the latter first as colonies and later as states—were the leaders in transporting the slaves to America.

In dealing with the Negro problem in the United States—including the colonial period—certain facts having to do with the "politics" of the whole course of North American history must be considered. It is not always possible to distinguish clearly between the two uses made of the word politics. In the first use it is closely related to the term statesmanship; in the second and popular use the term implies individual, and party, and sectional effort to secure advantages, or to carry through a sectional or a partisan program. The reference is frequently to those processes of manipulation by which parties, often sectional in origin and in interest, have sought control of government. It is needless to point out the fact that the clash of interests, national, sectional, or otherwise, has not created a situation in American political life in which great moral and great social and great racial issues could always receive calm and thorough and constructive consideration.

Negro slavery was fastened upon English America at a time when "slavery touched no man's conscience," and when the rights of the individual were but imperfectly recognized or respected even by his own government, and when the foremost nations of the world gave but little protection to their citizens abroad. Las Casas, the priest and "Protector of the Indians," approved the introduction of Negro slaves into the Spanish colonies during the earlier years of the sixteenth century. Leading ministers of the gospel of the Protestant churches, from New England to Georgia, later approved the introduction of Negro slaves into this part of the New World. White men, *and women,* citizens of the United States and of England, were held in slavery by the Moors of North Africa as late as 1816, a fact which shows clearly that the ideals of the present in reference to the rights of the individual and the protection extended to the individual by his government are of very recent origin. These had little place anywhere until 1800, or later.

No consideration of the political aspects of the Negro problem can be at all complete if it ignores the slave trade and the wars which grew out of it. There were, in many instances, other causes underlying the European conflicts of the sixteenth, seventeenth, and eighteenth centuries; but the slave trade unquestionably became the sole cause of grave conflicts between the nations engaged in it, and many wars sprang from it as one of the contributing causes. These earlier conflicts were not due, however, to any scruples, or convictions, concerning the immorality of the slave trade, but rather to attempts to monopolize the trade and its profits. During the colonial period neither slavery nor the slave trade was a source of serious division, or even controversy, nor did either become so until the nation was fairly well established. It is certain that slavery was, both directly and indirectly, the cause of the Civil War.

It is significant that much of the earlier opposition to slavery developed in the South, especially in the Virginia area. So long as the profits of the transportation of slaves were large, so long there were available for the trade ships of the various nations and men to operate these ships. The Virginia group, led by Washington, Jefferson, and other famous early leaders, made possible the first attempt to limit slavery through the cutting off of the importation of slaves. These men were too far in advance of their day. Too much money had been invested in the trade and the profits made were too great and too many nations were profiting by it, so nothing came of the efforts made by the Virginia group. Bancroft's statement in reference to New York is equally true of other sections of the North. He wrote: "That New York is not a slave state like Carolina is due to climate and not to the superior humanity of its founders." Slavery was profitable in the South. It was not profitable in the North. Consequently, there was a shifting of the Negroes southward, sold South rather than emancipated.

The course of events, especially that under the earlier colonial administration, forms an interesting study, yet one with but an indirect bearing upon present conditions. Later developments, showing the manner of life of the two races in America and the consequences of their racial contacts, are vastly more important for our study than are the conditions under which Negro slavery came to be fastened upon America. It was climatic and economic conditions which finally localized slavery to the South. It was the superior humanity of the Southern slave owner that created the slave family and thus bred enough slaves to render the overseas slave trade unnecessary. This completed the isolation, the localization, of slavery and thus paved the way for its destruction.

The developments preceding the Civil War, especially following 1850, are very important. It was at this time that the political situation, in the hands of partisan politicians and fanatical religionists, became such that armed conflict ensued. Opposition to the acquisition of Texas, in less degree of California and the intervening lands, following the war with

Mexico, had a profound influence upon the North and the East, and had given the Abolitionists abundant material for antislavery agitation. In this period the student of history may find abundant material illustrating the dangers inherent in such antagonisms, especially how sectional issues may be intensified until reason is dethroned and appeal to force follows. Force may provide a temporary method of dealing with a situation but this is not likely to be a constructive method.

The conduct of the Negro during the Civil War is one of the marvels of all the range of history. With his freedom in the balance, he did not strike a blow against his masters until, in sections of the South already overrun by the Northern armies, he was used by the Union forces. Even so, he was later the tool of unprincipled white men rather than the originator of the wrongs done by him. Despite opportunity to do so, those escaping to the North or to the Union forces were not relatively numerous. While the Civil War was in progress there was little or no opportunity for the Negro to participate in the political activities of the country, even in the Northern States. Mr. Lincoln had given expression to sentiments and to his convictions which leads students to believe that he, had he lived, would not have approved, or permitted, the course of his party following the close of the Civil War.

The fundamental mistake made by the North at this time was that of thrusting the power to vote, the full responsibilities of citizenship, upon a group which had no preparation for intelligent use of that power. The ballot, unquestionably demanding intelligence and preparation for its constructive use, was here treated as a magical wonder-worker, capable of transforming the slave at once into an intelligent citizen. This was, of course, impossible. The orgy of corruption following the Civil War cannot justly be charged to the Negro except as a tool in the hands of others. The real responsibility for the evils of the Reconstruction period in the South rests upon the white men who, supported by the Federal Govern-

147

ment and by the misguided sentiment existing in the North, of which they took full advantage, directed and used the Negro in carrying through their evil designs. With the return to power of the Southern whites, the Negro lost all political place in the State and local governmental agencies. He has, however, held certain political positions under the Federal Government. In this sphere the fullblood Negro has had but a pitifully small share of what patronage has come to the Negro group. Virtually everything worth while has gone to the mulatto group.

The educational and the property qualifications for suffrage, as well as other safeguards found necessary throughout the United States, and elsewhere, have in the South forced upon the Negro who would vote the necessity of making adequate preparation and have, therefore, proved a stimulus to many. These tests have virtually eliminated from the political situation those Negroes who are glaringly unfit for such participation. Unfairness in the administration of these tests there has doubtless been in many instances, but the marvel is that matters have not been infinitely worse in this respect.

The crux of the matter is this: out of these requirements, out of the situation as a whole is emerging a class of Negroes, a few of them full bloods, who are making substantial progress; and an increasing number of these are now able to participate intelligently in government. There have been, and still are, many features of the political situation which are exceedingly unfortunate and which go far to prevent the development of the independence and the self-respect of the American Negro. *It is in respect to his racial integrity that the American Negro has suffered most severely through politics.* Here, as elsewhere, there has been no effort to preserve the ideals of the race, as such. Its political representatives, with very few exceptions, have been in the past and are still mulattoes.

During the decade before the Civil War, while antislavery agitation was keen and bitter, several mulattoes became very

148

prominent. For the greater part their blood mixture was a cross between the fullblood Negro woman and a white male. The fact that the mother was a slave made such men and women a telling exhibit against slavery. Very few fullblood Negroes attained prominence at this time.

A logical result of this situation under slavery was that when the race was set free its political leadership was composed almost exclusively of mulattoes. It may be readily seen now that this was a time of supreme crisis for the Negro race in America, determining, as it did, the ideals and the practices which were to prevail. This mixed-blood leadership was accepted, both by the white and by the Negro. That there was any conscious preference for the mulatto was probably not the case. He was on the ground; he had whatever advantage his white blood involved; and no one was concerned about his illegitimacy or its effect upon the Negro race. The fullblood Negro made no objection; the whites made no effective objection; and so the leadership of the mulatto became established and confirmed under freedom.

It would be difficult, in the whole range of history, to find a war more needless than that between the States in 1861-1865. Left without outside interference, there were latent forces in the South which would have soon brought the institution of slavery to an end. Slavery was everywhere a doomed institution, and the factors which destroyed it elsewhere were operative in the South. Had the South been an independent nation and free to deal with her own affairs without outside interference, there would certainly have arisen a division concerning slavery and, in the nature of the case, the anti-slavery forces, greatly outnumbering the slaveholders, must have won. As it was, the radical attacks came from sources outside the South and hostile to it. New England had the lion's share of the profits derived from the slave trade. It was New England that took the lead in denouncing the South for holding in slavery the Negro group purchased originally largely from New England slavers.

149

Instead of recognizing the evolutionary process through which all permanent, and especially all natural, unforced progress is made, the radical agitators carried on a prolonged campaign of vilification that united the South and, taking away all possibility of a peaceful extinction of slavery or of a constructive program for the disposition of the Negro population once free, drove the South to seek means by which to defend itself and its inherited Constitutional rights. Then followed the struggle for territory and the struggle to decide whether that territory should be slave or free. No one proposed any adequate plan for the adjustment of the plight of the slaveholder, whose rights had been recognized throughout the colonial period and had not been seriously questioned during the first sixty years of national history.

The situation demanded the highest type of conservatively constructive statesmanship. The exigencies of practical politics as applied to this situation called out too many leaders of radical tendencies, and the North mistook the Southern radical for the South and, in so doing, came perilously near to putting the radical in power in the South. The North, too, had its radicals, and these were mistaken in the South for the real North. Garrison's denunciations were not just. They ignored too many hard, unyielding facts in the past history of American slavery, and they misrepresented the facts of his own day. John Brown was, by every legal principle bearing upon such cases, guilty of insurrection, inciting to insurrection, and of murder through insurrection. His record in Kansas bears the same general stamp of lawlessness as that made in the East. That such a man should become a popular hero throughout the North through such crimes necessarily had its influence throughout the South. Not so much the crimes of a fanatic as the popular attitude of the North toward these crimes and toward the criminal personally made the John Brown raid significant.

Denunciation of a people because of an inherited situation, created largely by the ancestors of those now indulging in such denunciation, is not the part of a just, or conservative, or constructive people. Its most marked tendency is to create unity in resistance, and this is what happened throughout the South. The "poor whites" of the South, although suffering terribly from slavery, willingly took their places in the Southern armies and fought bravely and well to uphold a social order in which they had but a small share and an institution which condemned them and their children to a lot necessarily hopeless as it was hard. Every radical utterance of the North awakened its response in the South, and so antagonisms grew and ripened into bloody conflict. This conflict was able to destroy slavery. It did not solve the race problem. Rather it intensified that problem by forcing it into complications and into associations which made a wise and just settlement a very remote possibility, certainly an unrealized possibility.

It is hardly possible for the Federal Government to escape responsibility for conditions which it has not only permitted to prevail but which, by its own attitudes and activities, it has created and still fosters. Perhaps nowhere else does representative government fail more utterly than when, in the exigencies of party politics, fundamental moral considerations clash with a prospect of gaining—or a certainty of losing— votes! The play for Negro support, especially in the national party conventions and in preparation for these conventions, has often been manifest, and sometimes not on a high moral plane. Mr. Theodore Roosevelt gained, or held, the support of Southern Negro delegates to the national convention of his party by the Booker T. Washington incident and by closing—in an utterly lawless manner—the Indianola post office. According to newspaper reports, a much more recent gesture in the same direction was made when, on the eve of a national convention, an aspirant for the nomination for the Presidency is reported to have directed that separation of white and Negro clerks, previously obtaining in the department over which he presided, should cease. For years past, the Southern delegates to the Republican National Conven-

151

tion, although unable to deliver a single electoral vote, were able to wield a deciding influence in the bestowal of the nomination.

The more recent migration of Negroes from the South and their massing in a few Northern cities have introduced this feature of the race problem into the North, giving the Negro politician there a leverage, a power in both local and national affairs, which he had not known since the Reconstruction era. Walter White claims that the Negro now holds the balance of power in at least seventeen states with 281 electoral votes, provided there is a near equal division in the strength of the two dominant political parties.[1] Thus it may appear logical that the race should come to command, with both political parties and with the national government, a dominant influence in national affairs, if not in state and in local government.

It is, however, very doubtful whether the securing of an occasional office or the wielding of an influence—not always wholesome—in political campaigns does not result in more harm than good to the Negro masses. It certainly tends to unify the white group and may, in the North, as is the case in the South, tend to drive the whites into one political party. Here is a set of facts which the Negro should consider very carefully in connection with the matter of repatriation— colonization. As an alien element here, no amount of manipulation can secure for him permanently anything which is not conceded by the white group. When his vote defeats one-half of the white group, he has antagonized that element of the whites involved. When he has shifted his vote but once, he has antagonized practically the whole white group involved. The Negro cannot assume the role of the independent voter without provoking antagonism. Neither can he assist in the victory of a white political party without arousing more or less of antagonism, even when blindly and permanently allied with that party. In view of the problems involved, it is fairly

[1] See *A Man Called White*, White, p. 262.

certain that, where Negroes become sufficiently numerous, divisions will be along racial, rather than political, lines.

It is not, however, in the exigencies of practical politics that the real significance of the political situation of the Negro appears. It is rather in the relation of politics to his higher interests, especially to the matter of his racial integrity. Politically the Negro is under the domination of the mulatto. Here as elsewhere whatever of success the mulatto achieves has a direct influence upon the whole group of Negroes acquainted with the facts of the case. The prominence, the success, of a mulatto in political life is, therefore, calculated to affect adversely the outlook, the ideals, of the fullblood Negro. In the political field the leadership of the mulatto has, from the beginning, been quite as pronounced and as complete as in other fields.

The work of Professor Reuter is again very valuable because of the accurate information furnished at this point. Of the two Negroes who have been members of the United States Senate, one is classed as a mulatto and the other as a Croatan Indian—Negro-Indian. Of the twenty members of this race who have held seats in the national House of Representatives, three were black and seventeen were mulatto. Of nineteen members of the race who were prominent during Reconstruction, four are classed as black and fifteen as mulattoes. Of six lieutenant governors furnished by this race during Reconstruction, all were mulattoes. Under President Taft, according to the *Negro Year book,* there were fourteen "more important political positions" allotted to this race, all of which were filled by mulattoes.

These figures are quite sufficient to show that *the National Government has thrown the weight of its influence into the scale against whatever of effort the fullblood Negro might have made to preserve his racial integrity.* This has been done—*is still being done*—through the distribution of patronage at the disposal of the victorious party, especially when this party is the one making the stronger historical appeal to the Negro voter. The mulatto dominates completely the political organizations of the Negro. He is, therefore, in position to control the share of patronage allotted to this race. Whether it be on account of superior ability found in the mulatto group, or for some other reason, *it is unquestionably true that virtually all of the more important appointive positions in government service set apart for the Negro race in the United States fall to the mulatto.* The figures are not available and it is, therefore, not possible to give a definite statement of the relative number of Negroes and mulattoes in government service. It is true, however, that except in less important positions and in those requiring little more than manual labor, fullblood Negroes are virtually not employed in government service.

Conditions in Washington City afford an easily grasped demonstration of the truth of the closing sentence of the preceding paragraph. A tour of any one of the Government buildings will furnish a concrete example, especially one in which any considerable number of Negroes are employed, as is the case in the Bureau of Printing and Engraving. Washington City seems especially attractive to the mulatto. Here schools for the Negro are of creditable construction and equipment. Not only are the public high schools attractive, but there are higher educational institutions ample for those Negroes who wish to use them. Howard University is one of the really great institutions of the race.

While conditions in Washington City, New York, and Chicago are very discouraging to those who wish to preserve the purity of either race, perhaps the most hurtful instances of the practice of appointing mulattoes to Federal offices are to be found in the postal service and in such other positions as bring them prominently before large numbers of Negroes throughout the country. The possibilities of such situations are suggested by a typical case which came under the personal observation of the writer. It is that of a mulatto whose mother, a fullblood Negress, was notorious in the town of which the

154

son became postmaster. The father was an unidentified white man.

When this appointment was first contemplated, a determined effort was made to prevent it, prominent white men, representing the political party in office at that time, doing all that they could to prevent it. The local and the state party organizations, composed almost wholly of mulattoes, had endorsed the mulatto and he was appointed, holding the office sixteen of the succeeding twenty years. This case is typical of a large class of Federal appointments made throughout the South since the Civil War. It is, therefore, of special interest to note that, in my investigations of conditions obtaining in the Negro public schools of this small Southern town, an investigation made after the close of the twenty-year period, the ratio of mulatto to fullblood Negro children was found to be higher than in any other Southern Negro public school investigated. *Sixty-four per cent of the total in attendance were mulattoes!* There is, of course, room for speculation as to the extent of the cause-and-effect relationship existing between the position of this initial increment mulatto and the number of mixed-blood children born in this community. Since his illegitimate origin was known, his prominence, especially his official position, certainly did nothing to elevate the morals or the ideals of the Negroes of the community! This investigation was made more than twenty years ago. A recent check on this area showed that a very large percentage of these people had gone North, for the most part to Chicago.

It is quite common in certain circles to attribute any local objection that may be made to such an appointment as that here mentioned to the unwillingness of the Southern white people to have the Negro placed over them in any official capacity. It cannot be said that the average Southern community always bases its objections to such an appointment upon high moral grounds. Yet the moral and the racial issues are, in a very general way, understood, and the better element of the Southern people do deplore the situation because of

155

its effect upon the fullblood Negro, especially as shown in the stimulus given to the evil of amalgamation. It is not racial pride nor racial prejudice alone but these, reënforced by fundamental moral considerations, which cause the deep resentment upon the part of the Southern people that those of such origin and of such social and racial import should be placed over them in any official capacity, or otherwise. The popular attitude toward such a case, North or South, may be taken as an index to the moral sentiment and to the moral perceptions prevailing in any community. So much depends upon the strength and the purity of moral perception and moral sentiment in any community that these should be respected by all, including the political parties, and even the Federal Government!

In such a case as that given above, it is customary to consider only the white people involved. Such disregard of local interests, sentiments, and convictions, is naturally regarded by the victims as little short of tyranny, and as utterly inconsistent with the principles upon which our government was founded. Yet, when all that concerns the white race has been expressed in the strongest terms possible, it still remains true that *the fullblood Negro is the chief sufferer*. With the average Negro, an object lesson is worth vastly more than any amount of abstract discussion. Everywhere the Negro is, in so far as his race is concerned, confronted by examples of utter disregard of moral sanctions.

To claim that the present situation is not understood by the Negro people is hardly creditable to their intelligence. It is rather generally understood, perhaps more clearly and more generally by the Negro than by the white people. It is certainly understood by many of the mulattoes. Even under Civil Service rules, the hurtfulness of this predominance of the mulatto in public service is not diminished. The example remains, rather strengthened than weakened by the fact that personal merit, rather than political or party considerations, has been the deciding factor. The effect upon the ideals of

the Negro, in such cases, is little different whether the successful mulatto be the product of an initial amalgamation or
whether he represent a racial mixture of several generations'
standing. The vital fact affecting the racial integrity of the
American Negro is that everywhere the political representatives of the race are not fullblood Negroes but mulattoes.

*With such object lessons constantly before Negro mother-
hood and before every aspiring Negro and every aspiring
mulatto, it is inevitable that ethical sanctions should suffer.
So long as the advantage of the mulatto child over the fullblood Negro child may be seriously given as thirty-four to
one, now fifty to one hundred to one, Negro womanhood will
continue to be subjected to a destructively unfair stress, and
racial self-respect and racial self-sufficiency can hardly come
to characterize the fullblood Negro group.*

Thus the crux of the race problem in the United States is
the same from whatever standpoint it is approached. As in all
other interests of the two races, the political forces of the
United States have not endeavored in the past, and are not
now endeavoring, to conserve the higher interests of either
race. There has been no ultimate analysis of the situation
confronting the two races here; no comprehensive grasp of
the needs of the Negro race—as a race; no final analysis of
the interests or of the situation of the white race throughout
the Americas. Thought, insight, seem to have been turned
largely to political advantage and to political manipulation.
The exigencies of practical politics—the politics of temporary
party interests and sectional advantage—should not be allowed to imperil the higher interests of two races. This is now
certainly being done and, of the two groups, the fullblood
Negro is the greater sufferer!

In dealing with the political aspects of the race problem,
some reference to the matter of crime should be made. There
are indications that the Negro throughout the United States
is more criminal at present than at any time since his coming
to America. It is certainly true that he now commits a more

serious grade of crime than formerly. Petty thievery was once characteristic of the Negro criminal. While still prominent in the commission of minor crimes against property, the Negro is now involved very largely in murders and in other major offenses. The Negro in the North is, judged by prison statistics, more criminal than is the Southern Negro. Such statistics, however, do not really prove the Negro more criminal in the North. Northern Negroes are much more certain to be caught and convicted and punished for crime than is a Negro in the South—provided the crimes of the latter wrong only members of his own race, as is largely the case with crimes of violence committed by Negroes. Often in the South minor crimes and misdemeanors within the race receive as little attention as it is possible to give them. Sometimes officers are said to use the crimes of the Negro to increase their fees, but such cases are rare. If the Negro is a worker, he can usually count on his employer's help and influence in his favor when he is in trouble with the law. On the whole, the North has regarded the Negro as a "dark-skinned white man" and has dealt with him as a citizen on that basis. This is especially true of those who have undertaken his education and his manual training. The South knows well that the Negro has not the background of the white race and, while disparaging in other respects, has been much more indulgent in dealing with the Negro criminal—too much so for the good of the race. In reference to certain crimes this·is not the case, but as a general proposition greater efficiency upon the part of the courts and greater certainty of punishment would have proved wholesome for the Southern Negro. The failure to consider the antecedents of the Negro group is one of the most serious errors of the North in its dealings with the race. The "equalitarian" theorist, in his efforts to apply his theories consistently in dealing with the Negro, becomes enmeshed in many difficulties.

In concluding this chapter, a word should be added in reference to the problems created in Washington City, especially in official and diplomatic circles, by race. The diplomatic representatives and other agents chosen and duly commissioned by any country must be received by official Washington. Matters of precedence and other details of official etiquette are controlled by certain rules governing such matters, and the question of race is not considered. A sharply defined line of distinction should be recognized as between the official and the nonofficial in Washington City. In the former, there is little freedom possible; in the latter, the case is quite different. It is certainly true, however, that the socially nonofficial reacts powerfully upon the official and the personality of the diplomatic agent counts greatly in fixing the limits of his usefulness.

The ideals and the customs and the institutions of the country sending the representative may differ widely from those prevailing in the United States and may not agree with even the more cosmopolitan views of nonofficial Washington. In several of the Latin-American states "one drop of white blood makes a white man." When, therefore, a representative appears in Washington, duly accredited as such by one of these countries, he must be received officially and must be accorded every official courtesy due his position and his rank. Only for some serious breach of propriety may he become *"persona non grata"* to this government and his recall be requested. Doubtless, however, men of pure white stock, with wives of pure white stock, are able to accomplish more here than can those of mixed blood. In view of the problems of race already confronting the white people in the United States, it is the part of tact and of wisdom for foreign countries to send as representatives to Washington only those who will neither create racial problems nor intensify those already existing.

There is not the same obligation resting upon the various social groups of the capital city as rests upon official Washington; but no one wishes to be other than duly courteous to representatives of other countries. Certain social functions

159

approach very nearly to official status because of the personalities involved, and it is through these various social groups that foreign diplomats may get a semiofficial contact with the people of the United States. It is this feature of Washington life which limits the usefulness, the activities, of the man of confused racial antecedents. In the future it is probable that the relations between the United States and some of the Latin-American groups may be affected by this question of race. Socially, as concerns these countries and their people, differences exist and should be frankly recognized. It is not by denying or by ignoring fact that constructive results may be obtained. It is rather by arriving at that course of action which, in view of existing fact, promises best results.

Official Washington is not expected to impose any restrictions in the recognition of, or in its dealings with, congressmen or with the wives of congressmen. When, therefore, a Chicago district sends a Negro to Congress, he has the same rights in official circles as has any other representative so chosen. It is not a personal matter, but distinctly official. This does not imply recognition in nonofficial circles; nor does it imply recognition in nonofficial social relations.

Much of the racial antagonism of the past has grown up around the political interests of the two races. It is probable that such will be the case as long as the two races remain in contact. For the present it is a problem of such adjustment as will remove, as far as possible, the hurtfulness of racial contacts. With every constructive effort, all right-thinking people must sympathize. Essentially, constructive effort must tend to strengthen the Negro race, as such, and to elevate the morals of both races. May we hope to see the political parties, the political leaders in each race, conscious of what is involved in the present situation and earnestly endeavoring to protect both races, rise above party and local and sectional strifes and interests and prejudices in an earnest effort to conserve the higher interests of both races? We are indebted to the late General Smuts, of South Africa, for an expression

160

born of his efforts in behalf of the South African natives. It is: "Parallel development." Not racial destruction through amalgamation, but racial development through intelligent conservation and development of each race as a race. Mulatto leadership in politics, as in every other interest of the Negro race, must react disastrously upon the fullblood Negro. The supreme tragedy of the situation lies in the fact that the greater the achievements of the mulatto leader, the finer his personality, the nobler his character, the more skillful his leadership—by just so much the more must he constitute a destructive racial threat to the fullblood Negro people!

CHAPTER VIII

RACE AND RELIGION

D UE to the improved means of travel and of communication, there is now a contact of races more general and more intimate than has previously prevailed or has been previously possible. Except in a few remote or otherwise inaccessible regions, there are few groups of people who are not brought into contact with people of other races. Such racial or group contacts have created many problems, some of which are of minor importance, while others are not only vitally important but must be met and, whether consciously or not, decided in so far as present programs and attitudes are concerned. The insistent nature of race contacts and of the problems growing out of them appears when it is realized that failure to face these problems, to learn their deeper meaning, refusal to analyze them, is as truly a program for dealing with them as would be any other course of action adopted after the most thorough investigation and the most exhaustive analysis. It is, however, the program of indolent indifference or of satisfied ignorance rather than a program based upon accurate knowledge and honest constructive effort.

One of the vital issues created by this contact of the various peoples, the consideration which is really fundamental to all others, is whether or not the present divisions of mankind should be preserved, or whether they should be disregarded and thus permitted to disappear ultimately through a general amalgamation, racial selection yielding to an individual "survival of the fittest.")

It is characteristic of racial contacts that the present only is considered. Desire for cheap labor; immediate profit; for personal ease; for prestige; for a willing servile class quite willing to remain servile—these and similar considerations have often led the more advanced and the more powerful groups to introduce people of diverse race; of low economic efficiency; of backward development generally. The only question that has arisen or that has been considered by the dominant element of a given group seems to have been whether or not the unfortunate alien, along with the un-privileged of their own race, could be exploited immediately and successfully. The future of the dominant group; the atmosphere in which its children must be reared; the im-possibility of any such arrangement proving permanent or satisfactory—such considerations have been subordinated to the profit, the pleasure, the convenience, of the present hour. An acquaintance with ancient or medieval history will furnish abundant examples. Quite universally, what was admitted to the group, even though in servile status, was quickly ab-sorbed and thus modified the dominant race stock. In mod-ern times the introduction of the Negro slave into America is the outstanding example of this shortsighted policy with some of the older immigration policies a close second.

It is inevitable that the problems growing out of this in-creased racial contact should react powerfully upon the various religious systems of the world. It was inevitable that the various religions should be brought into contrast as to their teachings, their organization, their effects as seen in the status of their votaries, in the degree and in the character of the aspirations they kindle and in the elements of aspiration they bring. For the most part, the various religious systems have been restricted to a given area or people. It is, however, neither possible nor desirable to enter upon a discussion of the various religious systems or their social value. The Amer-ican Negro is too far removed from Africa and from the native religions of Africa to know, or to care, what they are or what they teach, although he has not yet outgrown fully his African heritage. Only Christianity now enters directly into the racial situation in America.)

Christianity is an ethical religion. By this statement is

meant that it is essentially concerned with conduct rather than with ritual, and with life rather than with forms and ceremonies. It is this characteristic which gives to the Christian religion a social value far surpassing that of any other system. It is this fact which gives to Christianity its universality.

Not only is Christianity an ethical religion, but it is a religion of general principle rather than one of specific statute. The contrast between the Old Testament codes, regulating the details of conduct by "thou shalt" and "thou shalt not," and the teachings of the Christ, expressed in principle rather than in statutory form, is very sharp and instructive. This characteristic of Christianity assures that it will never be outgrown. Whatever the progress of mankind, the problem of intelligent interpretation and that of the consistent application of Christianity will retain their power to stimulate thought and to direct the moral conduct of mankind. The Christian, definitely committed to what is highest and noblest, finds a wide field of choice, of personal initiative, a wide latitude for personal initiative within definitely constructive bounds.

Christianity is not antagonistic to race. Since racial divisions existed at the time the Christ was on earth, He could not have been ignorant of them or indifferent to them. Indeed, He belonged to possibly the most exclusive of all racial groups and kept, with few exceptions, within the limits of this group. Christianity was made universal by the apostles, especially by St. Paul, in an effort to obey the command: "Go ye therefore into all the world and preach the gospel to every creature."

The general principles as applied in the gospel commit the Christian, then, not to the destruction of race and racial distinctions but to interracial respect and fair dealing. These terms are very inclusive and involve a vast deal more than men generally are in the habit of associating with them. Negatively, *Christian brotherhood no more involves race destruction than brotherly love involves the destruction of the fam-*

164

ily. Properly understood and applied, Christian brotherhood protects race just as brotherly love protects the family.

There are two general planes of contact as between the non-Christian and the Christian world. The great missionary movement of the past hundred years has sent many Christian laymen, teachers, and preachers, avowed propagandists, into non-Christian lands. Along with these—usually following them—have gone the soldiers, the sailors, the traders, and the travelers, and these have influenced the prevailing conception of Christianity, sometimes interfering seriously with the work of the first group. There is a non-Christian white who, finding himself in a situation "where there ain't no ten commandments," proceeds to live accordingly and who succeeds in discrediting both himself and the religion he is supposed to hold; also his race. It is this element of the white race which has created the Eurasian problem in the East, just as it has created the mulatto problem throughout the Americas and Africa.

In view of the increased racial contacts in modern life, the relation between race and religion becomes a matter of prime importance. There are those who, carefully observing the practical activities of the Christian churches at present, reach the conclusion that Christianity is a "race-destroying" influence, and so it unquestionably is in some instances. Possibly at no other point is there a more insistent need for careful and accurate thinking and for correction of unreasoned attitudes and activities that exists just here. The gravest feature of this situation, its greatest danger, lies in failure to deal constructively with the matter of illicit racial intermixture. It is this feature of racial contact everywhere which calls most loudly for constructive control.

For those seeking a solution of race problems and who attempt to study the present situation here, a multitude of questions arise. A fundamental one is this: Is it right, or just, that those who, by foresight and industry, based upon superior ability effectively used, have created for themselves a situa-

165

tion in which they may enjoy, in high degree, the advantages of civilization, should be denied the right to protect themselves and their achievements? Or must such a group achieve its status only to have both status and themselves overwhelmed by an inrush of those who, upon a distinctly lower plane, would quickly reduce all to a common low level? Unrestrained, certain interests in colonial America introduced the Negro slaves. Later, industrial interests combed Europe for its cheapest, most easily controlled labor elements. But for the revolt of white labor and kindred interests, the West would have been flooded with cheap Oriental labor. Mexico is now being drawn upon for a supply of cheap labor, despite the fact that there are, in ideals, in antecedents, and in race, fundamental differences between the Mexican and the typical citizen of the United States.

No fact is more self-evident than that the people of a modern nation, holding a given territory for their future needs and growth, and being of a reasonable racial unity, cannot trust their racial interests to their industrial leaders or to those whose interests demand cheap labor. In some instances, due to the character, patriotism, and intelligence of individuals, this might be done safely, but such cases do not alter the situation as a whole, nor do they justify any alteration of plan or any relaxation of that eternal vigilance required if the highest types of mankind are to be preserved.

In this contact, this conflict, of races there is but one just and constructive attitude. This must recognize the rights of all others and must respect the principle of the exclusive occupancy of that part of the earth held by each group. Trade contacts and all other relations between different peoples should be such as would not only protect, respect, territorial limits, but such as would protect peoples also. Within these limits all necessary or desirable contacts are possible. There could be abundant interchange of ideas through travel, through educational agencies, through commercial dealings, and especially through the printed page as mediating the thought and the achievements of each group to all other groups. Thus it is possible that the various divisions of mankind may prove mutually helpful without subordination or exploitation anywhere. Backward peoples, so often exploited to the point of destruction in the past, should have a fair chance to develop to the limit of their capacity and in harmony with the peculiar genius of each. The logic of the situation demands for each race a homeland, not to be taken from it even on the specious plea of aiding in the education and the uplift, or even in the economic advancement, of the people involved.

Another source of questioning arises from a general survey of the work and of the attitudes of the missionaries. What has been the attitude of the missionary toward race, toward the family, and especially toward illicit racial intermixture?

The missionary occupies a position at once strategic and delicate. However the fact may be minimized by tact or obscured by personality, the missionary implies a system of religion designed to displace the religion, or religions, held by the people to whom he goes. He assumes to offer something better than the system which he attempts to supplant, whether that something is an entirely different faith or a different, a rival, interpretation of Christianity. The resentment kindled is the natural reaction of those asked to accept a foreign faith or to repudiate the faith of their ancestors, or to repudiate a historic interpretation of Christianity and to accept another, usually a rival interpretation.

Another consideration is important. The difficulties confronting the would-be missionary are sufficient to discourage quickly and finally those who are not deeply in earnest and held to their task by strong convictions. In the homeland there may be glamour and enthusiasm likely to attract the emotionally unstable, but the long period of preparation and the careful training now given tend to eliminate all who can be discouraged or diverted from the mission fields. It is, therefore, quite reasonable to assume that, as the facts clearly

167

demonstrate, missionaries, as a class, are people of deep religious conviction and experience, and that their training prepares them to mediate the Christian faith in its purity and in an intelligent and effective manner.

Few non-Christian peoples have developed anything approaching the high type of family life recognized as the ideal by Christians, and actually realized in the manner of life of consistent exemplars of Christian ethics. It is, therefore, an important part of the work of the missionary to establish the Christian family where this does not exist, and to raise the standard of moral living where this is deficient.

There is a tendency, however, in certain quarters for the missionary to accept a situation as found and thus, unconsciously perhaps, to lower the standards of Christianity by accepting, if not sanctioning, that which is really opposed to Christian ethics. Among a people where a very considerable percentage of the population are of illegitimate birth; where the family is regarded as of minor importance; where the birth rate of illegitimates is high, and where racial lines are growing dim, the religious teacher who would demand conformity to Christian ethics and endeavor to establish and to enforce Christian ideals would meet with bitter antagonism. In all such situations there are forces making for compromise and this compromise, especially when this situation has developed under conditions nominally Christian, may be such as to rob Christianity of a large element of its moral and social value. On the other hand, where such racial intermixture does not exist, or the step is from heathenism to Christianity, the ideal of the Christian home is more easily established and the results more satisfactory.

The mixed blood constitutes a problem now world-wide in scope. Even where the product of legal intermarriage, he is still a problem. Relatively, however, there are not a large number of interracial marriages but there are many illicit and many casual unions and many children are born of such. The status of such children is universally unfortunate, in most instances origin proving a barrier in their relation to both races. The plight of the Eurasians, as of all illegitimates, is destructive in direct proportion to the ideals, the outlook, the patriotism, the racial self-respect, of the group in which he finds himself.

This problem of the races, with the inevitable contacts involved, constitutes possibly the most perplexing, in some respects the most ominous, feature of the situation now facing the world. Railway, ship, and plane; telegraph, telephone, and wireless; papers, magazines, and books—all these operate to bring together the uttermost parts of the earth, either in personal or in intellectual contacts. The problem of race, once involving only the groups occupying contiguous or easily accessible areas, now includes all peoples. Radical readjustments are suggested, if not made imperative, by this wider range of contacts.

Among the perplexities growing out of, and inevitably connected with, this wider range of contacts is the outstanding question concerning the perpetuity of race. Should the world program, rendered necessary by the improved means of communication and travel, disregarding the conditions under which alone such fusion must occur, encourage such confusion of groups and races as will most quickly obliterate all racial lines, or should there be a definite and intelligent effort to preserve each racial group? This latter course has the merit of conserving each of those units most worthy of preservation and best able to contribute to the welfare of all. It would give to each unit an opportunity to realize fully its possibilities.

While greatly intensified and extended by modern conditions, the problems of amalgamation of the races is not new. Migrations, wars, conquests, involving entire peoples, have occurred within the range of written records. The skeletal remains of prehistoric man yield proof that in the more remote periods one race superseded another, great migrations sweeping over whole continents and changing the physical

169

characteristics of the people of these areas through fusion of conqueror and conquered. These movements and their consequences constitute an intensely interesting study for the scientist, especially for the anthropologist. The scientist brings to this study one set of interests, and these interests are often quite different from those of the eugenist, the moralist, or the student of religions.

For the Christian student additional problems arise, and these problems grow, in part, out of the fact that Christianity is a universal religion and, as such, proposes a world program as opposed to the many group or national programs growing out of local or national interests. The Christian religion is essentially a religion of brotherhood and must be interpreted in terms of universal brotherhood. It stands for the same things for all peoples and demands the same things of all peoples. It rebukes aggression in all its forms. It promotes kindliness toward all humanity. Essentially, it fosters the self-respect of every group and of every individual accepting it. Unfortunately, some of these facts and their implications have not been clearly grasped by many of the most zealous advocates of Christianity, while others have been hopelessly confused in their application to the race problem.

Turning now from this very incomplete, but possibly suggestive, discussion of the wider range of racial contacts in which religion has often been tribal in character and has sometimes served as a powerful agent in preserving the group intact, and as a determining force directing the group development and group achievement, let us note some of the vital features of the Negro problem as this problem has been affected by the type of Christianity mediated to the Negro here in the United States and exemplified by the resulting status of the race at the present time. More specifically, the influence of religion upon the matter of racial integrity of the American Negro will be discussed. The census returns for the United States as a whole are of prime value, but local situations are also important, especially conditions existing in the District of Columbia. Statistics furnished by the Federal Census for this area are supplemented by much more frequent enumerations made by the Police Department and by very highly valuable contributions made by the District Board of Health.

One of the most valuable studies yet made of the race problem in the United States is that made by Professor E. B. Reuter in 1916. The volume gives the results of extended investigations and furnishes a statement of the racial status of Negroes who have attained to special eminence. Summing up his investigations as these bear upon the relative achievements of the fullblood Negro and the mulatto, the conclusion is reached that: *"On the basis accepted for the purposes of this study, the chances of the mulatto developing into a leader of the race are thirty-four times as great as are the chances of the black child."* [1] The vital importance of this statement justifies its repetition elsewhere. It covers the whole field.

In a table entitled "Relative Prominence of the Negro and the Mulatto in Selected Fields of Endeavor"—twelve in number—Professor Reuter finds 2,129 names worthy of mention, 1,844 men and 285 women. Of the men, 206 are listed as black and 1,638 as mulatto. Summarizing his investigations upon this point, covering in all 4,291 cases of those prominent enough to merit consideration, he finds 447 blacks and 3,844 mulattoes! In twenty-five colleges and universities with Negro students exclusively he found 9,172 students enrolled in 1916. Of these, 1,605 were classed as black, or apparently fullblood Negroes, while 7,567 were classed as mulattoes! [2]

The above is a fair example of the directness with which Professor Reuter approaches his subject, and the definiteness of the information he supplies. For present purposes, the information given in reference to the Negro ministry is most important. The activities and the practices of the churches

[1] *The Mulattoes in the United States,* Reuter, p. 314. See also his later study: *Race Mixtures.*
[2] *The Mulattoes in the United States,* Reuter, p. 277.

are open to the same adverse criticism as are all other agencies and forces working with, or for, the Negro. In so far as we have been able to ascertain, no religious body, North or South, now makes, or ever has made, any consistent distinction between the Negro and the mulatto on moral grounds. Neither has any distinction been made in dealing with the Negro group between those of legitimate and those of illegitimate birth. As a direct result of this "hands-off" policy, this failure to protect the Negro at this vital point, the domination of the mulatto is quite as marked, as complete, in the religious interests of the race as in any other field. Without inquiry into family history, mulattoes, even those representing known initial amalgamations, are employed as teachers in those schools under the control of the various churches. Men of such origin are likewise employed as preachers.

A few references to Professor Reuter's comprehensive investigations will show how complete is this domination of the mulatto in the various Negro churches, especially in administrative affairs. In 1914 the nine bishops of the Colored Methodist Episcopal Church were all mulatto. Of the eleven general officers of this church, nine were mulatto, with two unclassified. Of twenty-seven bishops of the African Methodist Episcopal Church, four are classed as black and twenty-three as mulatto. Of the eight bishops of the African Methodist Episcopal Zion Church, two are classed as black and six as mulatto. The officers of the National Baptist Convention (Colored), twelve in number, are all given as mulatto, as is the case with the five general officers of the New England Baptist Convention (Colored).[3]

It is not necessary to give further details, as is done in the thorough presentation characteristic of Professor Reuter's book. His "Study has brought together the names of six hundred and forty-three members of the Negro ministry. . . . When the names previously mentioned are removed there remain the names of five hundred and eighty persons. Ninety-

---

[3] *The Mulatto in the United States,* Reuter, pp. 274-282.

five of these are considered full-bloods and four hundred and eighty-five are known to be mulattoes." [4] Let it be remembered that these figures represent the most prominent men of the Negro ministry in the United States. Here, as elsewhere, the mulatto greatly outnumbers the fullblood Negro, but the ninety-five fullblood Negroes who are worthy of a place in a group so small, relatively, are quite sufficient to show what might have been accomplished had right ideals prevailed and had practical effort been made to realize such ideals. The few fullblood Negroes who have, even under the prevailing adverse conditions, made good in the various callings, demonstrate the fact that a sufficient number of capable fullblood Negroes might have been found and trained for the leadership of the race. The fullblood Negro does not have a fair chance in those educational institutions where the teachers are wholly or partially white and the student body overwhelmingly mulatto. *The Negro is unconscious of this situation, or wholly indifferent to it, only to the degree that his education has failed dismally in the matter of implanting personal and racial self-respect.* Under present conditions, especially under present leadership, *there is little to convince the fullblood Negro that his racial integrity is worth preserving!*

Some years ago a mulatto published a book which was very severe upon the Negro, abounding in sweeping statements concerning his moral weaknesses and his moral lapses in general. He failed utterly to discriminate between the different levels of the race and thus did a gross injustice to that element of the race which stands for its moral uplift. This mulatto has, however, left a paragraph which contains a vital truth in reference to the effect upon Negro womanhood of the matter now under discussion. That there is a conscious desire upon the part of Negro and of mulatto motherhood to improve the condition of their offspring and that this desire affects vitally the matter of initial amalgamation, is clearly stated, as fol-

[4] *The Mulatto in the United States,* Reuter, p. 282.

lows: "That Negroes have a conscious sense of degradation, which they falsely attribute to their color, is shown by their eagerness to get as far as possible away from black shades. *It is this craving for a light color and better hair for their offspring which is responsible for many of the illegitimate children of Negro motherhood.*" [5] The italics are ours.

It will be noted that Thomas, himself a diffusion mulatto, places the incentive promoting initial amalgamation on the basis of physical characteristics of the offspring—color, hair, etc. Other considerations are certainly present. Beyond mere physical characteristics, Negro and mulatto motherhood may well begin to see possibilities before children of mixed blood denied to children of pure Negro descent. More or less generally, Negroes, and especially mulattoes, are coming to look upon racial intermixture as a means of thwarting the exclusiveness of the white race. Upon the part of many, present conditions and the present status of racial intermixture are cause for unconcealed exultation!

Discussing the racial integrity of the American Negro several years ago, the following passages having to do primarily with the activities of the religious organizations, were written: "So far as we have been able to ascertain, no religious organization, North or South, makes, or has ever made, any consistent distinction between the Negro and the mulatto. Without reference to family history or individual origin, mulattoes are employed as teachers and as preachers. The result is what might be expected. The mulatto avails himself of the opportunities offered. What type of morality can he inculcate? Will not every success achieved and every honor won by the mulatto react unfavorably upon the fullblood Negro? If the reader will take the pains to ascertain the complexion of the ministry of any of the religious organizations of the Negroes, he will find that where the Negro is weakest and his need greatest the least foresight has been exercised in his behalf, and that the moral and regenerating forces of

[5] *The American Negro*, Thomas, p. 408.

Christianity have been largely neutralized by the object lessons thus furnished. Religion should give a healthful moral atmosphere, as well as correct moral ideals. Otherwise, what is built with one hand is torn down by the other. Certainly religion should not vie with political parties and interests for the first place as patron, if not promoter, of social impurity. Here, as elsewhere, patronage must be considered as actual endorsement."

Again: "Mistakes have been made in the past and are still being made, and the interests of both races demand that such changes shall be made in dealing with the Negro race as shall hold it rigidly to the same moral and ethical standards as are applied in other races. In dealing with the moral lapses of the Negro, there is call for abounding charity. In the exercise of that charity in the past, the friends of the race, as well as others, have vitiated the moral standards of the race, robbed Christianity itself largely of its moral and regenerating power for the race, and have left but little to furnish that imperative incentive to right living of which the race, as a whole, stands so desperately in need. With the moral and the ethical standards practically suspended in the case of the Negro by those who attempt to conduct his education and his moral training, it is not strange that the Negro himself suspends them—on occasion. With mulattoes as its political leaders, as the teachers of its youth, and dominating its pulpits, we see no hope whatever of any marked improvement or moral uplift in the character of the race—as a race."

These paragraphs were written more than twenty years ago. There is a directness, even a harshness, about them which tends to excite pity for the mulatto and which may seem to contravene the spirit of Christianity. No one has, however, during these years attempted to show that any detail set forth is not true. The paragraphs are repeated here because they set forth the actual situation. If harsh, it is the harshness of definite recognition of fact; if offensive, it is the offense of truth to those unable to justify and unwilling to modify their actions and their attitudes.

In the writing of these paragraphs the effect of this strange attitude of its white friends—and enemies—upon the Negro race in the particular matter of its racial integrity, was chiefly in mind, but it becomes increasingly evident that this suspension of standards in the sex life of the Negro influences the race here in its whole outlook and strikes destructively at Negro character everywhere.

There are those who rise above these unfavorable conditions, but these conditions undoubtedly make the struggle of the race for ideal homes and a satisfying home life infinitely more difficult than it should be.

Mr. Earnest Sevier Cox, in a recently published pamphlet, thus evaluates the practical influence of Christianity as now mediated to the American Negro: "The most subtle, as it is the most dangerous, miscegenationist trend in the South at the present time, operates under the cloak of Christianity." [6] Others are being driven to the same conclusion here expressed by Mr. Cox. It is inevitable that the position of leadership enjoyed by the churches must suffer because of the record they have made in dealing with this aspect of race relations. No one need question the sincerity of those members of the white race who have sought to assist the Negro race, but their efforts, their work done, must be evaluated both by the insight shown and by the results achieved. The results are manifest to all. *The outstanding result is this failure to give to the race a sane racial pride and outlook, together with a compelling religious zeal for its racial preservation.*

The generally recognized characteristics of the race, together with the experiences through which the American Negro has passed, make it all the more necessary that those details of right living which may be safely left to the individual consciences in other groups having different antecedents, should, with the majority of Negroes, be explicitly

[6] *The South's Part in Mongrelizing the Nation,* Cox, p. 69.

taught both by precept and by example, especially by the latter. As it now is, the matter never having been laid upon the conscience of the race directly and unequivocally, it is not just to hold the Negro as wholly responsible. Censure must fall upon those, North and South, who have, in matters vital alike to character and to godliness, vitiated the ideals of the Negro by tacitly accepting and virtually approving his moral lapses instead of impressing, by practical and energetic disapprobation of their breach, fundamental moral principles. That is a mistaken kindness which results in moral confusion. *Under present conditions, especially under present leadership, there is little to convince the fullblood Negro that his racial integrity is worth preserving!*

From any general survey of the situation of the American Negro it may be seen that the influences radiating from the political, the educational, the philanthropic and the religious activities and institutions, in so far as these affect the Negro, unite in forming a subtle, but constant, menace to Negro character, as well as to the racial integrity of the Negro, a menace none the less destructive because largely negative, or indirect. Too much has been attributed to "race and previous condition of servitude," forgetting that, in so far as these had proved confusing to Negro thought and degrading to practical conduct, the need for clear-cut ethical instruction and correct moral example were indicated. Race, social status, and other disadvantages are still quite generally accepted as sufficient excuse for most of the wrongs to which the Negro race is especially disposed. *Thus its ethical code, primitive enough at best, is vitiated; religion becomes, for the mass of the Negroes, painfully near to being nonmoral; and the great body of the race loses the elevating effect of an all but compulsory effort to realize high moral ideals in daily living.* There can be no question but *the chief burden of this situation falls upon the fullblood Negro.*

Religion and the organizations growing out of religion occupy a very prominent place with the Negroes of the United

177

States. Large numbers of Negroes who have had but meager educational advantages, if any at all, have been very definitely influenced by some form of church association and by some school of Christian doctrine. The Methodist and the Baptist Churches have been most acceptable to the Negro and have been most influential with him. Throughout the Latin-American countries the Negro has been largely under the influence of the Roman Catholic Church. There seems no essential difference in the attitudes of these churches in so far as race is concerned. Conditions are vastly worse in at least some of the Latin-American countries, but the womanless colony at Isabella, typical of Spanish and Portugese contacts with the Indians and, later, with the Negroes, introduced a state of affairs very different from that existing in the North European settlements and made the problem confronting the Catholics an infinitely more difficult one than that confronting the Protestants later in North America. The fundamental error of both Catholic and Protestant was in that neither foresaw or made any effort to control the situation as to race.

A definitely neutral attitude is quickly recognized as characterizing all the churches and all the other agencies active in behalf of the Negro in so far as his racial integrity is concerned. There has been no general effort to bring this matter under control, or even to concentrate upon it the attention of either race. Historically, it may be readily seen how present conditions came to prevail. It may also be seen why present attitudes are wholly inadequate. It is fair to assume that a matter to which recognized moral and religious leaders give little or no attention, is a matter of no serious consequence, and such is the popular attitude toward the mulatto. By neither the white nor the Negro has there been any general or outspoken attempt to discredit or to prevent the amalgamation of these races. For the most part, there has been no clear conception of what is occurring, certainly not of its deeper significance.

In view of this utter failure of American Christianity, as

178

represented by all branches of the Christian Church, to deal definitely and constructively with the matter of race mixture as between the white and the black races here, it is well to note another factor which has been operative. *Race Prejudice* is, in many of its manifestations, exceedingly unfortunate, and some of its effects are very hurtful. In many respects both parties suffer seriously, but the less favorably situated individual or group suffers most. Anything, however, which forces upon a race the necessity of becoming self-sufficient, and of developing its own civilization and culture, challenges the best that is in the given race. The exclusiveness of the white race has forced upon the Negro many steps which he would probably not have taken otherwise. Because the Negro has had his own churches, he now has a religious leadership from his own group; because he has had separate schools and colleges, he now has trained teachers of his own blood; because of a dawning loyalty to his own group, the race now has professional men and business enterprises. As a constructive force, prejudice has united the Negro group and, in a measure, has forced upon it an independent life, a racial self-sufficiency. May not this prove a Providential training preparatory to the day when the American Negro shall build a civilization of his own? Upon the part of that type of white man morally capable of debauching Negro womanhood, prejudice has doubtless often proved effective when other restraints were absent or ineffective.

Usually it is not well to complicate a great moral and social issue by any introduction of a matter which has proved as unfortunate as has the prolonged struggle between Catholicism and Protestantism. A careful comparison of the place of the two systems in the settlement of America shows that there was far greater activity upon the part of the Catholic forces. Indeed, the first settlement in America was made when Martin Luther was ten years old, and the Spanish conquests in America were well under way before the "Reformation" began with the incident at Wittenberg. Later the Protestant

179

forces entered the field by the colonization of that part of North America now composing the United States. Catholics, however, settled in the valley of the St. Lawrence, in the Ohio valley, in the Mississippi Valley, in Florida, in Maryland, in Louisiana, and in the Mexican territory later annexed. These, however, were not, in racial attitudes, essentially different from the English, or the Dutch, or the French Protestants and, in many respects, differ as much from the Spanish Catholics as from the Protestants. In a large measure, therefore, adverse criticism of the Latin-American method of dealing with race is a criticism of the Spanish and the Portuguese groups quite as much as of the failure of the Church to protect the race of the natives.

With this qualification, a careful comparison of the two systems in the settlement of America and in the resulting social order created by each is of great value. Indeed, such a comparison is necessary in order that the student may understand fully some of the problems of the present day but which look back to Isabella as their origin. In a general way, in the light of present conditions, both Catholic and Protestant are subject to adverse criticism, for neither has dealt constructively with the race problems confronting them in America. The Catholic group in Latin-America has had to deal with by far the more difficult situation.

The Spaniard did not come to America primarily as a home-building permanent settler. He came rather for the purpose of exploitation, expecting to find mineral wealth to be had for the taking and, in lesser degree, he expected to gain wealth quickly by trading with the natives and by exploiting both the country and the peoples of the New World. In the chapter comparing the settlement at Isabella with that at Jamestown are pointed out the chief differences between the Latin and the English as colonizers. The fundamental difference between the two settlements, it is pointed out, lies in the total absence of Spanish women in the Spanish settlement and the presence of English or Dutch women either at the founding of the settlement or very soon after the beginning of a colony by the English or by the Dutch.

Priests were present in the major Spanish settlements and accompanied the armies on their various expeditions. It is possible to gain a fairly full and accurate knowledge of early Spanish conquests and colonization through the writings of Las Casas and those of other ecclesiastics. It is through Las Casas that the full significance of the Spanish Conquest in the destruction of the Indians is realized. Renteria and Las Casas were men who came to conclusions and developed convictions resulting in attitudes at once greatly in advance of the age in which they lived and productive of conflict with that type of ecclesiastic subservient to the military and characterized by the views and the attitudes of the age. The priest-chaplain to a Spanish official, civil or military, was hardly free to censure his commander, a fact which doubtless had its influence upon many. Las Casas was of the type that would not be subservient, and his life was one of protest and conflict. His appeals direct to the Spanish Crown and his efforts to influence the Church and the masses of the Spanish people won for him the title: "Protector of the Indians." The practical benefits he was able to secure for the Indians were not great. He approved Negro slavery for a time, but this was done in the hope that thus the Indians might be protected. Later he recognized this approval as a capital mistake, but this realization came too late to have practical value in either relieving the Indian or limiting the enslaving of the Negro.

From conditions obtaining in the settlement at Isabella have developed the unfortunate racial conditions characteristic of so much of Latin America at the present time. The work of Professor Foerster points out the logical results of these conditions after the lapse of more than four hundred years. The situation shows the inevitable results of leaving such matters to take their own course rather than to bring them definitely under the control of the character and the intelligence of the peoples involved. It is here that we recog-

181

nize the fundamental error underlying the whole of the settlement of America. There has been no just evaluation of population elements and no effort to preserve the best, as judged from any standpoint whatever. The possibility of making a homogeneous people, of the highest type possible, the basis of the State and of civilization has not been appreciated.

In passing judgment upon the Spaniard at Isabella, and everywhere else that they founded colonies, justice requires that full consideration be given to the age in which these things occurred. It is not fully just to say that the ideals of the age were low. They seem both low and cruel to those of the present. The ideals of the age certainly sanctioned wanton cruelty and utter lack of recognition of the rights of man, rights now recognized as fundamental and inalienable. The lot of the Indian was made worse because of the rather widespread belief upon the part of the Spaniard that, since the Indian was not mentioned in the Scriptures, he was not human in the same sense as are those so honored! In Europe the stage was being set for the tragedy of the Inquisition and for the destructive wars between Catholic and Protestant.

In the Spanish conquest of America, neither personal nor property rights were regarded in so far as the Indians were concerned. It was the custom to enslave the Indians and to force them to labor in the mines and upon the plantations. As the men were killed in war, or otherwise, the women were frequently bestowed upon the soldiers. In this there was nothing new. The custom was old and well established, Julius Caesar giving repeated instances, as do other writers.

Against this situation and against the intellectual and the spiritual attitudes underlying it, a few religious men protested vigorously and valiantly, as did Renteria and Las Casas; but protest from these was not sufficient to change the situation. Other ecclesiastics sanctioned the acts of the military and the civil authorities and approved the enslavement of the Indians and, later, of the Negroes.

Possibly nowhere in modern history can there be found a

182

situation out of which have arisen more unfortunate results, either in quantity or in quality, than can be traced to this womanless colony at Isabella. As the Spanish army extended its conquests throughout the Islands and to the Continental areas, the demoralization of the Indians kept pace and, with the introduction of Negro slaves, conditions became worse. Professor Foerster's findings may well be taken as the statement of the results—moral and social, and racial—of the failure of the Latin-American to transplant his home to the New World! He committed the racially unpardonable sin of leaving his own women behind!

Little need be said of the English and the Dutch settlements. Between the settlement at Isabella and that at Jamestown 114 years elapsed. These were years of intense struggle, but also years of very substantial progress. When the English, followed by the Dutch, began the colonization of North America, they had the advantage of all the progress that Europe had made during these 114 years. Europe had not outgrown slavery, and this institution was fastened upon North America, as it had already been fastened upon Spanish and Portuguese territories, but with this difference: Indians were not, to any appreciable degree, reduced to slavery. They were forced from their lands; they were debauched through alcoholic liquors; they were wronged in many ways; but their race existence was quite generally respected and there has been remarkably little mixture of red and white blood in the area now constituting the United States. It is chiefly in Mexican immigration that the mixed-blood Indian is coming to find a place in the population of the United States.

Most of the colonists coming to the English settlements were men of family, and with them came wife and children. The colonists at Jamestown sent back to England for wives, and thus early into the history of the first permanent English settlement in America was introduced the English home. The United States and Canada owe vastly more than is generally realized to the pioneer white woman who has kept pace with the white man on every frontier, and who has thus at once saved the manhood and the blood-purity of her race. Could the Spanish woman have done as much for the Latin-American?

Yet, into North America, and among those enjoying the benefits of more than an additional century of world progress, the Negro slave was brought in such numbers as to determine the course development was to take in a large part of North America. He came, in most instances, into close association with his white master and with the family of his white master as well. This arrangement had its advantages, as well as its perils. A goodly proportion of the slaves brought to Continental North America were women, making possible a semblance of family life among these people. Considering his antecedents, the advantages fell largely to the slave but at the close of 250 years of racial contact—1619 to 1870—the Census reported 584,049 mulattoes, by far the most unfortunate result of the period of slavery here.

No defense can be made for this mingling of the two races here. Theoretically, the slave woman was helpless. In some cases she was actually so. That there were influences which restrained the progress of racial intermixture under slavery is clearly shown by results following emancipation. Each twenty-year period is virtually duplicating in racial intermixture the results of the whole preceding time the races had been in contact. These figures show clearly what has occurred, what is occurring here, and that without protest, or even understanding, upon the part of those in positions of leadership in State, or even in Church.

In the face of the ideals and the outlook of 1950, defense of slavery is impossible; yet justice demands that facts be duly considered in their time and place setting whenever judgement is to be passed upon the Southern slave-holder. There is to be found nowhere else in the world an instance of 250 years of contact between an equal number of Negroes and an equal number of Caucasians, lasting so long and involving an equally close association, that did not result in a vastly greater racial intermixture than was shown by the Census of 1870. It would be difficult, if not impossible, to find an instance of symbiosis of the Negro and the Caucasian elsewhere under which blood mixture has occurred more rapidly than has been the case in the United States since 1865.

There is a widely prevalent assumption that those who carry on and those who support present activities in behalf of the American Negro, especially the Negro in the United States, are the champions, the expositors, the exemplars, of Christian brotherhood. This assumption often carries with it the implication that those unable to sanction the methods used or the principles underlying the past and the present activities in behalf of the Negro are deficient in "brotherliness," if not in all essential Christian qualities. Thus an issue is fairly joined.

This issue cannot be settled wholly by reference to abstract principles, nor yet by theories based upon such principles. The moral perception of one race and the ideals, the self-respect, of another race are being dulled, if not destroyed. The blood-purity of two races is being destroyed! These are facts which must be met by blind indifference or by constructive intelligence. Present attitudes toward these facts cannot change the past or its fruitage in the present; but the present and the future are not yet utterly hopeless. There is no better method in planning to safeguard the future than that of a careful study, analysis, of the past and the present. Factors active in the past have their fruitage in the present, results which may be recognized and classified and referred to their causes or to their sources. It is quite certain that factors producing recognized results in the past will, unless conditions are changed, continue to produce the same results in the future. Factors that persist tend to produce cumulative results, and that is certainly the case in racial intermixture.

In the chapter dealing with the near-white may be found a discussion of those influences which tend to urge on to completion the process of amalgamation once this process is begun. In this respect the forces affecting the individual mulatto affect likewise the whole Negro race, varying in degree rather than in moral quality. Throughout this volume may be found various references to, and discussions of, those factors and those influences bringing to bear upon the full-blood Negro woman a stress often all but driving her into the ranks of the practical amalgamators.

There has been pointed out, especially in this chapter, the danger that, through practical example, moral and ethical principles may, by their imperfect exemplification, if not perversion, lose their force and their value as applied to a given situation. This is what has occurred in reference to the Negro race in the United States. Precedent has been established. The Negro is now dominated, in all the higher interests of his race, by the mulatto. Above all is the imminent danger that religion itself may become nonmoral in its social aspects, if not in the whole range of its social-control values. *In the problem of the illegitimate child and in the problem of racial integrity, as these confront the American Negro, religion comes painfully near to being nonmoral.*

For this unfortunate situation the Negro is not primarily responsible. No higher ideal has been mediated to the race here. It is wholly unreasonable to have expected the Negro—the pupil—to develop a moral, a religious standard higher than that set for him in these respects by the practical attitudes and in the manifest approvals of those white religionists—his teachers—with whom he has had to deal. These teachers have, without notable exception, suspended 'moral and ethical and social and racial safeguards in the interest of those who have, in their immediate ancestry, from one to five or six cases of illegitimacy and initial amalgamation! In the face of this situation how could the ideals of the millions—Negroes and mulattoes—be preserved? Escape from racial proscription and from racial limitations, realization of all desirable opportunities and possibilities, have been made to lie not in the direction of racial development and racial self-sufficiency and racial self-respect but rather in escape, partial or complete, from race itself, even by those avenues most revolting to the moral sense and most destructive to all constructive forces in so far as these affect family and race. Upon existing conditions, the Clergy of the United States have, by their silence, their failure to protest, put the stamp of virtual approval. *There is real danger that the moral leadership of the churches will be gravely discredited as a result of this situation.* Against one of the gravest wrongs possible, the Southern churches have interposed chiefly silence; the Northern churches have permitted present conditions to develop without protest or effort to control the situation. Protestantism has not protected North America. It has made no persistent effort to do so. Catholicism has not protected race in those countries where its sway has been uncontested.

In view of this situation, so plainly manifest to all who consent to give it unbiased attention, it is inevitable that the attitude of the white clergy of America; individually, by denomination, and collectively, shall pass in review before the awakened laity .and before the great body of the American people. American Christianity is certainly subject to adverse criticism because of the fact that it has failed to advance right racial ideals in a wholesome and an ineffective manner. It has educated the mulatto rather than the fullblood Negro; it has approved the leadership of the mulatto in every field of endeavor. There is nothing in the direct attitude of any of the religious agencies assisting the Negro which gives to the race an unequivocal challenge to preserve its racial integrity. Religion may well seem positively against, instead of for, every effort to keep the races pure. Yet there are, unquestionably, a host of racially protective agencies which owe their existence to the teachings of Christianity and to the conscience created by Christianity. Thus indirectly Christianity is a highly constructive force even in the race problem. Its force is, however, exerted in a negative, an indirect way, whereas

187

it might be made positive and thus vastly more effective. Adverse criticism tends to ignore this atmospheric, this indirect value of Christianity, but society has the right to demand direct and positive action upon racial, as well as upon other problems.

Christian Brotherhood, it should be clearly understood, is not synonymous with lax or indefinite moral and ethical sanctions. Properly understood, it is not a "race-destroying" influence. The least it can approve is the extension to other peoples and to other races of the same protective influences characterizing its best intra-racial manifestations. In this endeavor there should be no unreasoned sentimentality, but rather careful analysis and moral certainty in its approvals. Issues now plastic must soon become rigid and unchangeable. The individuals of the present generation of the two races have in their keeping the issues of the future. The Chinese proverb, "Every day a new beginning," has in it for the individual a vital truth. For race, it also has much destructive error. It is possible to mend the broken life. It is not possible to restore the destroyed race.

Christian Brotherhood, the whole body of Christian teaching, meets its severest interracial tests when concerned with the so-called "backward" races. Possibly the greatest world-problem now to be met, the most urgent reform in world policies and world politics, lies in the direction of conceding to the less fortunately situated peoples a fair chance to work out their own destiny, stimulated indeed by the achievements of the more progressive, but undisturbed by aggressions, or exploitations at the hands of the more fortunate and the more powerful groups. This is not quite the same as the problem of the smaller nations. It is essentially a problem of racial contacts. Unless there can be implanted in the backward group, in the individuals composing it, a laudable race pride, it is certain that the highest results are impossible. If an extreme position must be taken in order to direct attention to matters of such vital importance, a frankly brutal attitude, forcing upon a group or a race the necessity for self-development, is vastly more helpful and more wholesome than an attitude approving a spineless morality and adapting itself to conditions as found rather than insisting upon strenuous effort to attain to the higher possibilities.

What does Christian Brotherhood demand of American Christianity—every name and order included—in reference to the Negro and from the Negro? Among such demands two matters are certainly fundamental:

I—*The blood-purity of the Negro should be respected and, in every practical way, maintained by every element of the white race.* Upon the part of those members of the white race directly concerned in the education and the training of the leaders of the Negro race, in America as elsewhere, a definite effort should be made to discover and to train capable full-blood Negro youth, in order that the race may have fullblood Negro leadership. A mixed-blood leadership will not, possibly cannot, stimulate to the full racial self-respect, racial self-sufficiency, or racial integrity.

II—*The matter of blood-purity should be stressed by all the agencies of education and of religion, whether controlled by the white or by the Negro race.* Certainly special emphasis should be given to all that is calculated to discourage initial amalgamation. Even the mulatto may render a helpful service in combatting this feature of race amalgamation. It is not, however, an easy matter for the mulatto to take an effective stand against initial amalgamation. It is very difficult for the near-white to do so. What he is tends to be more influential than anything he may say.

Let it be remembered that Christian Brotherhood finds its highest and its noblest expression not in a kindliness that has no power of analysis and no sharpness of ethical distinction but rather in arriving at ultimate rectitude, kindly indeed but uncompromisingly, even in dealing with race. The Golden Rule and Christian Brotherhood, properly understood and applied, are not racially destructive forces. They

189

are essentially conservative, preservative forces racially. The Negro has no more right to engraft himself upon, to lose himself within, the white stock than the white has to destroy the Negro through amalgamation.

In reference to the percentage of Negro ministers who are of mixed blood, this may be noted. Theoretically there is no distinction made between the Negro and the mulatto. Membership lists of the various organizations, conferences, etc. are, therefore, useless except as a basis for classification. It is immediately evident, however, that very few fullblood Negroes are found as pastors of the stronger Negro churches. The number increases as the smaller and weaker churches are considered, especially the rural churches, but throughout there is a preponderance of the mulatto in those situations requiring the higher types of service. Here, as elsewhere, there are enough fullblood Negroes actually filling exacting positions to demonstrate what might have been achieved had any persistent effort been made to discover and to train competent fullblood Negroes for religious leadership. With so high a percentage of the Negro population showing clearly the infusion of white blood, it is quite natural that their churches should reflect this situation in their membership. This, however, does not account for the manifest fact of mulatto leadership.

Close observation, extending over many years, has convinced the writer that those influences most widely operative and most hurtful to the Negro in the United States are directly and definitely associated with the religious interests of the race. It has been pointed out that the mulatto dominates the religious organizations of the race and that he largely monopolizes those positions in the Negro churches which are most desirable because of the possibilities associated with them, especially in the matter of financial support and the cultural opportunities dependent upon adequate income. Professor Reuter has provided the statistics fundamental to a study of this matter, and anyone wishing to do so may ascertain the situation within the range of his personal observation. This predominance of the mulatto has practical bearing in two directions. It affects, adversely and that in many ways, the fullblood Negro minister; and it affects, adversely and in direct proportion to the ability and the popularity of the mulatto minister, the congregation and the local community to which he ministers.

It is manifest that there is usually present no consciousness of the situation here discussed; and, it is argued, that therefore the situation is not essentially hurtful. In such reasoning there is a fatal fallacy. Moral soundness is not achieved by resolutely shutting out from a given situation all investigation, all analysis, nor yet by a sophistic seizing upon what supports a given predetermined program, without assurance that this program is sound and that its ultimate results are desirable. The *laissez faire* theory in economics has long been discredited, as have most of its modifications. Not "hands off" policies but intelligent understanding and purposive, constructive control are required if the character and the intelligence of America are to be brought to bear directly and helpfully, upon the matter of race protection and race purity. In all thinking upon this matter it should be remembered that *the situation must be dealt with and that everyone, in both races, is actually dealing with it.* The great majority, in both races, are dealing with it negatively because either not conscious that such a problem exists or, if conscious of it, fail to give to it sufficient thought or attention to cause them to realize its issues as vital. The few who have realized something of the hurtfulness of past and present conditions, something of the results which these conditions, unchanged, must produce in future, have been unable to arouse any general interest in this matter. Outstanding in the ranks of the indifferent are the clergy of the Americas.

A precedent of prime value, but one totally ignored in the case of the American Negro, is furnished in the history of the Hebrew people. At the close of centuries of slavery in Egypt

191

and as this people was being prepared, under Divine guidance, for an independent national existence, the estimate placed upon a pure family life is clearly demonstrated by the statute recorded in Deuteronomy 23:2, viz.: "A bastard shall not enter into the congregation of the Lord; even to his tenth generation shall he not enter into the congregation of the Lord." This 3,401 years ago; 3,316 years before the emancipation of the American Negro! From 1865 to 1950 this lesson seems completely lost.

The Negro of 1865 had a desperate need for the development of a strong and pure home life, a strong and pure type of family life. Slavery had taken him from centuries of African barbarism and, by association—contact—had imposed a semblance of civilization. There was grave need for any and for all influences calculated to impose right ideals and to secure the practice of Christian principles. Instead of insisting upon such ideals and principles, existing conditions were accepted—without analysis. All those forces strengthening race and all those safeguards necessary to right moral conduct as reflected in social and family and personel sex mores were ignored; illegitimacy was practically approved; and the leadership of the mixed blood was established along with emancipation. Eighty-five years of such leadership, with the antecedents of the Negro group, could not have produced other than the present racial confusion. The contrasts between the statute of Deuteronomy—1451 B.C.—and the practices of 1950 Christianity as these affect the Negro race should be carefully studied, analyzed, and evaluated.

CHAPTER IX

Colonization as a Solution of the American Race Problem

AT VARIOUS times during the past century there developed an interest in the matter of the separation of the Negro and the white races in the United States through colonization of the Negro. The methods proposed at various times were not essentially different, but the locations proposed differed widely. One group favored the setting apart, exclusively for Negroes, a definite part of the then unoccupied territory held by the United States; another group proposed to remove them to some part of the Western Hemisphere other than that held, or likely to be acquired, by the United States; but the only serious attempts to solve the Negro Problem by colonization have contemplated the return of the Negro to Africa. The more recent Garvey movement [1] proposed a return to Africa, Liberia being the location proposed for the beginnings of the movement. Among the Negroes of the United States, however, was a strong party favoring colonization, but opposing Garvey. This party favored Abyssinia as the part of Africa to be colonized. Neither Garvey nor the "Abyssinians" seem to have considered the interests or the wishes of those already occupying these areas.

Sharp clashes occurred between the two groups, and these differences and the divisions and antagonisms growing out of them did much to prevent the program of either party from being given a fair trial. Indeed, neither program, except as it affected Negro ideals and indicated Negro attitudes, seems to have produced any appreciable permanent results. Garvey and his activities will be discussed later. Despite the seeming failure of both, these movements give refreshing evidence of the easily aroused longing of the American Negro for a homeland of his own. They have, unquestionably, con-

[1] See Index.

tributed much toward the creation of group-consciousness and racial self-respect upon the part of the American Negro. Abyssinia, in the Northeastern part of Africa, and Liberia, on the Western Coast, are the only independent political division of Africa, the first a Monarchy, the second a Republic.

Two colonies for those Negroes who were returned to Africa were established, but neither was the result of Negro effort. Indeed, had these efforts been dependent upon Negro initiative, neither would have been founded. The records show clearly that both came into being by an effort of white people to protect their own interests, whatever of benefit accruing to the Negro through these colonies being incidental rather than of design or intent.

The first of these colonies was founded by England at Sierra Leone[2] and was designed to provide for certain liberated slaves and for those Negroes later captured in the efforts to break up the slave trade. Doubtless the latter class would have been permitted to return to their former homes had they so desired. However, as slavery existed throughout Africa, and such return usually meant reënslavement, with probable sale to the nearest slave-dealer, there was no incentive for the liberated slave to return to his own tribe. Owing to conditions obtaining throughout Africa at this time, few were thus returned, and Sierra Leone is, therefore, a tribal composite of all those sections of Africa from which slaves were transported to America.

Freetown, in the British colony of Sierra Leone, was founded in the year 1786. The immediate, if not the ultimate, purpose in founding it at this time was wholly remote from the suppression of Negro slavery. When the defeated British armies returned to England at the close of the Revolutionary War, a thousand or more Negroes, who had escaped to the British and thus secured their freedom, accompanied them and, for the most part, found their way to London. Soon many of these were "in destitute circumstances and were found

² *Liberia, New and Old,* Sibley and Westerman, p. 9.

begging on the streets of London. This aroused the sympathy of English leaders, who sought to found an asylum for them on the West Coast of Africa." [3]

"In 1815, when the British army again left American shores after its attack on the city of Washington and its defeat at New Orleans, it was accompanied by another body of refugee slaves. Some of them eventually found their way to London. So a second colony was sent out to Sierra Leone." [4] As the British cruisers became active in the suppression of the slave trade, considerable numbers of Negroes from captured slave ships were settled in Sierra Leone, giving to this area an African population but a population without tribal affiliations.

In the year 1816 [5] The American Colonization Society was chartered by Act of Congress. The purpose of this Society was to assist "freed men of color to return to the African Continent." It was not intended, at least by many of its supporters, as an instrument for the ultimate extinction of slavery in America, or elsewhere. Among the Negroes "there was often a superior group, who through personal worth and strength of character had acquired their freedom." These groups of free Negroes were a source of anxiety in a society founded upon slavery. They necessarily occasioned dissatisfaction upon the part of the slaves, especially since among them were to be found so many of the most capable and efficient, as well as the most prosperous, individuals of the Negro group. Whatever was likely to produce dissatisfaction and unrest upon the part of the slave group could not long continue a matter of indifference to the masters. While some of the supporters of The American Colonization Society undoubtedly hoped that thus the ability of the Negro to govern himself would be demonstrated and that a prosperous and successful Negro State would prove the ultimate solution of the problems created by slavery in America, as well as of great benefit to

[3] *Ibid.*
[4] *Ibid.*
[5] *Liberia, New and Old,* Sibley and Westerman, p. 7.

the Native Africans, others looked upon it as a means of prolonging the institution of slavery indefinitely, but quietly and peacefully, by removing from the United States a class that necessarily involved friction. Another fact must be recognized, a fact that tended to promote the interests of the Colonization Society. There was small place for freedmen among slaves. The latter exercised upon freedmen an influence similar to that of the slave upon the poor-white and, while some of the free Negroes were successful and lived creditably, many fared badly. The qualities leading to the emancipation of the parents were not assured to their children and many of these "fell into vice and shiftlessness." It is not surprising, then, that we find among the supporters of The American Colonization Society men of widely differing views and aims. Jefferson and Lincoln were among its most intelligent and patriotic supporters, while Garrison and the extreme abolitionists later attacked the Society, bitterly and effectively, as a deception calculated to perpetuate slavery.

It is not our purpose here to tell the story of Liberia. As a solution of the problem of Negro slavery, colonization in Africa proved a failure. As a means of meeting the problems of the free Negroes in a social order based upon slavery, colonization proved wholly inadequate. In the matter of kindling hope upon the part of a limited number of Negroes, it had value; but in the matter of kindling hope upon the part of the American slave and a desire for some realization of his racial possibilities, colonization and the discussions growing out of it have had very great value. The hope of its realization awakened and stimulated, upon the part of many Negroes, a race consciousness and a belief that some day a creditable race-life would be possible to the Negro, as to other peoples.

The outstanding fact in reference to colonization, as proposed by the Colonization Society, is that it was not designed either to destroy slavery or to remove the Negro *en masse* from contact with the whites. In purpose, therefore, except in the minds of a few, such colonization was quite inadequate

196

as a solution of the race problem in the United States. Had the Liberian venture proved a decided and an immediate success, it is possible that its scope might have been widened even to the point of the extinction of slavery through the return to Africa of the entire Negro group. Only as colonization promises relief from hurtful racial conditions and offers wider racial possibilities can it now have a place in racial plans.

Attempts to assign reasons for the relative failure of colonization in Liberia as a solution for the Negro problem in the United States may well lead to a study of this whole matter. Such a study no longer leads to the conclusion that the case is a physically hopeless one, especially in the matter of transportation. One hundred forty-seven voyages, each consuming months of time and involving great discomfort and even intense suffering, were required to remove 12,000 emigrants. Two trips of the Leviathan, requiring little more than six weeks of time could now, with vastly less of suffering and with less of sicknes or crowding than occurred on any one of these 147 voyages, transport the entire 12,000. Despite the fact that numbers have increased so greatly, transportation, with modern equipment, is not now an insurmountable obstacle, as it certainly was during the entire time the Colonization Society was active.

The matter of health was possibly the most discouraging of the obstacles encountered in the earlier efforts to colonize Liberia. Most of the white men going there sickened quickly and many died. The long list of white agents, missionaries, teachers, and others who either died or were forced to leave the country because of illness, warranted the belief that Liberia is a place where white people cannot live and where even the Negro is unable to thrive. There can be no question but that, with the knoweldge then possessed in reference to the transmission of disease and to sanitation, this impression was, in 1816, correct. At a much later date the French, although with much greater knowledge to guide them, failed

197

in their efforts to construct the Panama Canal, largely because of bad health conditions.

During the first fifty years after colonization began, scarcely one white man was able to remain in Liberia long enough to accomplish any thing of permanent value. The native Negroes seem to have suffered very little, but the immigrant Negro fared but little better than did the whites. The terrible fevers and other disorders which swept the colony warranted the conclusion that Liberia was impossible for the white man and but little kindlier toward the Americanized black man. The experience of Ashmun is very illuminative at this point. Of marked ability, of indominable energy, and sincerely loyal to his task, his life was literally sacrificed in the cause of colonization.

Speculation as to the results which would have followed a marked success upon Liberian soil is of little value. As it was, the total number of Negroes emigrating to Africa was not more than 25,000. The fact that more than three hundred voyages were made by parties of Negro emigrants shows a very real interest on the part of the Negro in his return to his native land. Concerning 12,000 returned this is said: "Of this number approximately 4,500 were born free, 344 purchased their freedom, and nearly 6,000"—value near $3 million—were set free in order that they might return to Africa. Mr. Lincoln was confronted by the failure of all previous efforts to colonize even the free Negroes. No one had proposed any other workable plan for the solution of the Negro problem as a whole.

We may digress here, in order to call attention to certain facts which seem well established by the records. What Mr. Lincoln's plans were, in detail, is a matter of doubt. He had given expression on several occasions to his conviction that, for their mutual benefit, the races should be separated. Taking all of these utterances into consideration, it seems clear that, once the Civil War was concluded, he would have proposed a plan for the separation of the races. It seems a great calamity that, in the face of such a crisis, the assassin's bullet should have removed from the Presidency and from the moral guidance of the nation the one man who saw clearly what was involved in the race problem of 1865 and whose position made possible conservative and constructive action. His removal by assassination cleared the way for the domination of the distinctly radical element in the Government and for the Reconstruction program inflicted upon the South. In the program which prevailed matters of far less import held a larger place than did considerations looking to the preservation of either race.

While the matter of health was unquestionably the most discouraging feature of the earlier efforts to colonize American Negroes in Liberia, it is not now a serious obstacle to such colonization. It was, for a long time, the sincere belief that the tropics are impossible for the white man and terribly destructive to the black man, a conviction fully borne out by all the facts as formerly existing. Until very recently, even a brief sojourn in the tropics was fraught with gravest danger to anyone from the temperate zone.

The progress of science has done much to change all this. "Tropical medicine," with knowledge of the causes of disease and with effective methods of prevention, has made it possible to live in the tropics in health. Further, various inventions have contributed greatly to the comfort of living in the tropics. It is highly probable that, in future, great states and great civilizations will develop and flourish in the tropics and that life there will prove pleasant and far easier than is the case in the temperate zones. The example of Panama, changed under the direction of Gorgas and his aids from one of the most deadly situations to one of the most pleasant and healthful of localities to be found, demonstrates what may be done throughout the tropics. Modern sanitation, with sane methods of living, has made it possible for the American Negro to return safely to any part of Africa suitable for habitation. The central plateau has decided advantages over the lower coastal

199

regions. Further developments may be expected in "tropical medicine," each advance assisting materially in rendering available the rich lands and the lavish resources of what is known as the torrid zone.

Successful colonization demands at least three conditions, viz.:

I—A place available and adequate in size and capable of supporting the transferred people;

II—A location either already healthful or capable of being made so; and

III—The possibility of transferring the colonists to the new location.

There can be no question concerning the adequacy of Africa. In area it is adequate, and the present population is, relative to the potential production of food supplies, very small indeed. In the earlier stages of the movement the immigrants should form compact settlements in order to achieve quickly roads, schools, etc., and to be mutually helpful. From one such center, settlement could expand outward as numbers increased. It would, of course, work a great hardship and great injustice upon the resident natives should the entire group of American Negroes be placed in any one section of Africa and this be done so rapidly as to preclude fusion between the two groups. Fortunately, this is not possible.

Africa, as a whole, is very rich in resources and has almost unlimited possibilities. In area, in resources, and in essential homogeneity of the native peoples, Africa, and Africa alone, presents a most inviting field for colonization by the American Negro. Tact would be required; but the American Negro, permanently located in Africa, would have virtually unlimited opportunity to mediate to the natives, in a single generation, the civilization the race has acquired in the United States, including its industries, its education, and its religion. Should groups of American Negroes desire to hold aloof from the natives, there are areas still available having

200

no Negro inhabitants or, at most, with very few such occupants.

Taking into consideration the available parts of Africa and assuming the distribution of the American Negroes throughout these areas as conditions would suggest, a vast increase in trade, an immense advance in the production of raw materials and substantial progress in all that goes to make up civilization should quickly follow. The American Negro, thus located and inspired by right ideals, should be in position to mediate all that he has gained by his stay in America and to give such an impetus to African development, industrial, social, moral, and religious, as would go far toward the regeneration of Africa.

While the interests of the African Negroes would suggest the diffusion of the American Negro throughout those parts of Africa now occupied by the Negro, it would be best to concentrate upon one or more areas and to develop these as demonstrations of what may be accomplished.

A fundamental weakness of the "Garvey movement" lay in the fact that it gave but little consideration to conditions actually existing in Africa. The Negroes already settled in Liberia came to feel that due consideration was not shown them. The announced program of "Africa for the Africans," involving the ultimate wresting of all territory from the Europeans, necessarily provoked a defensive antagonism upon the part of all European states now holding colonies and having business interests in Africa. Since the Garvey program included armies and navies to be used in wresting Africa from European domination, and since this was openly declared as the goal of Negro achievement, no encouragement and no assistance could be expected from Europe or from Europeans making their homes in Africa or financially interested in its development.

Europe is now vitally interested in Africa and, once the way is opened, stands ready to further its development. The interests of all the more powerful nations of Europe, the manufacturing nations, demand the development of Africa, especially in the production of raw materials and as a market for the products of European industries. The American Negro, judiciously placed, could at once greatly increase the production of such materials and vastly increase the demand for, and the consumption of, manufactured articles. A colonization movement, therefore, constructive in character and without antagonistic program, would unquestionably be welcomed and substantially assisted by Europe. Not only this; the European governments would, undoubtedly, give to the various areas held by each a measure of self-government commensurate with the demonstrated ability of the Negroes in each area to govern successfully.

Another fact which should have great weight is that the American Negro has nothing to lose, rather much to gain, by fusion with the native African. This is true especially in the matter of physical development. Throughout native Africa natural selection has had uninterrupted sway, and authorities agree quite generally that in physical characteristics the native African has a decided advantage over the American Negro. There the weak have perished, usually in infancy. In America, though to a lesser extent than has been the case among the white people, the weak have survived and have contributed their share to the future of the race group here. The American Negro could contribute much to the African Negro by a fusion of the two groups, but would himself gain greatly in physical qualities. Of the same blood, such fusion would involve no race problem, no racial change, except as among American Negroes tribal organization and tribal associations and differentials have been lost.

The diffusion of the American Negro throughout Africa would afford the opportunity for the greatest possible service to the natives. Unquestionably, it would prove more pleasant for the repatriates to remain together and to build their community life apart from the natives. It may also be argued that each such settlement would constitute an object lesson in civilization for the native and thus assist in his progress. From such centers, teachers and religious leaders might be sent to the native Negroes, and thus the main benefits arising from diffusion might still come to the native.

Africa, as a whole, has a relatively sparse population. For the whole continent it is given as 175,000,000 against 446,-800,000 for Europe. Henry M. Stanley long ago pointed out the possibilities of that region which might be occupied by the American Negro. It is the Upper Congo Basin. In area, in potential productivity, in climate, in present population, this part of Africa fulfills every reasonable, every essential, condition. In a celebrated letter, quoted by Mallison at pages 289-290 of *Color at Home and Abroad,* Stanley writes:

"There is space enough in one section of the Upper Congo Basin to locate double the number of Negroes of the United States without disturbing a single tribe of the aborigines now inhabiting it. I refer to the immense Upper Congo forest country, 350,000 square miles in extent, which is three times larger than the Argentine Republic, and one and a half times larger than the entire German Empire, embracing 224,000,000 acres of umbrageous forest land, wherein every unit of the 7,000,000 Negroes might become owner of nearly a quarter square mile of land. Five acres of this, planted with bananas and plantains, would furnish every soul with sufficient subsistance. . . . The remaining twenty-seven acres of his estate would furnish him with timber, rubber, gums, dyestuffs, for sale. There are 150 days of rain throughout the year. There is a clear stream every few hundred yards. In a day's journey we have crossed as many as thirty-two streams. The climate is healthy and equable, owing to the impervious forest which protects the land from chilly winds and draughts. All my white officers passed through the wide area safely. Eight navigable rivers course through it. Hills and ridges diversify the scenery and give magnificent prospects. To those Negroes of the South accustomed to Arkansas, Mississippi, and Louisiana, it would be a reminder of their own plantations without

203

the swamps and the depressing influence of cypress forests. Anything and everything might be grown in it, from the oranges, guavas, sugar cane, and cotton of subtropical lands to the wheat of California and the rice of South Carolina. If the immigration were prudently conceived and carried out, the glowing accounts sent home by the first settlers would soon dissipate all fear and reluctance upon the part of others. But it is all a dream. The American capitalists, like other leaders of men, are more engaged in decorating their wives with diamonds than in busying themselves with national questions of such import as removing the barrier between the North and the South. The 'open sore' of America—the race question—will ever remain an incurable fester. While we are all convinced that the Nessus shirt which clings to the Republic has maddened her, and may madden her again, it is quite certain that the small effort needed to free themselves for ever from it will never be made." [6]

This letter was written many years ago. Meantime the number of Negroes has more than doubled. Still, if every one of the 15,000,000 Negroes now in the United States could be removed to this area, there would still be ample acreage for their support. Removing only the productive element of the race, the area is generously ample. Immediately east of the Upper Congo Basin is the central plateau, several times the area of the basin and, in many respects, a more desirable region. It also is sparsely populated. It is here, rather than in Liberia, that the American Negro should seek his future home.

Mr. William Archer, a clear-thinking Englishman, who gave much time to a study of the American race problem and who advocated colonization of the Negro in some part of America, or elsewhere, believed that thus the Negro problem could be justly and permanently settled. A telling paragraph is quoted by Mr. Mallison in *Color at Home and Abroad*, page 290, from Mr. Archer's *Through Afro-America*, page

---

[6] See *Color at Home and Abroad*, Mallison, pp. 289-90.

233, as follows: "Lastly, we have to consider the fourth eventuality, geographical segregation of the Negro race, whether within or without the limits of the United States.

"This is usually ridiculed as an absolutely Utopian scheme, and at the outset of my investigations I myself regarded it in that light. But the more I saw and read and thought, the oftener and the more urgently did segregation recur to me as the one possible way of escape from an otherwise intolerable situation. Not, of course, the instant, and wholesale, and violent deportation of ten million people—that is a rank impossibility. Between that and inert acquiescence in the ubiquity of the Negro throughout the Southern States, there are many middle courses; and I cannot but believe that the first really great statesman who arises in America will prove his greatness by grappling with this vast but not insoluble problem. And, assuredly, the sooner he comes the better."

There are, then, three sections of Africa to be considered in the matter of the repatriation of the American Negro. Abyssinia has been considered but there are serious obstacles. The people are of mixed blood and are, in their origin, partly Semitic. The ruling house claims blood descent from King Solomon, and much is heard of "black Jews." While of considerable area, much of the country is too dry to support a dense population. Abyssinia may be dismissed except as it might attract the mulatto.

Liberia has been the only area seriously considered in all past efforts at colonization. This is a hot area, much of the country being but little above sea level. The native population is considerable, and the area is quite limited. It can accommodate part, but not all, the Negroes now in America. By arrangement, Liberia could supply seaports needed for the interior lands. Liberia would share in the benefits of the whole development, and American Negroes might settle there to the limit that the land would bear. It is certainly inadequate to accommodate all the Negroes now in the United States.

It would appear that, in the Upper Congo Basin and on the Central Plateau lying eastward from the Basin, is the prepared land for the American Negro, the land in which he may live his own life and from which, once established in it, he may render the greatest service to his race throughout Africa. Both the Upper Congo Basin and the Central Plateau have sufficient elevation to insure a desirable climate. The sparse population of both these areas affords an opportunity to build a fiat civilization, enabling the American immigrant to carry through his plans. The backward state of the present occupants makes it impossible for the natives to wield a deciding influence. This is an area which could be conceded to the Negro by international agreement and guaranteed to him by the same authority.

In all discussions of colonization—or repatriation, as it should be called—the difficulties loom large, and many take refuge in the thought that the idea is visionary, impracticable, impossible. The moving of 15,000,000 people is regarded as a task to be immediately accomplished, together with all provision to be made for them in their new home immediately, and all losses to America due to the removal of Negro labor as an immediate calamity to be borne in a day. As a matter of fact, no one approaching the problem calmly and in a practical way fears any of these matters. Only those members of the race actually contributing to its numerical increase should be assisted to go to Africa. Others—and there would certainly be many wishing to migrate—may be permitted to do so by paying part or all the cost of transportation and of getting established in the new land.

A rigid program of selection would be suggested. Only the part of the race capable of reproduction should be considered. Two plans are possible. Arrangements could be made for all Negroes reaching a given age to emigrate to Africa, with such assistance as would give them a fair chance to find a place in the new economy. This plan would, however, call for the transportation of many who, for a wide variety of reasons, cannot contribute to the numerical increase of the race. The plan most reasonable and still effective would require the sending of those only who are actually in process of breeding. For the most part this would involve young married couples. If the general rule was adopted to remove all the productive element of the race as soon after marriage as reproductive capacity became evident, the number removed in any one year would not be impracticable as to transportation; adequate provision could be made for their settlement in their new homes; and no serious interference with the economic situation in the United States would result. Little change would be noticeable during the first years of the program; but a single generation would see the problem solved. *A Negro state would be founded under the most favorable conditions possible. The defectives, the delinquents, the hopelessly diseased, would be left behind.* Provision for the indigent aged and for the helpless would have to be made by the states but this would hardly exceed the present crime cost of the race in the United States.

If once the race problem were assuredly in process of final extinction, it is reasonable to assume that kindlier feelings would prevail between the races. Competitions would be recognized as but temporary. Political antagonisms would be useless. All America could join, with good will, in fitting the young Negroes for the independent life possible in their own land. Farseeing whites would no longer suffer because of the depressing influence of the Negro upon the poor of their race; because of the threat of amalgamation for the white race; nor yet because of the bitter wrongs suffered by the fullblood Negro because of the present status and progress of racial intermixture. Christian brotherhood would no longer cower here before the problem of racial self-protection. A nation, honest and generous at heart, might thus pay the debt it assuredly owes to this people, so strangely thrust upon America.

Fourteen million immigrants came to the United States

207

during the ten years preceding the First World War. Their transportation did not interfere with normal travel. Several million transoceanic passages were provided in a relatively short time during each of the World Wars, and this in addition to the transport of enormous quantities of supplies, arms, and munitions. *The transportation of the Negroes, extending thus over a generation, is not an impossible task!* After the first few years it would be a rapidly decreasing task.

Like all others who face facts squarely, Henry M. Stanley, traveler and explorer rather than statesman, recognized the difficulties then surrounding transportation and may well have regarded them as insuperable. In the world as he knew it at that time, his conclusions were correct but the progress in ships, in machinery, in mechanical invention generally, has changed all this. *Transportation is now possible.*

The willingness of the Negro to leave the United States is, of course, a vital factor. Today there are many more ready and anxious to migrate than it is possible to transport and establish. Assured of right conditions, there will be little difficulty from the Negro's reluctance. Garvey demonstrated this. Trustful Negroes, moved by the hope of a land of their own, furnished large sums of money to an unorganized, incomplete, unbusinesslike venture, depending upon the personality of one man and that man without the training or the personal qualities needed for so grave an undertaking. Inevitably, the money was lost and Garvey was imprisoned and, upon the termination of his sentence, deported. Repatriation, the fate of two races, should not depend upon any one individual!

The unwillingness of whites to see the Negro go to a land of his own is a far more serious obstacle to colonization. The demand for cheap labor begins with the humblest domestic servant and extends through every field of employment. "Big Business" is especially insistent and "coddles the Negro for the temporary advantage that may come from the use of his cheap labor, and is not interested in the fact that white labor is destroyed in so doing, and that cheap labor is often the most expensive kind." [7]

In the title of this chapter, colonization is given as "a" solution of the American race problem. This is because there are other possible solutions, as amalgamation or segregation. After years of observation and study, the conviction is firmly established that colonization, repatriation, is *the* solution, *the only solution* possible that is at all consistent with the higher interests of both races. Before these interests all selfish concern of individuals, of politicians, of "Big Business," should yield voluntarily *or be coerced.* In view of the vital interests involved, there should be but one purpose characterizing both races. *That purpose should be to see the American Negro established in a land of his own and in the enjoyment of the fullest possible opportunity to build his own home, his own state, his own civilization.*

In making a plea for colonization—repatriation—of the American Negro, several vital considerations may be urged. Several facts must be recognized.

One of the hard inescapable facts is that there is an element of the white race that is lawless, without respect for the principles of morality, and wholly without respect or regard for the preservation of either race. Analyzing this group, it is found to consist in part of youths, immature, reckless, irresponsible, often morally depraved, but in natural endowment and in social status representing every stratum of the white race in America. To these passion is the dominating force. They pay a terrible price in disease and in premature death, as they inflict upon their own race the inescapable disease and physical degradation associated with interracial sex immoralities. This group also includes those of maturer years whose moral qualities permit them, while debauching members of the Negro race, to betray their own race. It is only just that, in all thought concerning this class of whites, a clear line of demarcation be preserved. The acts and the attitudes of this type of the whites are characteristic of a very small section of the white group. Always morally, and usually socially and otherwise, known practical amalgamators are locally recognized for what they really are—too low in the moral scale to be amenable to other than coercion. The white race in the United States, however, even in its best elements, is terribly at fault in its universal failure in the matter of the control of its own vicious elements.

Growing out of this hard, inescapable fact characteristic of the white is the corresponding fact that *the Negro race cannot hope to escape here wholly the devastating inroads of the depraved white.* The Negro cannot secure for his race complete protection so long as there is contact with this type of the white. The higher the Negro rises, the greater his self-respect; the greater his regard for his race, the less the danger becomes; but the stress put upon the race in its less fortunate strata by the dissolute white is wholly unfair, but equally inevitable so long as present conditions continue. This fact, along with kindred facts, is the logical basis for an unanswerable appeal to the Negro in favor of repatriation.

What is said of the corrupting influence of the depraved and vicious white upon the Negro suggests another of the hard and inescapable facts of present racial contacts. *The depraved Negro constitutes a terribly destructive force for the white.* It is needless here to repeat what is given elsewhere concerning the economic features of race contacts and competitions and the evils arising from these. Nor is it necessary to point out all the ways in which the Negro injures the white. In the one item of racial integrity we arrive at the heart of the matter. The virtual denial to the Negro woman of that legal redress theoretically available to the white woman, mother of an illegitimate child, gives to the offending white male an immunity tending to destroy restraint. Various influences combine not only to weaken restraints already achieved by the Negro but, a more serious matter, also to

210

prevent the development of those attitudes and those personal qualities essentially protective.

What has been said concerning the necessity for discrimination between the depraved and the honorable, the guilty and the innocent individuals in the white race needs to be said in reference to the Negro race. Lines of cleavage based upon moral and upon intellectual stratification exist in this race also and sweeping generalizations can no more be made in reference to Negroes as individuals than in reference to whites. However, just as the better, the representative, elements of the white race are terribly at fault in their lack of effort to control the baser white, so the better element of the Negro race is terribly at fault in their lack of effort to control the baser elements of their own race. The moral and the racial wrongs are not all initiated by the vicious white. There is a depraved, vicious element in the Negro race, and this element is constantly recruited by the inroads of the vicious white upon the Negro. This element in turn works havoc in the white race, especially among the young and the otherwise immature men. In this reciprocal degradation there is an unanswerable argument for separation of the lower elements of the two races, if not for complete racial separation. Major Cox has given a sentence which has a vital message at this point. He writes: "In saving our race from the Negro, we must save the Negro from our race." [8] The vast majority of the individuals composing the white race in the United States—in every part of the United States—are innocent in the matter of this race amalgamation and are sound in theory concerning it. In scarcely less degree this may be said of the representative Negroes, both in theory and in practice; but there is upon the part of the better classes in each race this strange indifference concerning the part played in race relations and in racial interests by the vicious and the lawless elements in each of the races. The courts, reflecting this general indifference, fail utterly in reference to race protection.

[8] *The South's Part in Mongrelizing the Nation,* Cox, p. 86.

Religion has failed to control the situation. Race prejudice, however effective, has failed as a complete control, and will continue so to fail. Only absolute separation of the races can prove a complete protection for either race.

To a group of free Negroes calling upon him in 1862, Mr. Lincoln, fully conscious of this feature of racial contact, said: "Your race suffers very greatly, many of them, by living among us, and ours suffers from your presence. In a word, we suffer on each side. If this is admitted, it affords a reason, at least, why we should be separated." [9] On June 25 ,1857, Mr. Lincoln had said: "Colonization is the only perfect preventative of amalgamation." [9] The progress of amalgamation since 1870 shows that Mr. Lincoln was correct in his statements. It is frankly impossible that all the individuals of the Negro-mulatto group and all the individuals of the white group should be brought to right racial attitudes and to right practices affecting race purity. Proper instruction upon the matter would, especially if properly and practically enforced, prove a wholesome restraint. Only absolute racial separation can afford complete and permanent relief from the threat of amalgamation.

It is difficult to determine the real attitude of the Negroes of the District of Columbia toward colonization. There was a response to the Garvey movement and this persisted even after Garvey was imprisoned and, later, deported. In so far as actual emigration is concerned, the Garvey movement was a complete failure. Its value lay in the quickening of race consciousness and the beginnings of a new hope among the Negroes. The collapse of the Garvey program almost at its inception; the loss of large sums of money contributed by the toilers of the race; the conviction and the imprisonment of Garvey, followed by deportation from the United States— that all this, and more, has failed to extinguish completely the hopes expressed in the Garvey movement shows that there is, among the Negroes here, the mass of the race, a longing

[9] Mr. Lincoln, quoted by Major Cox.

for a country of their own and a government administered by themselves.

The headquarters of the American Colonization Society are still located in Washington City. Its small income is not used in assisting colonists to emigrate to Liberia—the purpose of its endowment—but has been directed to certain interests of the Negroes already there, especially the schools. The society is not now in the hands of those who are at all enthusiastic in the matter of promoting emigration to Liberia, or to any other part of Africa. Its resources are so small and its attitudes so chilling that one is led to feel that it has no vital part to perform in the solution of the race problem in the United States. There seems to be no vital interest among the Negroes, even those of Washington City, in the Colonization Society or in its original purpose. Neither is there any general interest in any special part of Africa.

Among those Negroes who hold government positions, one can hardly expect to find a general eagerness to embark upon a wholly untried venture. The positions they hold are permanent, with pensions following sufficiently long terms of service. Yet it is here that we find the only group of Negroes who have had the practical experience and the training necessary to direct the affairs of the immigrants, especially as the numbers would increase and the problems of administration become correspondingly complicated. Business leadership is being developed elsewhere, but nowhere else in America is there any considerable group of Negroes having any immediate contact with the problems of governmental administration. It is from the District of Columbia that the governing personnel of any independent group in Africa should come, indeed, must come largely for the details of administration. It would remain to be seen whether or not race pride and the opportunity to render pioneer service to their race would outweigh that personal ease promised by position and assured support. There is reason to believe that there would be those who would meet the demands of the

213

situation in the true spirit of the missionary crusader, and that there would be a sufficient number of such to provide the services needed. With the passing of time and increase in population, in schools, and in resources, a competent leadership should arise among those born in the new homeland. The prosperous Negro in Washington, and elsewhere, should consider the future of his children.

The reluctance to leave the United States to be expected among Negroes in government service would likely appear also among those Negroes successfully engaged in business or in professional pursuits. These two classes would be essential to the success of any colonization plan, and it is quite certain that enough Negroes trained in these fields to meet the needs of the transplanted people would be willing to go to the new race home. The plan would logically involve very few already established. It would enlist that element of the race having received professional training but not yet established in the practice of a profession. Just as there would be an appeal to the race loyalty and the idealism of the trained expert government worker, so there would be an appeal to all the prepared leadership of the race, an appeal which would certainly have great weight and influence with those entering upon the practice of any calling or profession.

In contemplating colonization the problem of the mulatto looms large. Washington City has a very high percentage of mixed bloods, many of whom are "near-white." In lesser degree, the same is true of the United States as a whole. These are all arbitrarily classed as Negroes. Taking into consideration all the factors involved, especially that of ultimate escape from the Negro race through amalgamation, and the salaries received in government employ, these could hardly be expected to prove enthusiastically willing to emigrate to Africa.

On the other hand, no class of people is more insistently race conscious than are the mulattoes generally, and nowhere is the mulatto more insistently race conscious than is the case in Washington City. Professor Kelly Miller, of Howard

University, discussing the low birth rate of the families of teachers in a department of this university, attributed it, in part, to their unwillingness to bring children into the world subject to the proscriptions to which they themselves are subjected, and which are certain to be the lot of their children. Surely, where a matter has so serious a consequence and is consciously felt and recognized, there are those who would welcome, gladly, an opportunity to pass into a situation where there would be complete freedom and where unlimited opportunity would await each man to realize all his possibilities and where none could enforce racial discrimination because only one race would be present. Racial separation alone promises complete removal of the ills of interracial contacts as between the white and the black. What of the Negro and the mulatto?

Under existing conditions there might well arise friction between the black and the yellow people. That such friction has been so completely absent in America in the past is due to a set of circumstances driving the Negro and the mulatto to stand—or fall—together. Once in Africa, with the hope of further "bleaching" removed, it is wholly reasonable to assume that the near-white would, in a few generations, disappear as the white blood would become generally diffused and group unity approximated. Indeed, such diffusion would be wholly desirable and might be promoted until racial unity was completely secured. Thus the problem of the relation of the Negro and the mulatto would cease to hinder the development or to disturb the peace of the repatriate group.

The plea for colonization—repatriation—gains immensely when its alternatives are considered and the contrasts in the possibilities open to the Negro in America and in Africa are duly considered. In America the Negro is a hopeless minority in so far as numbers are concerned. He is more or less proscribed in so far as all other elements of the population are concerned. He has not here developed racial independence and those other qualities conditioning the highest manhood,

215

and possibly cannot do so here. His protests, his demands, in the face of existing conditions, are often pathetic—possibly never more so than when they include a threat of retaliation. Walter White claims that the Negro now holds the balance of power in any reasonably close election in seventeen states and controls 281 votes in the Electoral College. The inference is that the Negro is now in position to decide what individuals shall be nominated by the national political parties and which national party shall be placed in power. He does not seem to see that the exercise of such power must antagonize the defeated party, thus creating grave problems. A minority group, standing upon principle, commands respect; standing for patronage or for group advantage, it cannot long command respect either for itself or for the political unit bargaining with it. In Africa, as a free people, the American Negro would open the pages of a great blank book. Upon these pages he would write the record of his own achievements. No people need ask for more than a fair chance, and this the repatriate Negro assuredly may have.

The central theme of this volume suggests the one alternative to the separation of the races. *Either the races must separate or ultimately amalgamate.* This is the conclusion indicated by all the facts available, and it is the conclusion of those who have made a careful study of racial contacts here and elsewhere. In the earlier part of the past century De Toqueville wrote his great book, *Democracy in America.* In this he gave careful attention to the race question and to the anomaly of the existence of slavery among that people who had developed the form of government allowing the greatest freedom to the individual and which imposed the least restriction upon mass action. The conclusion reached by this brilliant Frenchman is thus stated:

"There are two alternatives for the future—the Negroes and the whites must either wholly part or wholly mingle." [10]

[10] Quoted by Major Cox. *The South's Part,* etc.

Mr. Lincoln, under date of June 25, 1857, is quoted as saying:

"Colonization is the only perfect preventative of amalgamation." [11]

Again, addressing a committee of free Negroes, August 14, 1862, Mr. Lincoln said:

"Your race suffers very greatly, many of them, by living among us, and ours suffers from your presence. In a word, we suffer on each side. If this be admitted, it affords a reason, at least, why we should be separated." [12]

"The greatest error the North made was in permitting Congress to repudiate Lincoln's plan for the solution of the Negro problem." [13]

"There are but two possible outcomes to the American Negro problem—separation or amalgamation. As a nation we are confronted with these alternatives and from them there is no escape." [14]

"If the purity of the two races is to be maintained they cannot continue to live side by side, and this is a problem from which there can be no escape." [15]

These quotations state the situation fairly and accurately. In the context the authors give the grounds upon which their conclusions are based. Here no proof is offered in support of the assertions made. There is no analysis of the situation to determine the forces operative, nor is there a statement in detail of the factors here active. There is no attempt to specify how, or why, the races suffer, each from the presence of the other, nor why the hurtful features of this racial contact are necessarily continuous so long as the races remain in contact. There is a sense of regret that Mr. Lincoln, and others, did not discuss more fully the details of certain features of racial contact, stating their views more in detail.

Had there been, along with emancipation, any general

---

[11] Quoted by Major Cox. *The South's Part,* etc.
[12] Mr. Lincoln, as quoted by Cox.
[13] *The South's Part,* etc., Cox, p. 80.
[14] *White America,* Cox.
[15] *The South's Part,* etc., Cox, p. 60.

and rational effort made to protect the Negro race, as such, and to hold the race to right ideals, it is reasonable to assume that vastly better conditions would now prevail and that the progress of racial intermixture would have been greatly retarded. Even so, it could only have been held in check, not prevented wholly. *So long as the advantage of the mulatto over the fullblood Negro is markedly evident, so long will the incentive to racial intermixture continue.* Separation of the races alone can control wholly the matter of amalgamation.

There are other aspects of the race problem which plainly demand the separation of the races. Many of these details, considered alone, seem of but little moment. Others are of graver significance. The chapter dealing with *The Poor White* should be consulted here, for it gives the case of the white people forced to earn their living in competition with Negro labor. Considerations, of little importance within themselves, may assume grave significance because of their relation to, and their influence upon, the matter of racial integrity. It is impossible to discuss, or even to formulate, the host of reasons and of arguments supporting the proposition that the races should separate. What follows is not offered as complete, but rather as suggestive of some of the vital issues involved.

The frequent use made of the terms *self-respect* and *racial self-respect* has been ridiculed in certain quarters, as has the insistent demand that there be the utmost consideration given to all possible means of developing these upon the part of the Negro race as a whole. Possibly it would be more accurate to say that the use of these terms has been resented, since they point out at once the most glaring defect in the attitudes characterizing the Negro and a most grievous failure upon the part of those attempting to direct his education and his training. Only as the Negro can be brought to right attitudes toward himself and toward his race may there be a constructive program. The white race throughout the Americas, and elsewhere, needs the lash of discriminating publicity so applied as to bring it, individually and collectively, to a just regard for the Negro's race life and a sane use of those means and those attitudes tending to strengthen and to purify the Negro home. Repatriation would put these matters into the keeping of the Negro himself.

Two vital considerations, or rather the application of the same principle to each of the races, result in a strong argument in favor of the separation of the races. It is in the matter of schools that these considerations are most apparent, but they are present in every feature of racial contact. It is not best that Negro and white children should be permitted to attend the same schools. It is hurtful to the children of both races. Two quotations, from the late Edgar Gardner Murphy, state the case so well that they are given here:

"It is an injury to the children of the weaker race to be educated in an environment which is constantly subjecting them to adverse feeling and opinion. The result must be the development of a morbid race consciousness without any compensating increase in racial self-respect." [16]

It is well to note that here Mr. Murphy states the case of the Negro child presumably of the public school age. He might have made his case much stronger without going beyond the facts and he might have extended his field to include the experience of the Negro student in those colleges and universities attended by white students. Even where the number of Negro students is small, unfortunate attitudes are pretty sure to arise, especially if these Negroes are forced upon such schools by order of the Federal Courts. As the number of such students increases, the danger of open clashes increases, while that disparagement which is atmospheric grows more hurtful. It is interesting to note the tendency of the races to remain apart even in the Northern cities. It is unquestionably better for the Negro child that he should be educated in company with children of his own race and that his higher education should be in institutions from which the white is excluded.

When the interests of the white child are studied, all considerations favor the separation of the races. The Negroes have not the ideals of the whites, nor have they attained either the moral or the cultural plane of the whites. Despite individual exceptions, this statement is certainly true of the mass of Negro children. In the main, in so far as association with the white child is possible to the Negro child in school, it is likely to be with that type of white child not helpful to the Negro child. For the normal white child coming from a representative white home, if not for all white children, Mr. Murphy is right when he says: ". . . the point of helpful contact must not be placed among the masses of the young and the leverage of interracial cooperation must not seek its fulcrum upon the tender receptivities and the unguarded immaturies of childhood." [17]

A number of instances of clashes between the white and the colored children attending the same school have occurred in the North, in which racial lines have been sharply drawn. These riots and clashes are sufficient to demonstrate the fact that the Negro may expect trouble wherever and so long as he is in contact with the white. The recent migration of Negroes into the North is quite sufficient to remove all hope that the North will escape its share of the burdens created by the Negro.

Another matter, which the North should consider very carefully, is that discussed in the chapter on the near-white. The *New York World,* of Sunday, July 28, 1929, has a very valuable article dealing with the number of Negroes—near-whites—now "crossing the line" annually into the white race. The author fixes the number at 5,000. Walter White, in 1948, claims that every year approximately 12,000 "white-skinned Negroes" [18] cross the line and disappear into the white race.

[17] *The Present South,* Murphy, p. 36.
[18] *A Man Called White,* White, p. 3.

We have no means of checking upon either of these statements and the authorities are not given. Such cases necessarily
involve secrecy and a breaking with Negro and Negroid associations and associates. Undoubtedly there are many instances in the North today—many of them recent arrivals
from the South—of men and women belonging to the border
line group. Behind these people are from three to six or
seven generations of disregard for social conventions and
disregard for moral law. It is thus that they have reached the
degree of whiteness which enables them to "cross the line" by
deceiving the white people with whom they associate.
This "crossing the line" may be regarded as a victory for
the Negro group, and many do so regard it. As a matter of
fact, this is one of the clearest proofs of the unfortunate situation of the Negro in the United States at the present time.
That he should so despise his own race that he is willing to
abet escape from it by the route of illegitimacy—surely this
is an evil of the first magnitude. That the Negro and the
mulatto women should be driven to regard initial amalgamation as the means of improving the prospects of their offspring—surely this is an evil certain, if unrestrained, to work
the total undoing of the race!

It is possible, even probable, that the full significance of
conditions now obtaining in America will yet find a place
in the conscious thinking of the white people of the United
States. If so, this will influence their attitude toward the
Negro. That he will be helped here to a fuller and more
satisfactory life is by no means assured. What he may be able
to gain will rather emphasize his limitations and will probably tend to embitter him because of what is withheld. If,
however, through his experiences here, he receives a fuller
training, a better preparation for an independent life elsewhere, these experiences will prove helpful. If here he loses
his race consciousness and is himself lost in that stratum of
the Caucasian that is lacking in race pride, his destruction
through absorption will follow and the hope that his ex-

periences and his training in America may yet prove of great benefit to the Continent of Africa will vanish.

There is a hopeful aspect to all racial conflict here. It is an evidence that racial lines still exist and are consciously recognized. Such conflicts indicate that the Negro is gaining group, if not race, consciousness. May it not well be that antagonisms shall become sufficiently general and sufficiently sharp to force upon both races a realization of what is now but imperfectly understood by either? What could prove more helpful to the American Negro than such a development along the lines of personal and group and racial self-respect as would make his situation in the United States intolerable and lead—or drive—him to seek a land of his own? What reaction to present conditions could be more creditable to the American Negro?

A large part of the energy of a certain class of Negroes, many of whom should be constructive leaders of their race here, is now expended in setting forth the wrongs which they believe to be inflicted upon the race by the white group in America, especially in the United States. Wherever a real racial awakening occurs, consciousness of the unfavorable conditions surrounding the race here, and especially of the adverse attitudes against which the race here must contend, immediately arises. The degree, the energy, of this consciousness depends upon the higher qualities possessed by the individual Negro, qualities enabling him to appreciate the ideal and to realize the true significance of his deprivations in reference to cultural privilege. While but a small part of the Negro group—chiefly mulattoes in the North—give expression to the feelings aroused by this situation, the race, as a whole, has some understanding of the situation and is adversely affected by it. The development of race consciousness, not always understood by the Negro, is the compensating aspect of this situation.

It is not necessary here to attempt to give details covering and illustrating this feature of racial contacts. Almost every autobiography written by a Negro residing in any part of the United States records the experience which brought to the author a distinctly personal realization of the line of racial cleavage and of his own disadvantage because of race. Negroes and mulattoes reared in the South are loud in their praises of those in other sections who do not discriminate against them as do the white people of the South. Possibly the day may come when, in view of what has befallen the Negro in Latin America and everywhere else that race prejudice is wanting, even the Negro will realize that had the Southern white man been less exclusive, had he possessed less of character and less of race pride, this section would have differed in no essential respect from those sections of America looking to Isabella as the people of the United States look to Jamestown, to Plymouth Rock, and to Manhattan Island. That the Negro of the United States is now still a Negro at all; that he has before him racial possibilities at all; that he has a chance to serve his race in Africa—all this, and vastly more, is due to the very characteristics of the representative whites against which the Negro now so loudly declaims. Much of this clamor from the modern Negro is, in its last analysis, a demand for the privilege of committing racial suicide! Further, it is a demand for respect while the process of his racial degradation, destruction, goes steadily on!

The final argument for colonization, for repatriation, of the American Negro is not in the negative features of his situation here, not in his deprivations, not in the discriminations he suffers here. These are real. Further, they are inevitable, in some degree, so long as two races so dissimilar as are the white and black remain in close contact. The final argument should lie in what the Negro may reasonably expect in the way of independence and possibility of independent development in a land of his own.

Here, again, it is not necessary to attempt an elaborate statement of details. It is sufficient to say that, once in a land of his own, opportunity would be given for the exercise of whatever intelligence, whatever skill, whatever efficiency, whatever industry the Negro may possess or may be able to develop. The situation would be in his hands, and he would set the limits of achievement. The fruits of the exercise of all his powers would be his to enjoy. That haunting sense of inferiority which, sooner or later, meets and blights in some degree every Negro child here would thus be removed, and in its stead would arise the possibility of racial self-respect and racial self-sufficiency.

Repatriation would, at best, involve hardship; it would, in some instances, involve real suffering. Yet, as compared to the settlement of America, the hardships and the sufferings of the repatriates would be insignificant. Transportation is now swift and without serious inconveniences. Disease is largely under control. There are no hostile tribes to be overcome and none waiting to take the lives of the immigrants, as did the Indians of America. There are world markets ready to absorb the products of the soil, of the forests, and of the mines, as there were not at the first settlement of America.

That the Negro should hesitate because of prospective hardship is not quite creditable to him. Hardship has ever been the lot of those daring spirits who have gone into new surroundings there to build for themselves and for their posterity what they could not have achieved in the older order out of which they came.

Finally, the American Negro should consider carefully what he may, by the exercise of tact and discretion, be able to do for the Negro race in Africa. Looking toward this great continent, the American Negro should not forget that its people are his people, 175,000,000 strong; that from this land his ancestors came and that here, and here alone, are the people with whom he is really one, and that, if ever his race is to make for itself a creditable place in the earth, that place must be Africa. In proportion to the estimate the American Negro places upon himself and upon what his stay in America has brought to him, should be his estimate of his ability to mediate the essentials of civilization and of religion to the members of his race in Africa. It becomes increasingly difficult to respect the Negro in America who clamors for recognition in the civilization of another race when he might expend his energy more profitably in carrying to his own people what he has gained here, and in assisting his own people to merit, rather than to clamor for, a creditable place among the peoples of the world. Respect is not generally or long withheld from those who genuinely respect themselves and, by worthy achievement, demonstrate their right to respect.

It is a strange Providence that has brought the Negro to America. It is likewise strange that here in the United States he has been preserved racially as nowhere else. Is it the Divine purpose that, through long ages of moral wrong, working through and upon the poor, the ignorant, the degraded of both races, the Negro here shall ultimately cease to be a Negro and, in his own destruction, degrade the moral standards of America; or that, equipped for the task, the American Negro is yet to prove the hope, the strength, of his race? If the latter, the ways of Providence "will have been made plain," and justified, in their ultimate results.

CHAPTER X

SOME CONCLUSIONS AND A FORWARD LOOK

IN THE concluding chapter of this study it seems logically necessary to bring together and to correlate the more important facts established, or discussed, and the conclusions reached in the preceding chapters. Each of these chapters deals with features of the race problem more or less distinct, giving to the discussion a unity of chapter gained sometimes at the expense of that element in the study as a whole. It is usually easier, and safer, to arrive at a just conclusion as to what is established fact than it is to correlate and to interpret facts when recognized as such.

The supreme need of the present is a thorough and an accurate understanding of the facts of the race problem in the United States, coupled with the unalterable purpose to deal constructively with this problem. No program can be regarded as truly constructive which ignores the higher interests of either race. Blood, purity, racial integrity, must be regarded as the highest interest involved for either the white or the black race in America. Each chapter, in its discussion of the past and the present, suggests the future, if only to raise questions in reference to it. It is necessary to the preservation of the two races here that the situation, past and present, be not only known but that this knowledge shall so permeate both groups as to become effective in the mutual protection and preservation of each.

It is of prime importance that the student of the race problem secure a clear conception of the extent to which racial intermixture has been carried. This is given in detail in Chapter I, *The Statement of the Case*. The reader is urged to secure a comprehensive grasp of the statistics of racial intermixture. Once this is done, a foundation is laid for an intelligent understanding of various other aspects of the problem. The popular attitude seems to assume that there is no occasion for alarm and that the initial increment in amalgamation is now negligible. Against this conclusion the findings of the Census are decisive. In 1870 there were 584,049 mulattoes returned; the result of 250 years of contact of the races here. The period covers the whole of slavery, the years of the Civil War and the first five years of freedom. No other figures are available for 1870, and these must be accepted for practical use, despite probability of error due to the unsettled conditions prevailing in the South at the time the enumeration was made.

In 1890 the Census returned 1,132,060 mulattoes. This is virtually double the number returned twenty years earlier. The significance of this increase should be carefully noted. It is due largely to the normal increase in the mulatto element and to the intermixture as between the fullblood Negro and the mulatto. There are those who would have it appear that this phenomenal increase of mulattoes, duplicating the results of the preceding 250 years, was wholly due to these two sources.

There is a manifest tendency, especially among Negro and mulatto writers, to deny that there has been, since the close of the slavery period, any appreciable initial increment in racial intermixture. Unquestionably there has been, especially in the earlier years of freedom, a very large number of such cases. There is still a very large element of such cases, possibly numerically greater than at any preceding time.

The increase in mulattoes during the twenty-year period between 1890 and 1910 was reported at practically the same rate as for the preceding twenty years. From 1,132,060 mulattoes reported in 1890, the number rose to 2,050,686 in 1910, an increase virtually duplicating the results of the preceding 270 years! Such are the figures collected and published by the Census Bureau and, within reasonable limits, these findings must be regarded as dependable. From these enumerations may be deduced the expectation for 1950, viz.: 584,-

049:2,050,686::2,050,686: (?) . Solving, the result is 7,200,274 mulattoes for 1950, or slightly less than one-half the present Negro population of the United States!

Unfortunately, for some reason, the returns for 1920 are worthless, if not positively misleading, in so far as racial intermixture is concerned, a fact frankly admitted by the Census Bureau. This enumeration, showing a decrease of 390,132 in the mulatto element of the population, as compared with the findings of 1910, is so inconsistent with preceding enumerations that it cannot be dependable.

The Census returns for 1920 have been used in an effort to prove that the mulatto problem is no longer acute and that discussion of it is unnecessary. Why the wide variation from the facts established by preceding enumerations is a matter for conjecture. Why the status of racial intermixture should be omitted in any Census enumeration likewise raises questions. There is no other item of population statistics more important. Upon the Census findings must be based whatever of definite statement is made concerning the present situation and any forecast as to the future. Is the political influence of the mulatto now sufficient to enable him to eliminate all reference to himself in the Census investigations? Has he been able to prevent the gathering of dependable information concerning racial intermixture? If he has done so, a serious mistake has been made. Without the findings of the Census everyone who observes and everyone who invokes his imagination is free to reach his own conclusions.

The significance of the mulatto problem is more easily grasped, possibly, when restricted areas are considered. The State of Virginia may serve as an example. In 1870 the Census returned 72,248 mulattoes for this State; in 1890, 122,141; in 1910, 222,910. This rate of increase gives an expectation of 685,250 for 1950! In addition to those mulattoes still in the State many have left the State, finding homes in the North and the Northeast. Many are in the District of Columbia. These figures call attention to two facts: the relatively small racial intermixture in this State under slavery—72,248 in 250 years, including the demoralization of the Civil War period and five years of freedom; and the astoundingly rapid progress of racial intermixture here since the full emancipation of the Negro. Virginia had the largest number of mulattoes returned for any state in 1910. Fourteen states and the District of Columbia showed a higher percentage of mulattoes in total Negro population than did the State of Virginia.

It has been pointed out elsewhere that this rapid increase of mulattoes is due to three factors. There is first the normal increase of the mulatto group, wholly within itself. For the most part, this now occurs within wedlock—and this should be recognized. Secondly, there is a mixture, a diffusion, of white blood through the interbreeding of the mulatto and the fullblood Negro. Much of this also occurs through marriage, and this fact should, in justice, be recognized. The third class of mulattoes springs from fullblood parents or from white and mulatto parentage. These we have designated as initial increment mulattoes, as contrasted with the diffusion mulattoes, composing the first and second classes here mentioned. It is true that this distinction between the two classes of mulattoes cannot usually be made. It can, however, be made in all individual cases brought under observation, for here ancestry may usually be ascertained. It may also be pointed out that, in so far as the ideals of the Negro race are concerned, mere recognition of these distinctions within the mulatto group does not wholly safeguard the moral issues involved. The mixed blood is everywhere known as such. He forms a group, the markings of which identify it and render recognition as a member of this group inevitable. Only by continuing this interbreeding until the physical markings of the Negro are obliterated may the individual hope to escape from the group; only by breaking down the standards, the ideals of the better elements of the two races can the mixed blood here hope to escape wholly the consequences of his origin. It is only when all the implications

229

of these facts are given due consideration that the real import of present conditions in the United States begins to appear. It is only then that the imperative need for a complete and a final separation of the two races appears.

Passing, then, from the matter of the presentation of the statistics of amalgamation, the impression upon the mind of any person who has grasped the facts must be that the situation presented, while utterly discouraging, is one of vital importance. What it involves beyond mere physical fact may not be realized but the student should, at this point, comprehend the seriousness of the figures presented by the Census. Also, why the Census Bureau has discontinued its investigations.

The statistics quoted above are the established facts, according to the Census, and a legitimate inference from these facts in reference to the situation in Continental United States and in that one of the States into which slaves were first introduced and where the economic situation has made the association of the races closest. It is inevitable that every thoughtful person, with the facts of the past and of the present before him, should turn to the future in anticipation of the working out, in their full fruition, of the factors entering into the past and the present. The prophecies of De Toqueville and the insight of Mr. Lincoln are being fully vindicated by the unquestioned facts of the present situation.[1] It requires neither prophetic insight nor even any unusual degree of mentality to forecast the future, once the past and the present are understood.

It will help in the realization of the seriousness of the present situation to recall at this point the fact that the findings of the United States Census fall below the actual facts in reference to racial intermixture. The presence of a wholly undetermined error is recognized and the fact frankly stated in those bulletins dealing with the mulatto. In all use of the Census returns, therefore, it is well to regard them as a

[1] See pp. 116-117.

minimum statement as concerns the actual number of mulattoes in the United States at the various enumerations taking account of the mulatto as a distinct element in the total Negro population.

Important as is this matter of racial intermixture it is the feature of the race problem which received least consideration during that period of readjustment immediately following the Civil War and the termination of slavery. No distinction was supposed to be made between the mulatto and the fullblood Negro and, in a supposedly free field, the foundation for the subsequent domination by the mulatto was laid. Growing out of this situation there is now a group of people numbering into the millions and standing between two races. The blood mixture, in its origin almost wholly illegitimate, ranges from so small an infusion of white blood as to be almost imperceptible to that group at the other extreme in which white blood predominates to such an extent that many surreptitiously enter the white race or, as the Negroes express it, "cross the line." The *New York World* of July 28, 1929, placed the number thus escaping the race annually at 5,000; Walter White, in 1948, places the number at 12,000.[2]

If, at the present time, the representative citizen of the United States were required to give expression to his response to this situation, it would be, first of all, to admit that he *knows* nothing concerning it and that it has not even entered into the realm of his conscious thought. Should the more specialized groups, the intellectuals, be questioned carefully—lawyers, doctors, teachers, journalists, and even the Catholic priests and the Protestant clergy—an appalling ignorance of the real facts and of their significance is immediately encountered. The majority have accepted the situation without analysis, and the details, the results, everywhere plainly apparent, without comparison or evaluation.

Many thousands have contributed to the founding and equipping of educational plants for the benefit of the Negro.

[2] *A Man Called White*, p. 3.

Many have contributed liberally to the support of such institutions, trusting wholly to the individuals in charge or to the organizations promoting the various enterprises and institutions, but who would be shocked to learn the practical attitude toward race of those employed in the actual administration of such benefactions and still more to learn that of 9,172 students enrolled in higher educational institutions for Negroes in 1916 as careful an investigator as Professor Reuter has shown himself to be classified 7,567—82.5 per cent—as mulattoes and 1,605—17.5 per cent—as "black," not necessarily all fullblood Negroes. It is safe to assume that the institutions investigated are fairly representative and that the fullblood Negro element receiving higher academic and higher technical training is now not above 17.5 per cent. Morgan College, of Baltimore, Md., was credited with 450 students, not one of whom was considered a fullblood Negro. There has been no improvement since 1916. The percentage of fullblood Negro students enrolled in higher educational institutions for Negroes and in the colleges and universities of the North and those of foreign countries is now less than the 17.5 per cent found by Professor Reuter in 1916.

The chapter dealing with the mulatto is not an exhaustive treatment of this feature of the race problem. In the nature of the case, it cannot be made more than suggestive of many matters of even grave importance. It does, however, call attention to some of the more vital wrongs and the more serious aspects of the present situation. The fact that what logically would fall in this chapter necessarily comes up for discussion in other chapters renders it impossible to make the chapter on the mulatto a complete treatment without undue repetition.

Closely associated with the estimate a race sets upon its continued existence as a race, involved in its extra-racial morality, is the type of morality developed within its own group—its intra-racial morality. This is a field in which it is very difficult to arrive at all the details. In the present study no attempt is made to reach definite conclusions as to the classes involved in the high rate of illegitimacy officially reported among the Negro population of the District of Columbia, or elsewhere. In the matter of illegimate births, however, there are official statistics available as a basis for conclusions concerning both ideals and practices.

The chapter dealing with the illegitimate child covers a much wider scope than the title of this study warrants. Conditions in Europe, especially in European cities, show the vital importance of an intelligent approach to the problem of the illegitimate child. This chapter should serve to emphasize the need for an honest and a thorough inquiry into conditions in America, especially as these conditions affect race. The two World Wars have affected adversely the ideals and the standards of a very large element of the population of the United States. This is apparent in the increase of divorces and in the number of illegitimate births.

The rate of illegitimacy among the Negroes in Washington City is very high. The statistics concerning it are gathered by the Health Department and may be fairly regarded as reasonably complete and, certainly, as uninfluenced by racial bias. For various reasons, however, the returns are to be taken as a minimum statement, as there are certainly unreported cases of illegitimacy occurring in both races. It may even be that a higher percentage of the illegitimate births among Negroes are reported than among the whites, for many of these occur under circumstances where there is little to be gained by concealment and little to be lost by publicity.

The lowest rate of Negro illegitimacy yet reported for the District of Columbia is 15.8 per cent, reported for the year 1926. For 1893 over 29 per cent of Negro births in the District were registered as illegitimate. Percentages are not given in Table II, but in an instance or two the figures given are greater than the 27 per cent of illegitimates as given by Mr. Evans, as quoted in Table VIII, at page 72.

There is nothing in the health reports to indicate the social stratum in which the birth of an illegitimate child occurs, nor are many other details available which would throw light upon the causes and the conditions producing this large number of cases of illegitimacy. Housing conditions must share the blame, but the one fact that is of practical value is the clear indication of the need of the Negroes in the District of Columbia for a higher type of family life, and for the stressing of all those agencies and forces calculated to meet the needs of the race at this point. The present situation in the District may well prove very discouraging to the fullblood Negro. There is no way by which the percentage of illegitimate Negro children representing initial amalgamations may be determined. From the highest to the lowest there is little in the way of utterance or of effort calculated to restrain this evil. There is much calculated to promote it. When any large number of children born in a group are registered as illegitimate, a situation is indicated calling for specific and drastic remedies. Why has the situation, throughout the nation as well as in Washington City, not received the attention from students and from writers and from publicists and from ecclesiastics which its importance demands?

The chief value of the chapter dealing with and comparing Latin and Teutonic ideals and methods of colonization lies in the fact that the former has, openly if not avowedly, applied the principles which the religious leaders in the United States, while repudiating them theoretically, are likewise applying in practice. Approaching the matter from almost opposite standpoints, the two agree in this, that neither has respected, or protected, the race life of the backward, the dependent groups. The difference has been in degree rather than in principle. The Teutonic ideal, with all its so-called brutality and lack of brotherhood, has, so far in the main, held the white of the United States and of Canada to race purity and has preserved a group in each race to which national, and especially racial, aspirations are still possible. The Latin ideals and practices have so far reduced the full-blood element that it is now often a hopeless minority and can exist only by sufferance of the mixed-blood groups in which it is submerged! Mr. Foerster finds only about 10 per cent of fullblood whites in several of the Latin-American groups. Under which group does the backward individual fare the better? Under one he is lost in a welter of moral and of racial confusion; under the other he maintains his racial identity and has the opportunity of working out his racial life and of realizing his racial possibilities.

For this study, the vital fact of early Latin-American colonization lies in the absence of the Latin woman and the resultant failure to transplant to America the home, as known in Latin Europe. The practice of enslaving the Indians and of conferring captured Indian women upon the Spanish soldiers—a custom derived directly from classical antiquity and from the practices of the Saracens, with whom the Spanish had now contended for several hundred years, a custom doubtless followed by the Spanish and the Portuguese elsewhere at this time—was fatal to race purity. It was these two features—the absence of white women and the enslaving of the Indian women—which determined other details and which so quickly led to the racial conditions characterizing much of Latin America. Introduced into this situation, the Negro tended quickly to lose his identity. The net result of the Latin method of colonization has been loss to Spain and Portugal—in scarcely less degree to France—of most of the men going out as colonists, and the peopling of Latin America with a mixed race, largely wanting in all those traditions conditioning stability and the achievements of highest order. Race tradition and race pride can hardly survive such fusion of three races as largely destroys each of the races involved! It is to this destruction of race that Professor Foerster attributes many of the unfortunate conditions exhibited by some of the Latin-American countries.

235

The matter of immigration from the Latin-American states takes its real significance from the facts here discussed. The admission of the mixed blood from these sources necessarily complicates the racial situation in the United States. These people have fertile lands, abundant undeveloped resources, and a reasonable degree of group unity. It should not be a hardship to them to remain at home and to work out a destiny there instead of coming into a situation necessarily involving more or less of humiliation, if not antagonism, because of efforts to preserve their identity by the whites already here, an effort leading to exclusiveness upon the part of the whites.

It is true that the contrasts here suggested seem most unfortunate for the Latin-American groups. Their hurtfulness is greatly increased when the individual finds himself among those unsympathetic and disposed to shut him out from their social life generally and especially to withhold from him the privileges of the more privileged social circles. The West Indians have the same general situation to face as confronts the Continental Latin American. Doubtless the political unrest in Mexico during the past few years, with resultant economic conditions, has driven many Mexican laborers into the United States. Most of these are of mixed origin.

Delicate as this situation undoubtedly is, there is no escape from it. Logically, the industrial interests must look to Latin America for raw materials and for markets for their manufactures. European competition must be met and good will is a vital factor here. A careful consideration of those social forces and those practices which grew out of the womanless settlement at Isabella may not minister to that commercial reciprocity so much desired by the business interests of the United States. It should not be forgotten, however, that some of the gravest problems confronting America today had their origin in such a desire for gain as obscured other and more vital interests.

The chapter dealing with the near-white requires little comment. It is here that America faces the completion of the process of racial intermixture, a process involving so much that is tragic. A limited number of mixed bloods achieve success and these loom large in the public view. Little is known of that vastly larger number whose white blood leads to unrealized ambitions and to inevitable frustrations. Mulatto womanhood is possibly the most unfortunately situated group in America. It is wholly reasonable to assume that, as the goal is approached, the desire for its attainment grows stronger and frustration more destructive.

The question arises here as to the extent to which the mass of the Negroes are conscious of what is occurring and, despairing of the future of their own race, look to escape from it as the only hope for betterment of their offspring. There are many such. Their number depends, in large part, upon the ability of the Negro to understand his present situation and his ability to interpret aright the prevailing attitudes toward the matter of his racial integrity. Behind the near-white there are several instances of initial amalgamation and, in the nature of the case, each of these steps involves not only racial intermixture but also illegitimacy. The cases occurring in wedlock are relatively negligible. A little honest thinking at this point must bring a measure of realization of the true meaning of this situation. Relatively, the number of cases of initial amalgamation may appear small. It is certainly sufficiently large to exert a most destructive influence upon the ideals and upon the morals of the whole Negro population. This influence is greatly strengthened by the advantageous status of the successful mulatto.

In the nature of the case, so long as racial contact continues, there can be no escape from the problems presented by the near-white. To refuse to face the facts is to leave the whole matter to take the course of least resistance, to remove largely from its ultimate solution the character and the intelligence of both races, thus accepting and, in the last analysis, approving the whole process of racial intermixture as this is now occurring and as it has occurred in the past.

One of the strongest arguments for the repatriation of the American Negro must be drawn from the near-white and his position, his significance, in the race problem in the United States.

The chapter dealing with the poor white calls attention to one of the vitally important problems of racial contact in the United States, although conditions here are not essentially different to those existing in other parts of the world. Wherever there is prosperity, with higher wages and desirable living conditions, there will be those from less progressive, less favorably situated peoples eager to share that prosperity. Wherever there is an employer of labor, his interests will prompt him to secure labor at once cheap and not too independent. Whether in industry or in domestic service, this demand for cheap labor arises and, if not met intelligently, will soon create conditions highly unfavorable to the poor, the laborers, of the more privileged group. These are facts having a direct bearing upon the matter of immigration, and they are just now of special importance because of the influx of Mexicans and of other Latin Americans. If restrictions were removed, the United States would quickly be overrun by people from every part of the world.

Many of the keenest and the strongest minds of England and of South Africa have dealt with the race problem in the latter area. Here the "bywoner" is full brother to the "poor white" of the United States. The effect upon the white race of the presence of the native and his employment in the lower and less exacting occupations is clearly set forth by several writers. Likewise the extension of this competition into the realms of the semi-skilled and of skilled labor has been recognized in South Africa as certain to have a depressing, if not destructive, effect upon white labor, extending into these fields the same hurtful influences as have so greatly augmented the "bywoner" group.

America may learn much from South Africa. The "bywoner," in the presence of the native Kaffir, is unwilling to perform "Kaffir's work," because of its effect upon his status and even upon his estimate of himself. Unquestionably, the attitude of the South toward manual labor has been affected unfavorably by the presence of the Negro. It is necessary to recognize this fact, if the whole truth is to be told. It is not, however, so much in those circles where this effect is recognized and resisted that the competition of Negro labor in the United States is found to work its gravest results. It is rather among those who must work in order to live but who, upon seeking employment, find that they must meet the conditions created by the Negro; that they must accept his wage; show his docility; do his work; or there is no place for them in a Negro-dominated industrial order. Behind the organized Negro group—should one come to exist—would be the unorganized Negro masses waiting to be drawn upon and in position to continue the depressing work of those who would have extended the field of racial competition.

Doubtless, there are those who will regard this chapter as radical, but the reader is urged to give the facts presented very careful and very thorough consideration. Well defined facts exist, and no one who would be at all thorough in dealing with the race problem in America can ignore these facts. It may suit the purpose of some to do so; but, except in the case of those definitely committed to a program or fettered by precedent, the thoughtful citizen, of either race may, and should, investigate these facts and reach his own conclusions concerning them.

Fortunately, the outstanding lessons of the past are available. Only as the whole range of history is surveyed and the rise and decline of nations and of racial groups carefully studied, will the full significance of the attitude of the group toward its own poor be clearly seen. However poor and however unprivileged socially and however depraved morally, the individual racial traitors have in their keeping the future purity of their race. The unprivileged, the despised, the social outcasts, if permitted to become sufficiently numerous, may turn upon and debase the race group deserting them and leaving them to the outcome of an all but hopeless racial competition.

If ever the poor-white comes to analyze his position and to tabulate the causes bringing it about, possibly the bitterest of all the factors promoting his resentment will not be the fact that he has had to compete with Negro labor but that, in the struggle for a chance for himself and for those dependent upon him to live the fuller and more satisfying life, he has found the privileged element of his own race at best indifferent but usually practically arrayed upon the side of the Negro. The Churches have demonstrated their teachings concerning human brotherhood by neglecting him for an alien race; the employers of labor have thought of their profits rather than of future conditions with which their own children, along with his, must contend; the politician has failed to make the State a source of protection at this point; the schools have made the Negro a keener competitor. He finds philanthropists openly and avowedly equipping the Negro for racial competition, while doing little or nothing, to prepare the poor and the unprivileged of their own race to meet the competition thus created. How shall white America answer him?

Objection to permitting competition as between white and black, or to control of such competition in the interest of the white, at once provokes one of two reactions. There are those whites who demand an equal opportunity for all and who seem pleased whenever a Negro succeeds in displacing, or in surpassing, a white person. There are those in this group who are pleased to have the competition of the Negro destroy the "independence" of the white laborer and thus "simplify" the labor problem. It was the packers in Chicago who introduced Negro labor for the purpose of breaking a strike. It is, however, by no means those only who profit personally by Negro labor who compose this group. There are those who approach the matter of such competition as detached theorists, many seeing in it proof of the progress of the Negro, but ignoring

240

completely the laborers and the poor of their own race. Until made to see the consequences of their attitude, usually a very difficult task, such people are often quite intolerant. Setting out with their views and their programs fixed and regarding themselves as champions of the race and exclusively the exponents of Christian Brotherhood, they miss the corrective influence of a really comprehensive grasp of the situation confronting them. A second class tends to become radical in attitude and needlessly harsh toward the Negro. Neither of these attitudes can be regarded as constructive.

It is in the field of religion that some of the most serious features of the American race problem are encountered. The contact of races has always involved antagonisms and these have usually extended into the realm of religion. It was not accidental that the religions of antiquity were largely national, even tribal. Even Christianity has not escaped this tendency toward appropriation by local groups and modification in its adaptation to the local situation. In this field mankind has the right to demand those attitudes which guarantee, if not ideal results, at least the approval of the highest and the realization of the highest possible under all the attendant circumstances. Christianity demands that these attitudes extend to all, rather than stop at national or racial boundaries.

This study reaches every essential value when, instead of furnishing too great a mass of details, it arrives at a clear statement of prevailing policy and practice through a general statement of fact. It is not necessary to ascertain the exact percentage of mulattoes composing the leadership of the various groups composing the successful element of the race. Thus it is not so necessary to ascertain what percentage of the Negro ministers are of mixed blood. The vital feature of the situation is that there is, theoretically or practically, no distinction made and that mixed bloods are prominent everywhere. The extent of such employment, the fact that so large a percentage of Negro ministers are mulattoes is a problem in degree rather than one of principle. The extent has its

241

force and value in showing the urgency of the matter and its ultimate outcome. It is quite evident that the Negro churches in the whole country, especially the stronger city churches, are largely dominated by the mulatto, and that these churches are not standing, with any enthusiasm or with any special determination, for the racial integrity of the Negro race, here or elsewhere.

Due to the greatly increased racial contacts at the present time the problem of making such contacts helpful, constructive rather than destructive, becomes highly important. The ill informed, unintelligent, emotional approach must be discarded. "Parallel development," not exploitation, should be the ideal. It is certainly of prime importance that the individual, the group, the race, shall reach that degree of self-respect which will lead to self-preservation, the realization of the possibilities of each. Whatever brings this about, has a very real and a permanent value. Whatever works in the opposite direction, must be recognized as destructive.

Most careful investigation fails to reveal any convincing evidence that the Negroes in the District of Columbia—the most highly privileged of the world—as represented even in their religious interests and institutions, give any serious thought to the matter of preserving their racial integrity. Nor is there any convincing evidence that the white people of the District have any definite knowledge of the situation confronting them or that this situation gives them any real concern. In this respect the entire nation is alike.

The Negro church organizations are, fortunately, completely independent of the white churches, and much is gained from the fact that the Negro is forced to plan and to act for himself. Except for a few individuals in each race, sympathetic contacts are now rare. The vast array of details bearing upon and constituting this situation need not be given here. For this study all practical purposes are served when it is ascertained, and its significance realized, that while no discrimination is consciously made against the fullblood

Negro in favor of the mulatto, yet the present situation throughout the United States does, in religion as in every other interest, involve such discrimination.

Thus is indicated the supreme social and the supreme religious needs of the Negro throughout America. Sixteen and one-half per cent of the children born of Negro and mulatto mothers in the District of Columbia in the year ending in 1928 were officially reported as illegitimate. Add to this that element of illegitimates born of married women of the race but rarely reported, and that element which is not reported at all because successfully concealed, and it becomes evident that, for 1928, at least twenty per cent, one in five, of the births among Negro and mulatto girls and women in the District occurred illegally. Certainly this is a situation which should challenge every leader in each race. It indicates a condition upon which should be focused the attention of the whole country, for it is not only in the District of Columbia that such conditions exist. No attempt is now made officially to determine what part of the illegitimate births in the District represent initial amalgamations.

The attitude of the religious white toward the Negro certainly calls for careful analysis. A group of irresponsible whites forms a mob and lynches an individual Negro, believed to be guilty of crime. Immediately, and justly, sometimes not wisely, there is an outburst of indignation, and the usual comments go the rounds of the press—the religious press especially. There is no disposition here to uphold the lawless, and there is an imperative need that such mobs should be put down pitilessly and their members punished adequately. Many do not seem to realize that there is such a thing as "lynching" the ideals of a people. Between the infrequent murder of an individual believed to be guilty of crime and an age-long assault upon the ideals, the racial self-respect, the blood purity, of a people, the latter is infinitely the more destructive. That this assault should come from a people who would die in defense of their own group rather than permit the conditions to prevail there which they thoughtlessly approve and promote among the Negroes, takes on the marks of a sickening if not a disgusting, inconsistency. The effect of this wrong upon those who perpetrate it requires careful analysis.

The casual observer, the average citizen, if his attention has been directed to the matter of the final and complete separation of the white and the black races in the United States, quickly dismisses the matter. He does not carry his investigations far enough to reach an intelligent decision concerning repatriation of the Negro or the conditions under which this may be brought about. At best, the task would prove a stupendous one and it is quite the popular thing to dismiss the matter comfortably by saying that it cannot be done.

The repatriation of the Negro is not impossible, nor is it impracticable. The best plan is that suggested in the chapter on Colonization. It is that of removing the productive element of the race only. The death rate among Negroes is high —in Washington City the death rate of Negro children is about twice that of the whites—and many children will not reach maturity. Many Negroes are diseased and cannot contribute to the numerical increase of the race. There are now about 15,000,000 Negroes in the United States. By the consistent removal of those reaching maturity and demonstrating reproductive capacity, after a few years the number would be reduced sharply and the whole matter would be settled within a half century. The greater part of the burden would fall within the first 15 years that the plan was in operation.

When the United States entered the World War, very little preparation had been made for moving men or munitions to Europe. The speed with which preparations were made and the magnitude of the task accomplished in the face of dangers from submarines and the general stress of war should set at rest all question of the possibility of transportation. The motive then was the winning of a great war. The objective here would be the protection of our own race from a calamity

244

infinitely greater than any that could have followed defeat at the hands of the Central powers. It would be the protection of the Negro from the vicious element of the white race; the giving to him the opportunity to build his own civilization; the freeing him from that proscription of which he so loudly complains here; and, finally, placing him in position to serve his race in Africa to the limit of his attainments and of his possibilities. Colonization, repatriation, alone promises these boons to the American Negro or protection to the white race.

A question of vital moment is this: What does the Negro think in reference to the race problem as a whole and, especially, the mixture of the blood of the two races? In the endeavor to arrive at an answer to this question there arises the difficulty of penetrating the racial reserve and of learning the secrets of a people schooled by centuries of servility in the art of concealment. Few white people have been able so to win the confidence of the Negro as to be able to penetrate the workings of the Negro mind, especially in its reaction to this feature of his life here. Whether through fear of the white, or through indifference, or through approval of race intermixture, *the Negro man has not opposed amalgamation.* So far as written statement is concerned, it is unquestionably true that the Negro and the mulatto writers do not care to discuss racial intermixture with any degree of thoroughness. It is a matter which seems, even with fullblood Negro writers, to produce heat rather than light. It is, however, hardly possible for any fullblood Negro to discuss the matter fully, for such discussion would affect adversely influential mulattoes and would certainly produce intense bitterness. The antagonism of the mulatto group would, in most cases, involve difficulties insurmountable by the fullblood Negro. His efforts to deal with the problem would likely result in loss of standing and in loss of position and of opportunity; so the few fullblood Negroes who rise decidedly above the racial level are not in position to speak frankly when something like nine out of ten of the group of educated and successful members of the Negro group are really mulattoes, who would not only take offense but make their resentment felt. It may well be that there are educated fullblood Negroes who really believe no good can now come from making a distinction between the mixed-blood and the fullblood Negro.

Nor is it reasonable to expect the mulatto to discuss thoroughly, certainly not to condemn vigorously, a situation which touches his vital interests adversely. He is interested not in thorough analysis and a true statement of conditions, a true evaluation of the forces bearing upon the mixture of the races, but rather in promoting those attitudes which will leave him in the peaceful enjoyment of the privileges he now has and in increasing rather than diminishing his hold upon, and his leadership of, the fullblood Negro. His attitude is necessarily defensive and, so far as he can prevent it, no agitation of the matter of amalgamation will occur.

Some twenty years ago there was published a book written by the late Professor R. R. Moton, President of Tuskegee Institute. In many respects this is one of the strongest and one of the most valuable books yet produced by a Negro and in the interest of the Negro race. His insight into the situation of the American Negro had come to the author largely through his own varied experiences in his struggle upward, in his association with the recognized leaders in Negro education, and his actual contacts with Negro students. Dr. Moton was himself a fullblood Negro, of fine physique, a man of recognized ability and, as successor to Dr. Booker T. Washington at Tuskegee, was in position to influence the Negroes of the United States as few others could have done. The book is, however, somewhat disappointing in that the references to racial intermixture are few and brief. It is condemned, but not with that energy and decision and precision that the situation demands. The references to amalgamation might have been made more numerous, more pointed, and better calculated to arouse the Negro group to a more energetic determination to protect itself at this point.

Certain facts should be remembered. Dr. Moton was at the head of an institution founded by the late Dr. Booker T. Washington, by his own published statement shown to have been an initial increment mulatto. Of the faculty of this institution two students of the race problem—neither Southern—Mr. William Archer, of England, and Professor E. B. Reuter, have given practically identical statements. Of 200 teachers, only nine, and at that time none of these in important positions, were regarded as fullblood Negroes. With Dr. Moton as President and with Professor Carver, an outstanding member of the teaching force, a practical demonstration was later afforded of what might have been done had any regard been shown since 1865 for the Negro as a race. The Negro might now have had a fullblood leadership.

At present it still remains true that both the teaching force and the student body of Tuskegee Institute are overwhelmingly mulatto. Under the conditions then existing it was necessary for Dr. Moton to avoid friction with the mulattoes on his faculty and with the mulattoes in the student body, or his position would have become insecure, even if he had not lost it promptly. It is hardly reasonable to have expected a man thus situated to imperil his personal interests and his prospects for future usefulness by speaking upon this matter with the fullness or with the force possible to a man detached and with no personal interests involved. There is probably not a fullblood Negro in America today, competent to deal constructively with the mulatto problem and now holding any desirable position in politics, in a school, or in the ministry, who would not promptly lose his position if he became actively outspoken in reference to the fullblood Negro's side of the mulatto problem.

In reference to the attitudes of the white people toward the Negro, there are passages in Dr. Moton's book which discriminate clearly between the different classes of white people, and there are others which treat the race as an undifferentiated unit. One such statement occurs at page 219 where, discussing the attitude of the Negro toward the views of the white man, he treats the white man's reference to "race integrity" as the "outstanding joke." There are white men whose practices deprive them of all right to speak upon any moral issue, but there are others who cannot be associated with any racial wrong, except it be through their silent acquiescence in the evil of amalgamation. Such silence upon the part of good men, and women, recognized moral leaders, has permitted present conditions to develop without serious restraint. Only as this evil is brought within the range of conscience through thorough understanding may we expect convictions to develop into purposive action.

So long as the mulatto can control the situation, his position will not be endangered. It is hardly to be expected that the mulatto should give much weight to the interests of either white or black at a point where these interests are in irreconcilable conflict with his own. If the full significance of this racial intermixture ever penetrates the American mind, it will do so because of the activities of the white group, with at best but indifferent support from the fullblood Negro. In some instances the fullblood Negro opposes discussion of these matters with more energy and with more feeling than are shown by either of the other two groups. The attitude of the fullblood Negro is very discouraging to all those fully conscious of the present situation and its significance.

There is another feature of the race problem which merits very careful consideration. In a general way it may be said that, in the past, the Negro in the United States has survived largely because he has not been self-assertive, but has rather accepted the position assigned him here with a readiness and even with a cheerfulness which not only made for him friends but also preserved him from any general molestation. There have been numerous instances of violence, ranging from personal encounters to mob action involving local communities or cities, but as yet none racial in extent. In virtually all these encounters the Negro has been at the gravest disadvantage

248

and has usually furnished far the larger part of the casualties. Organized attack or organized resistance upon the part of the Negro would, undoubtedly, have extended and intensified such conflicts. The race has "bent" and survived when an effort to stand erect would have invited disaster. In this respect the contrast to the course pursued by the American Indian is highly instructive.

Lynchings usually involve a single victim who has committed a crime or who is believed to have done so. Mob action is, therefore, to be distinguished from the race riot, approaching the status of racial conflict. Race riots have been confined to no one section of the United States. The most serious of these riots occurred when the movement of Negroes to the North first became sufficient to affect seriously the laboring class outside the South. Serious riots occurred in East St. Louis, in Chicago; in Springfield; in Washington City; and elsewhere. In all these riots there was much violence, often wanton brutality, upon the part of the white people involved. The lawless elements found in these occasions an opportunity to disregard law and order with little danger of being punished for what they might do. The gravest immediate dangers in all rioting grow out of the fact that the lawless, the depraved, find in the incident disorganization and confusion an opportunity to commit even grave crime with but little probability of being brought to account for it. Under the stress of a riot there are usually those who, law-abiding under normal conditions, become temporarily law-breakers.

In all these riots and clashes, the lawless element of the white group and their acts of violence loom largest. The fact that the Negroes were displacing white laborers, leaving white families in want; that they were forcing white laborers to abandon their homes or to remain in the midst of a Negro community; that the introduction of Negro labor was part of the scheme of industrial interests endeavoring to secure labor at once cheap and easily controlled—these and other vital matters were forgotten by the type of white men and women

249

who, assuming for themselves little less than a monopoly upon insight, upon brotherliness, and upon all the other virtues considered Christian, rushed in to defend the encroaching Negro, but to utter no word for, possibly not so much as to consider seriously, the white man being crushed by the situation. Such falacious supposed expression of Christian brotherhood does not help the Church in the estimation of the laboring classes of the white race.

Those who would understand fully the situation created by Negro labor in thus entering the North, its effect as demonstrating the power of the man on the lower plane to drive out or to degrade to his own level the man on the higher plane, should study the conflict between the Japanese and the Koreans and, even more illuminating, that between the Japanese and the Chinese, especially during the period that Japan occupied these countries. Here the Chinese were, in every respect except education and organization, quite the equals of the Japanese. Because of the low standard of living of the Koreans and of the Chinese, Japanese laborers found it impossible to compete succesfully with them, and, hence, the Japanese hope of colonization in these areas for the surplus population of Japan was not realized.

For a further example of a more advanced and privileged group having to deal with a primitive people, the experiences of the English and the Dutch in South Africa afford a situation which Americans should be able to study with some degree of detachment. Writers in England and those in South Africa have dealt rather exhaustively with the situation in this area, and the parallel between this and the conditions in the United States is so close that it is impossible to make a study of one without arriving at a clearer understanding of the other. About 10 per cent of the whites in South Africa are rated as "bywoners," a term nearly or quite synonomous with that of "poor-white" in the South.

There are now a considerable number of Negroes—virtually all mulattoes and many of these near-whites—residing in the North, who are advocating a complete change of policy upon the part of the Negro. These object to the peace policy advocated by the late Dr. Booker T. Washington and insist upon such assertion upon the part of the Negro as would be calculated to secure for him equal rights and privileges with the Caucasian in every respect. F. V. Calverton tells us that this new attitude of the Negro was first expresed by W. E. B. DuBois, in a speech at Atlanta in 1912. Some claim that the experiences of the Negro soldiers in the two World Wars have greatly intensified and extended this attitude. Undoubtedly, a section of the Negro press has proved very radical advocating measures and attitudes which, had they been put into practice, especially in the South, would have intensified racial antagonisms to the point necessitating final adjustment. On the whole, the masses of the Negro race in the United States have proved unwilling to follow the leadership of radicals of either race. It is a marvel that the Negro refrained from violence in 1861-1865. It is equally a marvel that in recent years the radical Negro press has failed to incite the blacks to organized crime and violence.

While there has been a general repudiation of all forms of radical leadership, there has been, especially in recent years, a decided gain in race consciousness and, as this has progressed, a drawing apart of the two races that has, while lacking in violent manifestations, carried some Negroes far toward racial self-respect and racial self-sufficiency. *The Negro's new belligerent attitude,* so long as it ministers to racial solidarity in a constructive way, is to be welcomed by all. Along with race prejudice upon the part of the white race, this new belligerent attitude of the Negro race, if both are wisely directed and sufficiently intensified, should register, first of all, in a greatly decreased number of initial amalgamations, thus proving helpful where philanthropy and even Christianity have succeeded but indifferently. Even bitter antagonism, with its constant danger of open hostility, is to be preferred to that indifference which permits gross wrongs

251

to pass unnoticed, even a wrong so grave as race destruction through illicit race amalgamation.

There is a hope, a possibility, that this new belligerent attitude will permeate the entire Negro group, and that its influence will prove definitely constructive. At present it exists almost wholly among mulattoes in the North and East. In the thought of the mulatto, it certainly has a place, a prominence, not found, as yet, in the thinking of the fullblood Negro. With the mulatto, it naturally leads to a consideration of his grievances and to demands for the removal of all that irritates him. Possibly this new belligerent attitude may yet develop to the point where it will force racial separation geographically. If so, it will have rendered the highest possible service to both races.

Any constructive program, looking to the preservation of the white race in the United States and Canada, must include rigid control of immigration. Earlier in the history of the United States there was little need for such restrictions. The quality of the immigrant was not always high but they were almost wholly of the same general racial group as were the original settlers and there were no serious problems in assimilation or in Americanization. Those coming came to make their homes here permanently, not for the purpose of a limited stay and an ultimate return to the homeland, enriched by what they had succeeded in accumulating here. Those coming to the United States represented the more progressive and enterprising classes of Europeans, shown by the fact of their willingness to make the adventure involved in leaving old associations and entering into new fields. The type of man who thus breaks with his natal situation and goes into a new land is usually a man of aggression and of initiative.

Thus the United States received in the earlier settlement a most favorable human element, not because of any restrictions imposed but because of existing conditions. The same is true of the earlier years of the Republic. The introduction of the Negro slave was the supreme mistake of the earlier period of settlement. Carelessness in the matter of immigration has later proved very hurtful, introducing further complications in the matter of race. Many evils might have been avoided had there been any rational system of permit-entry enforced and followed up by a rational system of registration, enabling officials to keep a record of each immigrant. As a protection from undesirable and illegal persons, such a system would have yielded valuable results.

In this later period, the country having been developed to the point where industries became prominent, began the demand not for homebuilders but for laborers; not for those elements which would quickly and completely merge into a population unity but for those elements offering a laborer, docile and dependable, a willing worker and one content to remain a laborer. Steamship lines, anxious to fill their steerage to capacity, contributed to some of the most unfortunate features of the situation. Thus, in later years, have come into the United States population elements differing widely from those coming earlier. The antecedents, the ideals, the outlook of North and Western Europe differ widely from those of South and of Eastern Europe. Possibly in no respect has there been greater difference, historically, than in the elements entering into the composition, the blood, the race, of these peoples. Due to extensive conquests and to the practice of slavery, the Greek people underwent such changes as worked their degradation as a world power. Rome later did the same. For Italy especially it is possible to study the results of compulsory cosmopolitan origin, especially the fate of the patrician in the midst of a situation created by him, and for his own ease and pleasure, but which proved his undoing.

Many of those, coming from areas having a population composit and cosmopolitan in origin, have subjected the American Negro to an undue stress, especially in the greater urban centers. Economically, they have had the training secured in a situation involving the practice of ultimate econ-

253

omies and the taking advantage of the smallest gains. Of cosmopolitan origin themselves, many lack pride of race, for to them race is a matter of too great confusion to form a supporting force adequate for group preservation. The gravest problem of the Negro in contact with these people, as in Latin America, is not that of industrial competition; it is rather the quickness and the completeness with which his racial identity is lost, and the moral and the social conditions prevailing while this destruction of his race is in progress.

A writer has called attention to the fact that the white peoples are a hopeless minority and that it is folly for them to provoke the enmity of the colored races. He writes: "The true situation seems to be that, of the total number of human beings alive today, about 1,700,000,000, only 550,000,000 of them are white, and the remaining 1,150,000,000 colored." He held that it is, therefore, folly for the whites to provoke needless racial antagonisms or to intensify needlessly those already existing. It should be necessary to do neither. Yet, it is impossible to study certain features of racial contacts without coming to recognize that the group, national or racial, has its value, and that out of both may come highly conservative, and hence valuable, results. Bitter prejudices may, and frequently do, produce more wholesome results than arise from "cosmopolitan spinelessness."

How may a white group, national or racial, more justly incur the animosity or intensify the hatred of any other group than by inflicting upon that group a class neither white nor colored and which constantly reminds the one group of the sins of the other? The basis of interracial goodwill and co-operation lies not in a refusal to face evils, actual or potential, in such racial contacts, but in mutual regard for race itself.

Some years ago the writer heard a prominent Southern clergyman, in a public discourse, make the statement, the assertion, that there is no Negro problem. What he had in mind was that the question of race relations is broader than any one race and that local instances of racial contacts should be interpreted in the light of this comprehensive view of human unity and through the higher conception of Christian Brotherhood. An inspirational speaker, his audience probably did not realize that such a statement had been made and, if noticed at all, the statement was quickly forgotten. The emotional impulse of the address constituted its real value.

With his explanation of the statement, his repudiation of the plain meaning of his words, his oratorical device for emphasizing a larger truth became clear. Yet, here was a man who had received the best that his people and his section were able to give him; a man who had grown up in the midst of the Negro people; a man whose own immediate circle had been twice invaded, and blighted, by outstanding interracial irregularities; a man to whom had come unusual opportunities to study world conditions. As a religious leader, the moral problems of many peoples had come under his observation.

The question arises as to how far this man is typical of his class, even of his race. In many respects he was far in advance of his section, and his work and influence were of real value to both races. Yet, knowing, as he certainly did, the darker side of racial contacts—a knowledge which had come to him, with terrible force, through the two experiences referred to above—it seems strange that he uttered no word; that he did nothing; that he wrote nothing calculated to bring the moral aspects of amalgamation within the range of conscious and specific purposive control. It is just here that this man becomes typical of the religious organizations and the ecclesiastics of America, if not of the world. These are not wielding the influence in behalf of the races and of interracial morality which it lies in their power to wield. In their personal and in their official attitudes, there is this manifest departure from the moral standards set for Christian guidance.

Very few white people openly advocate amalgamation as the final solution of the race problem involving the Caucasian and the Negro in the United States, or elsewhere. Attitudes may differ widely concerning other features of the situation here; but, theoretically, there is a near unity in opposing the fusion of the white and the black races. There is a wide range of reasons assigned for this attitude, some of which are fanciful; but, for the most part, the arguments advanced are valid. In the Negro race are those who are coming to respect their own race and who fully agree with the attitude of the white people in reference to amalgamation. It is not necessary that they should accept, or admit, the biological propositions upon which the white people base their attitude toward racial intermixture.

Those opposing amalgamation from the standpoint of the white race have usually advanced two groups of reasons for doing so. The first of these groups is based upon racial differences, mental, physical, and cultural; the second is based upon the moral and the social conditions inseparable from amalgamation as this has occurred in the past, is now occurring, and as it can reasonably be expected to occur in the future. The higher type of Negro, the race-respecting Negro, recognizes the second group as valid and opposes amalgamation, if for no other reason, because of the moral and the ethical conditions involved.

The science of Anthropology has a legitimate contribution to make in the settlement of all problems of race fusion. The anthropologist is not necessarily a moralist. Neither is he an equalitarian. Science, classified knowledge, is concerned essentially with *what is*, rather than with *what should be;* with the actual, rather than with the ideal. In a vital sense, therefore, ultimate morality waits ultimate fact.

The older schools of Anthropology devoted much time and study to the human brain. With great care and thoroughness they examined characteristics of the brain of the various races and of different classes within the various races, noting size, weight, structure, relative development of various areas of the brain, and other variable characteristics. Upon these findings it was sought to classify individuals, and even races. Great

umbers of human skulls were carefully measured and their
ɔrm and capacity were ascertained. Craniology has now, with
mprovements in technique and in instruments, become much
nore exact; yet the work of the older scientists retains a real
ʿalue. It has been proven incomplete rather than incorrect.
Modern psychology, with its many developments and sub-
livisions, may be said to establish the fact of racial variation
ɔn brain endowment and in brain development.

The older schools of anthropologists agreed among themselves in assigning to the Negro branch of the human race a
smaller and a less highly developed brain than is exhibited by
other races. By charts, and otherwise, some of them sought to
show the areas of the Negro brain not developed to the standard of the Caucasian. The logical results of the findings of
these scientists, with their prodigious industry and patience,
are distinctly discouraging to the Negro. Accepting their findings, there is provided an unanswerable argument against the
lowering of the Caucasian through absorption of the Negro.
Later researches have modified some of these findings but
have strengthened, rather than weakened, the evidences
pointing to essential racial differences, especially as between
the Caucasian and the Negro brain.

While this is true there are still those who object strenu-
ously to any classification of the races unfavorable to those
recognized as "backward," claiming that these are not necessarily of inferior endowment and that response to stimulus
and to opportunity may be a matter of personality as well as
of capacity. It is asserted that differences are compatible with
essential equality; that strength may lie in different endow-
ments, both physical and mental. It is pointed out that racial
groups now holding high rank were but recently nomads, or
but partly civilized. Thus doubt and uncertainty are introduced and many former conclusions reached by the older
anthropologists are now discarded or seriously questioned.
The division of the races upon the basis of advanced or
backward development—achievement—rather than that of

superior and inferior natural endowment is far kindlier and less discouraging than are the findings of the older anthropologists. By this division the argument against amalgamation would lose something of its sting but facts are not changed and the argument remains valid and final.

In the midst of the uncertain utterances of physical scientists, and the failure of the Anthropologist, the Ethnologist, the Craniologist to advance a constructive program, the practical man will turn to the facts as exhibited by the races—their relative achievements—and to the political, the social, the moral, the religious conditions marking their contacts. Here the argument against the fusion of the white and the black races finds abundant and unanswerable support. Mr. Reuter finds that the infusion of white blood increases the chances of the resulting group by thirty-four to one—later advanced to fifty to one hundred to one—over those of the fullblood Negro. Allowing for error in observation; error in the evaluation of evidence; error in the evaluation of achievements—the fact remains that, *functioning in a white man's civilization,* the infusion of white blood does greatly affect the race. If, as Professor Reuter finds, this difference in actual practical achievement be placed at over thirty-four to one, in favor of the mulatto as over the fullblood Negro, then the chasm separating the Caucasian and the fullblood Negro is a vast one, so vast that it is unfair to the awakened Negro that he be condemned to perpetual competition under such a handicap. This unfairness becomes the more galling when it is realized that there awaits the American Negro a place in the homeland of his race, and that the conditions of his return are now easier and vastly speedier than have ever before marked the migration of a people. The backwardness of the Negro peoples now in Africa places the future of this homeland in the hands of the American Negro—in so far as he proves able to use the equipment he has received during his sojourn here. His service to his race there would be measured finally in terms of his character, his tact, his economic efficiency, his devotion to his racial heritage.

The differences between the Caucasian and the Negro are such that there is no hope of the two coming together upon a basis fair and inspiring to both. Essentially, each group hurts and hinders the other. When the thrifty and industrious Negro, with his lower standard of living, has displaced the white laborer, in proportion to his degradation the displaced white becomes a menace to the less fortunate strata of the Negro group. Economically, socially, morally, religiously, each race suffers at the hands of the other. Mr. Lincoln was right, more than 80 years ago, in assigning this fact as a reason for the separation of the two races. Subsequent developments, nowhere more marked than in Washington City, have made of each passing year a vindication of the wisdom and of the insight of this plain, practical man. Justice to a race that has toiled for the white race—long and patiently, if not faithfully and well—and which now shows signs of racial awakening, demands for the Negro a chance. It demands for him a chance not merely as an individual but as a race. It demands for him something more than a chance to compete on equal terms in a white man's civilization and in a white man's industrial order. It demands for him something higher than the privilege of ultimate racial extinction through age-long immoralities, hanging ever gravely upon the lower strata of his race group!

Finally, the demands are not all *for* the American Negro. The situation requires much *of* him. Not the least of these requirements is that he shall face fairly his situation here and that he shall employ, to the full, all legitimate means to build up racial self-respect and racial self-sufficiency. He must protect his race from disintegrating forces. As his goal, he should not forget that Africa, the homeland of his race, holds for him an independence, a freedom, a chance, a racial status not possible elsewhere.

259

INDEX

www.ingramcontent.com/pod-product-compliance
Lightning Source LLC
Chambersburg PA
CBHW040140270326
41928CB00022B/3267